ECOPSYCHOLOGY AS ULTIMATE FORCE PSYCHOLOGY

ECOPSYCHOLOGY AS ULTIMATE FORCE PSYCHOLOGY

A Biosemiotic Approach To
Nature Estrangement And Nature Alienation

Jorge Conesa Sevilla, Ph.D.

CONTENTS

Acknowledgements

As in a Catalan human tower, a *castel*, I stand on the shoulders, hearts, and spirits of amazingly strong, diverse and creative people. As in a *castel*, the human at the top is both inconsequential and in incredible danger. This last climb is usually left to small children. The latecomer to any intellectual task, with a recognizable history and proven record, is usually the young and less experienced scholar. The danger of a child at the top of a *castel* is that of not being able to continue or finish the hard work of others and of tumbling down, often to injuries and bruises. I keep this humility and danger forefront in my mind when I acknowledge these great men and women, because acknowledging itself implies complicity and relationship. If I should fall, however, it would be due to my inexperience and not because they have failed at making an incredibly solid base of facts or ideas—of HEART.

Thanks to my parents, Antonio Conesa Carmona and Montserrat Sevilla Perez for allowing freedom when it was *desperately* needed. Thanks to the Dominican priests, and one in particular, Padre Losada, for sharing the joy of "wandering." It stuck! Thanks to Don Miguel for instructing and for injecting Venezuelan indigenous lore into my soul. Special thanks to William Devall, a noble giant, for putting up with insolence and for allowing a vision quest as part of my term project—thanks for Deep Ecology. Thanks to Joe Lesh for being a kind and patient California "Fish and Gamer." My special thanks to a remarkable woman and educator, *Florence Shepard*. Thanks to all the snow blizzards, poisonous snakes, gigantic bugs, sands, rocks, lightening, waves, bears, elk, and trees that did not kill me while I was learning my way through the wilderness and the natural spaces of Venezuela, Mount Lassen, the Blue Mountains, Mount Baker, the hills of Conesa, Kenai Peninsula, the Cascades, Swiss Alps, and the Sonora Desert. That was not luck—I was often overconfident or completely ignorant!

Thanks to my two foremen at Blossom Hill Ranch and at Creques' Greenhouse. Ranching-farming is tough work! Thanks to the *mega-kool* cynegetic Albrici family for their Swiss hospitality and for being the ambassadors to forests, animals, and secret natural places. More intimately or recently, thanks to my wife, Dick Brigham, Connie Veldink, Kaliana, and Jordi for reminding me and helping me, each in their own way, consciously or unconsciously, that I had lost my ecopsychological bearings and lens and that these needed updating. Particularly, thanks to my wife for laborious proofreading, to Jordi for his cover idea and images, and to Kaliana for contributing Chapter Nine. Thanks to so many others whom I am forgetting and deserve to be mentioned.

This living flowing
land is all there is, forever

We are it
it sings through us—

We could live on this Earth
without clothes or tools!

—Gary Snyder, *Turtle Island*

Forward

Jorge Conesa-Sevilla, in his book *Ecopsychology as Ultimate Force Psychology*, proposes that ecopsychology and biosemiotics provide the intellectual and moral framework for living harmoniously on Planet Earth. He tells us that to live rightly with others in society today, we must acknowledge in action and word our profound attachment to Nature. From the very first sentences to the final chapter Conesa lays out a convincing series of proofs, suggestions, and examples for living ecocentric rather than egocentric lives.

Conesa's book, which I read with fascination, took me on a three-fold ecopsychological journey: First, his careful elucidation of the growth and premises of the field, ecopsychology. Secondly, Conesa drew from the scholarship of my late husband, Paul Shepard, and this took me back once more to his creative speculations. I believe Paul would have greatly appreciated Conesa's interpretation, translation, and extension of his ideas. Paul would have found much food for thought in Conesa's original and discerning theory and explanations of matricial relationships. Lastly, and most importantly, reading Conesa's book was a very fascinating and personal experience for me. It demanded that I recapitulate and examine my past life and present practices and consider future self-correction in light of the premises he sets forth.

In his *Semiotic Matricial Theory* Conesa offers a convincing explanation for how living organisms are intricately entwined in complex organic matrices that are earth bound. Matrices express energy, safety, and possibility, "beta elements," which provide the fuel, scaffold, and potential for life. Conesa's profound rendition of our earthly relations caused me to visualize my life as part of a dynamic matrix orbiting and intersecting with other matrices emanating from the earth. The image holds like one of Conesa's lucid dreams and forces me to look back at my own ontogeny.

Raised during the Great Depression on a sheep ranch in Southwestern Wyoming, sagebrush steppe where unpredictable weather is a major determiner of survival, my sisters and I were an integral part of this ranch: working in the garden or hay fields, milking cows, feeding ranch animals, helping our mother with cooking and household chores. Free time in the summer, except for mandatory embroidering, was spent swimming in the river, wandering over the hills discovering Indian maidens, or gathering creatures in a verdant pond near the ranch house. I was always close to nature. During school and winter months we were freed from ranch chores to play in snow banks or wander through the old log house with many nooks and crannies for child contemplation and imaginative games. Using as a guide the insightful description of an experience on an organic farm written by Kaliana, Conesa's daughter, I could say that I WWOOFed my way through childhood (WWOOF= Willing Workers on Organic Farms). Our ranch was definitely organic, and there was much work and many mosquitoes.

My parents had a "native" sensibility honed by their peasant ancestors in Northern Italy. They lived frugal and sustainable lives out of necessity, but theirs was not an intentional back-to nature existence. Their view of land was a fine admixture of pragmatic and utilitarian considerations and aesthetic appreciation. Ranching successfully and making a living were their primary goals. Given the context of their lives, I do not fault my parents for a lack of consciousness; at base I know they loved the Earth. And I agree with Paul and Conesa that children should have intimate early childhood contact with nature, time to wander and explore. But, as Rachel Carson reminded us, caring adults are absolutely necessary. Children need guides that instill a deeper understanding of their relationship to the earth and responsibilities to nonhuman nature. Kaliana's wise rendition of her experience assures me that her parents fulfilled this obligation beautifully.

Through my childhood and youth, undergraduate university studies with a degree in zoology, training in physical therapy and practice with children with cerebral palsy, I did not consider myself in a *matricial* relationship with Nature or other living beings. I married and returned to the small, rural Wyoming town where I had attended school. Unaware of environmental consciousness building in society, I devoted my entire being to my four children who had come to me, via my Catholic ethic, one after another.

At the time, family, church, and community socialized women to be homemakers, not career women. Out of financial necessity, and with no opportunity to practice physical therapy except on my temporarily disabled husband who was recovering from surgery, I decided I'd try teaching. Finishing required education courses by correspondence in a summer, I began teaching junior high science, totally naive to the complexity of the process. Thanks to the intelligence, creativity, and patience of my first students, some of whom have remained life-long friends, I grew in understanding of the synergistic student/teacher relationship. My teaching, however, was text bound and detached from the real life of my students.

I moved on to teaching biology and one summer, needing re-certification credit, I attended a two-week field course offered by the Audubon Society in the Wind River Mountains in Wyoming. This was the early 60s when ecology and environmental activism were metamorphosing out of the turn of the century conservation ethic. Along with the place-based courses in geology, botany, vertebrates, invertebrates, and ecology, I was captivated by the other participants. Never before had I seen persons kneel in admiration of small blossoms, which I had stumbled over for most of my life; or stand agape at hawks soaring overhead; or marvel at the tiniest variation in the most inconspicuous little brown bird! The experience was an epiphany—heart, soul, and mind changing.

I returned to my classroom determined to make biology relevant to my students, to make the sagebrush steppe the base-line of their education. I convinced the administration to buy an over-grazed bull pasture with a small spring that adjoined the school and developed it into an outdoor lab. I abandoned the traditional biology text and fashioned a curriculum out of sagebrush, wind, mud, and the creatures of the Wyoming steppe. A source of ecological studies for all ages, the "outdoor laboratory" is still used to this day.

One day a notice for a book titled *The Subversive Science,* by Paul Shepard, came over my desk. Although it sounded interesting, I didn't order it. I was too busy defending my non-traditional teaching, which, considering the context of the conservative community, was about as subversive as one could get.

I had experienced a "Passing," about which Conesa writes, the transformation experienced when a person moves to a new state of consciousness. There was no turning back. My being was joined with the earth biosemiotically and ecopsychologically. The challenge of teaching and acquiring knowledge infused me with energy. I abandoned the safety net of community and home, and with four young children and a baby sitter in tow in summers I completed a masters degree in biology at a science institute for teachers at Washington State University.

After twelve years of teaching, with a failing marriage, and one daughter married and on her own, I abandoned the safety of home and community for good. With three teen-age children I moved to Salt Lake City and the University of Utah to seek a doctorate in education. Building on my background in the biological sciences, I sought a degree that would prepare me to teach environmental studies.

Now seen through the framework of Conesa's Semiotic Matrix Theory, I understand more fully the intricate intersections of many factors that initiated these changes. Love for my children and of the earth and its creatures were the primary matrices that brought cohesion to my life. My mother, who by then was widowed, and through her unconditional love, was always a safety net. Not fully understanding or agreeing with my decisions, she nonetheless provided an unconditional matriarchal, *matricial* bond that never wavered. Even now, fifteen years after her death, it steadies me. My children trusted in me and cooperated with me as we laid new plans. In this regard, and at an early age, they showed great maturity and sensitivity that formed the basis for the synergistic relationships we now share.

Unlike the planned and thoughtful interdisciplinary graduate studies program that Paul had designed to carry him into a scholarly life, my "advanced" studies, just as they are for many women, were patched together out of necessity, contingency, and a good bit of luck. Completing my doctorate, I was appointed as an assistant professor at the University of Utah when I was emerging from middle age, about twenty years behind my peers.

In the first part of my life, I had suffered through what Conesa describes as the "Singularization of Language," language that is "funneled" or restricted in meaning and leads to "false TEXT, false institutions, false meanings, false ideologies, and a host of materialistic narcotics." More importantly, it is language separated from its "telluric" origin. I spent my youth during World War II bombarded by war propaganda that, unfortunately, continues to this day. During my teaching I was required to write behavioral objectives. Although I resented reducing learning to a series of facts and behaviors that could be measured, I gave the process considerable thought and designed outcomes that would address affective and conceptual learning. Throughout my entire life I had been deluged with the distorted language of war and consumerism. As I entered graduate studies, the rhetoric, although idealistic, brought hope for peace and harmony in the world, reform to education, and a suggestion of sustainable populations and livelihoods.

The 60s revolution came to Utah in the early 70s as disaffected high school students stressed the patience of traditional schools. Paulo Freire's *Pedagogy of the Oppressed*, Ivan Illich's texts on social ecology, Edward Abbey's opus, *Desert Solitaire*, a guide to ecological ethics, John Dewey's philosophy, along with an array of books on humanistic education and self-actualizing psychology, helped me form my own brand of educational reform. I once more abandoned the safety of traditional education as I instituted alternative education programs in high schools for youth suffering from what Conesa terms *Lebensneid*, a feeling of being alienated from and misunderstood by the dominant culture. Together with dedicated alternative teachers, we created "generative thematic" curriculums, modeling Freire's methods, which immersed students in community and nature-based learning.

I developed a field course in environmental education taught each spring and environmental studies seminars offered each quarter for graduate students, many of them teachers in alternative programs. Summer courses included extended ecological and cultural field studies in such places as the Navajo Reservation, the canyons and rivers of Southern Utah, Teton National Park, and Alaska.

The deep ecology movement arrived on the scene as described by Conesa, imploring us to live as if "Nature mattered." At a seminar in Denver I met, among others, Bill Duvall, one of Conesa's teachers, and Dolores LaChapelle, a significant contributor to the movement who became a friend. She visited my home and classes every February when she joined her powder skiing associates at Alta and offered workshops on deep ecology for my students.

At the fairgrounds in Salt Lake City in a summer thunderstorm, I sat under an awning in the company of longhaired, damp smelling, Earth First advocates listening to the eco-poet Gary Snyder. I hesitated officially joining the group since I could not advocate some of their tactics. However, I became an activist and testified tirelessly on behalf of wilderness preservation. I invited Edward Abbey, anarchist and guru, to speak at the University on behalf of Utah wilderness and take part in a writing workshop in Arches National Parks, which he called "On the Rocks." A hero to many, he grounded ecological ethics in the red rock landscape. He clarified the meaning of true altruism, the generosity of spirit that motivates humans to defend wildness, the land and its non human creatures who cannot speak for themselves

To Conesa's rhetorical question, "Is ecopsychological education possible?" my answer agrees with his: Yes! But only with great effort on the part of teachers and cooperation from communities and traditional educators. "Alternative" programs for nontraditional students and wilderness experiences for high-risk youth are offered throughout the world today. The ecopsychological assumption is that if one begins with a safe and supportive milieu grounded in nature, the young person is then enabled to internalize his/her behaviors and build responsibility to others. But such programs are not usually available for the children of the poor. In polluted inner city environments or in desertified rural areas where people are starving or struggling for their own safety and energy for life, they are incapable of thinking of possibilities for a more equitable life for all creatures.

Among the texts chosen for my environmental field studies courses, seminars, and workshops were Paul Shepard's *Thinking Animals, The Tender Carnivore and the Sacred Game,* and *Nature and Madness.* I had ordered books from him for my courses several times. Having never met him I was surprised when in the winter of 1985 he wrote me a note from his home in Claremont, California, where he held an endowed chair in Human Ecology and Natural Philosophy at Pitzer College, one of the Claremont Colleges. He wondered if, on a stop-over in Salt Lake City on his way to a speaking engagement, I might meet him for lunch at the airport. At the time, we were reading *Nature and Madness* as the text for the seminar that would meet the evening before his scheduled arrival. I asked if for a small stipend he would come in one day early and speak to my class. He agreed.

This was our first meeting and the beginning of our life partnership that took me into yet another unexpected adventure of life. Older and nearing retirement, we planned to make these years meaningful. We phased out of our university positions and built a small cabin in the Hoback Basin in Wyoming where we hoped to spend most of our time writing and living close to the wild. As things turned out, we had only a decade together, abbreviated in time but rich in content.

Through those busy years I was privileged to observe the assiduous dedication of a visionary at his life work. His aim since writing his first book *Man in the Landscape* had never faltered. He was steadfastly devoted to uncovering the roots of our ecological madness. At base he, like Conesa, reviled ideological thinking and language that distorted the truth and aimed at mindless consumption. He believed that we are still genetically hunters and foragers and most content and harmonious when living close to nature. Paul would have taken seriously Jorge Conesa-Sevilla's proposals to mend our ways and live sane and sustainable lives. He would also have supported whole-heartedly Conesa's dedication to tracking and the textured meanings it holds. In a sense Paul followed a cynegetic method of research, much as Conesa tracks.

Moving into retirement and a new marriage with Paul was a joyous passing but not without difficulties. Energy, safety, and possibilities abounded, but firm matricial bonds to students and family had to be loosened in order for us to deepen our relationship. Students and children must have felt abandoned as we began extensive travels, mostly seeking evidence of our primal companion, the bear. I owe a debt of gratitude to Paul Shepard, who was the greatest teacher I've ever encountered. He taught not by rhetoric or exhortation but by example, patience, and diligence to his vision. One of his goals was to ask the right questions. He hoped others would seek answers. I sense similar dedication and vision in Jorge Conesa-Sevilla, who has eloquently met Paul's challenge and through his writing, work and teaching is helping us to achieve sanity, balance and harmony in our lives.

Since Paul's death, while editing his last books and archives, I have been privileged to revisit his ideas and trace the paths he followed. Everything I write since then is over-laid with his insights. Death disrupts and threatens matricial love bonds but doesn't destroy them. At such times we reach into another aspect of our being, the spiritual realm, about which Conesa writes as he completes his guide for mindful living. Faith in the fundamental wisdom of the earth and its cyclic processes of life and death provides the spiritual foundation of our life on earth. Death, that mysterious realm that cannot be known for certain by the living, is an aspect of our lives that must be accepted as we tend to our biophysical and ecopsychological needs. When energy fails and safety is threatened, when possibilities fade, the primal spiritual bond with the earth is our life-line until circumstances once more hold promise for this world or for what lies beyond.

A few days before Paul slipped into a coma, and ultimately into a peaceful death, he told me that the world suddenly appeared very different to him. He seemed to be in-between two states of being laced "into each other like fingers of clasped hands." Naively curious, I asked if he could tell me a little of what he saw, how he felt. He smiled patiently and said, "It is not anything I can describe, Flossie, but it's very interesting."

From my cabin window in early summer each year, I watch the birth of baby antelope. The fall to the ground from the mother's standing position forces their first breath. Within a short time, the fawn is standing and nursing. I watch the process for the next days marveling at the wonderful adaptations of these creatures: the wariness of the mother, their color and behavior, their perfect fit with the habitat where they evolved. Their instinctual knowledge, always available, shows me what we have lost, and what we "thinking animals" might hope to recover. (2984)

Florence R. Shepard
Professor Emerita
The Hoback Basin
Bondurant, Wyoming
USA

Preface

The future of our planet is too serious a matter to be left strictly to scientists and economists. Everyone has to participate in the discussion of environmental policies, which means that everyone should have at least a rudimentary understanding of how our planet maintains the conditions that allow us to prosper.

—S. George Philander

Ultimate Force Psychology: Ecopsychology

Pick up any book about psychology, from any area in psychology, written in the last one hundred years and it is very doubtful that you will find a significant number of references to *ecopsychology*. Even when this newly coined term is not directly used, the subject that it treats and addresses, *human estrangement and alienation from nature and its consequences to biospheric stability or self-health and happiness*, is not a major topic in orthodox, mainstream psychology. The absence of these insights and criticisms in mainstream psychology can be partly attributed to the narrow path[1] that western psychology has taken since the 1870's or so. This narrow path, in my view, has prevented deep ecological and/or ecopsychological ideas from becoming the overriding "ultimate force" psychological paradigm.

What the curious and unbiased reader will discover is that psychology's brief history shows the following:

1) In an insecure manner, psychologists over-scientized, oversimplified, or ignored human mentality, wellness, or illness.[2]
2) Psychology exaggerated the ill effects of Id processes without grounding the Id in more benign and necessary natural processes—in an *Ecopsychological Unconscious.*[3]
3) Psychology Christianized human psychology with idiosyncratic prejudice (e.g., eugenics) and then evangelized its bad science as true and unbiased. Its founders often mixed personal religious aims with their "science," diminishing generic spirituality at the detriment of good science and better religion.

4) Psychology's humanistic-existential side ignored, minimized, and replaced the real evolutionary processes of a natural world on human intelligence and emotions with surface "feel good" philosophy—"going back to an insane society" instead of "going back to the woods" counseling.

5) Psychology eagerly (given #1) assimilated information processing theory depreciating an evaluative and universal-totemic, mythical ape into a cold informational processing machine. To be compared to a machine instead of to an intelligent wolf is demeaning to human intelligence and wishful-thinking AI nerdy fantasies.

6) Psychology conveniently mistook the most profound and spiritual aspects of human-nature deep ecological connections for simplistic behavioral adaptations that could be studied while ignoring the "black box" of an embedded and naturally moral intellect.

7) Some psychologists took Environmental Psychology to be Deep Ecology or Ecopsychology, and good for the planet—*good* holistically so. They made a mistake.

8) Psychology focused its endeavors on "elephant anatomical parts," such as intelligence, memory, human development and personality, without ever thinking about these parts as belonging to a living planet—as the elephant having walked in the savannahs to begin with. Human beings walked in savannahs, let's start here, in a real context.

9) Given the fact that most societies are described as "insane" by a consensus of natural-peoples who are still impacted by a more natural biosemiosis, psychology itself has not bothered to follow up on their observations while seeking cures.

10) Psychology, much like Anthropology, has given up on the notion of a universal *normative psychology* grounded in the insights provided by natural existence as some sort of obscene prescription, mostly because its western arrogance maintains an insular and relativistic view of mental health.

11) Psychology thought and still thinks within the limited box of the status quo, it serves the status quo, it is economically dependent on the status quo.

The apologists for the above list of psychological historical emphases, criticisms, and ensuing sciences would argue that this is the natural progression found in many scientific fields or that "we are no different than anybody else." The fact that this argument is still made even when "psychology" continues to lack an overriding paradigm that is based not on idiosyncratic hyper-humanistic ideas or plastic computing devices but on natural history, suggests that there are far too many apologists or antiquarians and fewer evolutionary realists in the field. More precisely and less contestable, a planet that dies at the hands of a misguided or arrogant ape deserves a more credible effort from Psychology, and Psychology is obligated to produce a Best, or Ultimate Ecopsychology.

That over-culturized, anthropocentric psychology is partly responsible for this decay and demise should be sobering to any future student of psychology. The simple outcome of this new learning should be: *Humanity is but a mere appendage to natural processes. Humanity, now and in the past, being an appendage to LIFE as opposed to its human arbitrary and decontextualized intellectual designing force,*[4] *needs to be described and treated from a natural holistic perspective.* On the other hand, if the direction that humanity takes is one where LIFE, its totality, is supplanted by arbitrary and decontextualized intellectual definitions, then the future will be very different from the past, or as a correcting force, barbarians would enter the historical scene yet again, to undue the superfluous *text*.

The contemporary student of psychology, at least the student who feels deeply the *ecocentric calling*, must guide his/her studies and operate under revised evolutionary theory and accept the reasonable arguments and confirmable facts that are next summed up. In Stephen Jay Gould's words:

> Humans are not the end result of predictable evolutionary progress, but rather a fortuitous cosmic afterthought, a tiny little twig on the enormously arborescent bush of life, which, if replanted from seed, would almost surely not grow this twig again, or perhaps any twig with any property that we would care to call consciousness.

And if the above learning outcome is too long, then we could try a shorter one, also by Stephen Jay Gould, "The course of evolution is only the summation of fortuitous contingencies, not a pathway with predictable directions." Nevertheless, here we are, absolutely creating ecological mayhem. Thus the apes who moralize, and because they do, are absolutely responsible for what they do to the planet, should feel guilty and then rectify their transgressions and infantile regressions.

To be fair, Psychology, like any other agglomeration of fields, is affected by and moves along the path laid down by networking obligations, deference to dying or obsolete leaders, factions, and preferred "mini-paradigms."[5] To continue to be fair, because "psychology" is not unique in this, there is an invested interest in publishing certain ideas and not others, in training (cloning) graduate students to be like their mentors and not somebody else, and in investing money only in "momentum science," or in "momentum therapy."[6] Only in transpersonal psychology is there an ecopsychological focus and the genuine desire to expand its aims.

But for all the other reasons, a book such as this is not only subversive, but also necessary. It is subversive to the extent that its ideas overlap those of the subversive science, Ecology, and because it aligns itself with *normative psychology*—it aims, unapologetically and with science, to say something final and general about the human condition. Simply, in the midst of human-made planetary catastrophes, the often meaningless term "psychology" should be completely erased and replaced with Ecopsychology. Introducing "psychology as if" or "as it is" without an ongoing ecopsychological criticism is missguided at least, irresponsible at worst.

A Rose Has Thorns

A lot of the chapters in this book are highly critical of mainstream psychology, including this preface. But I prefer that the student or psychologist reading it see this criticism as an act of "tough love," as an example of how the sciences keep checks on themselves, at least. Chapters seven and eight are particularly stinging to our collective professional ego. As a scientist and psychologist, I have heard and defended similar or worst criticisms from laypersons and professionals in other fields as well. So I know how some of my words, phrases, and mortifying puns must feel at the end of your optic nerves and other neuronal pathways. I cannot be, however, apologetic. When an entire planet is at stake and we know who the criminals are—what acts are criminal—anybody assisting the criminal is an accomplice. I don't want to be an accomplice anymore and I don't think you do either.

Thus, this is a necessary book for the same reasons that it is subversive, a wonderful tautology. It aims at informing the denizen of struggling or dying "mini-paradigms" in psychology and in asking them to reconsider their often barren fruits in the presence of clear and unarguable environmental catastrophes, many of which can be traced to human beings who no longer bond 24-7 with a larger matrix of LIFE. The sentence, "I am doing basic research," cannot be accepted as an excuse or cop-out any longer when the world is going to pieces. If human-Nature estrangement or alienation continues at the present pace, if the deterioration of large and small ecosystems continues at the present pace, then it is very doubtful that there will be anybody left to read close-ended, or otherwise decontextualized "basic" psychological research.

This is a necessary book, along with other more important ecopsychology texts (see inclusive bibliographies), because time is simply running out. Psychology can ill afford posturing itself as a valid agglomeration of important fields if it does not wholeheartedly join other natural, environmental, ecological, and evolutionary sciences in rescuing what's left of the natural world, natural psychology, and in being a vociferous activist force against political and social trends that wish to ignore these ills. It would be almost criminal not to do so. Applied ecopsychology and activism must lead the way.

This book is structured as a revisiting of semiotic, biosemiotic, and ecopsychological articles already published with further explanations and clarifications. These writings were conceived and written as a sequence dovetailing ideas and hoping that in the future, I could present them under one book title. That time has arrived.

For example, in trying to illustrate the seriousness of the problem we are all facing, I conclude this preface with a "fictional" case study: *Meet Heinz Droz*. It might be helpful to have an impressionistic description, even if it is not all inclusive of nature-estrangement (ecopsychological estrangement) or nature-alienation (ecopsychological alienation), before we propose additional arguments in subsequent chapters. I will also continue referring to this case study throughout the book while I make these points. If the reader finds that "Meet Heinz Droz . . ." describes a social and psychological reality that has to be met by all of us, then he/she will discover additional, similar insight in successive chapters.

Adhering to the authentic dialectical, learning-teaching principle that students should be presented with original scholarly materials rather than study oversimplified versions of the same text, most chapters are structured around original articles. In order to facilitate reading and understanding, I often italicize key terms and material that advances important recurring points. The rest of the book is organized as follows. *Chapter One* starts out with basic ecopsychological definitions and then revisits Semiotic Matrix Theory (SMT) as a biosemiotic paradigm from which to study ecopsychological problems and to be used as an interdisciplinary tool to study *signification* in general. The terminology presented in Chapter One will be employed in subsequent chapters as well. *Chapter Two* introduces the problem of singularized language—*bad text*, and how this relates to ecopsychological illness. In addition to SMT, the problem of the singularization of language and its deconstruction in ecopsychological therapy is core to this book. *Chapter Three* is an application of both SMT and singularization to biosemiotics proper dealing with the problem of *passing* (umwelten—reality assimilation, accommodation, and re-structuring). It is perhaps the most intellectually demanding chapter and essay. *Chapter Four* is the more extended version of "Meet Heinz Droz . . ." while making additional observations of these problems plus identifying new ones—the role that organized religion plays in *ecopsychological becoming*. *Chapter Five* introduces tracking as an ecopsychological and transpersonal practice. *Chapter Six* is devoted to educators and presents an integration of Paul Shepard's and Maria Montessori's ideas of a nature-based education. Additionally, this chapter presents and elaborates ideas in ecopsychological education from an entrepreneurial and practical perspective. *Chapter Seven* is a short presentation of Deep Ecology and extends the definitions and descriptions of ecopsychology briefly presented in Chapter One, but now in the context of its parent philosophy. *Chapter Eight* introduces the central role of dreaming and specifically of lucid or shamanic dreaming as part of biosemiotic-totemic human *function circles* where ecopsychological practice, aesthetics, and dreaming are interactive forces contributing to *ecopsychological individuation*, *becoming* or *unfolding*. *Chapter Nine* presents a student's personal experience as a Willing Worker on Organic Farms (WWOOF). *Chapter Ten* is the conclusion of this work as a reiteration of all the chapters and also a revisiting of the role that organized religion MUST PLAY in order to contribute to complete spirituality and individuation. Because these chapters are highly modular and can be read almost independently of one another, I have not included an index. I have added plenty of appendices, which I value more than indices. Apropos, materials that relate to but do not quite fit into previous chapters (philosophical examinations of ecocentrism, practical exercises, summaries, or the application of Ecopsychology) are placed at the end as indexes.

Meet Heinz Droz

I wrote about the "fictional" character Heinz Droz as a shorthand profile, after attempting to deal with issues of ecopsychological estrangement or alienation and while trying to convey the urgency of what I see are the root causes of many of the environmental and social challenges we are facing. Being a shorthand description, therefore, it is not meant to be inclusive of the traits and behaviors we associate with ecopsychological estrangement or alienation. Neither does the description address specific and technical challenges that ecopsychology as counseling or therapy has to overcome in order to be admitted into the orthodoxy of grand psychology. Rather, our impressionistic case study is aimed at looking into a mirror that more or less describes our condition of nature estrangement or alienation.

For now, the reader should perhaps "meet" Heinz Droz as a case study, unrelated to any other considerations and see whether his condition merits further explanation, generates questions, identifies personal trends, and produces a vital existential resonance in need of addressing. If Heinz Droz proves to be an alien caricature, a person whom we cannot recognize, then perhaps you as a reader are ecopsychologically better off than the average "Joe," or in our case, "Heinz" or "Heidi."

Finally, "Meet Heinz Droz . . ." anticipates core aspects of personal responsibility, social and political activism, and of *deliberate action* identified in the Deep Ecology movement.

Meet Heinz Droz: An All-Too-Real "Fictional" Case Study of Ecopsychological Alienation and Singularization[7]

Key terms: *Ecopsychology, ecopsychological alienation, ecopsychological estrangement, Nature estrangement, Nature dissociation, Umwelten, Nature reality therapists, LIFE interruptible and unintegratable, funneled-semiosis, telluric connection, Estranged Labour, Commodity Fetishism.*

Abstract

The fictional character "Heinz Droz" is used as a mirror that reflects, more or less, depending on our unique existential situation, the *ecopsychological alienation* and *singularized* semiotic sub-realities of the industrialized man and woman. Purposely described as a fictional character, nevertheless, Heinz Droz stands for an easily confirmable and almost inescapable reality made worse by self-denial, materialistic, consumer-oriented, pernicious, spirit-empty, and pervasive *umwelten*. Successful ecopsychological therapy or counseling includes the clarity of having understood self-denial for what it does: over-protects the Ego and prevents it from maturing. An ecopsychologically successful therapy or counseling goes beyond that: it contradicts, critiques, challenges, and reforms the orthodoxy of and the typical assumptions of both clients and therapists. Ecopsychologically successful practices are eco-centric, cultural transcending, about social activism, about Paleo-anthropology, about community reformism and deliberate peaceful resistance against seemingly impossible societal odds. These progressive, communal, and self-informing practices are also Deep Ecological. Ecopsychological practice is fighting sub-realities with new and old mythologies. But without meeting Heinz Droz, and seeing "him" as a fatality and a caricature of ecopsychological alienation, our therapy cannot commence.

> "My daughter once asked me if I was alive when the world was black and white, because everything she saw that was old on TV was black and white."
>
> —Attributed to Chuck Close by Richard Kehl, *Breathing on Your Own*

Introduction

As in the film *Pleasantville*, most *Nature reality therapists* who exercise the practice of Ecopsychology believe themselves to be painting the world back to its original pristine rainbow conditions starting with human physiology and its spirit. When our son Jordi was six or seven, he asked us a question very similar to the opening quote attributed to Chuck Close: "Were you guys alive in the black and white days—when the world was black and white?" My answer today would be that the world is still "black and white" and that our planetary village and biosphere is still a *Pleasantville* that has yet to turn into colors.

For most of the planet, and increasingly so, it is a perpetual psychological winter without red fall colors, the radiant yellow sun of August, or the green energy of spring.

It is not easy to exist, day-to-day, under these clinical conditions or with full awareness that a malignant and cancerous psychological evil permeates the very reality one is a citizen and product of. Cynicism, depression, apathy, anger, anguish, are some of the dark cognitive states and emotions that the therapist, if he/she is, ecopsychologically speaking, fully coherent and deliberate about addressing the illnesses of *Nature estrangement* or dissociation,[8] is apt to encounter or experience. This angst is the price many others and we pay for such awareness.

"Meet Heinz Droz"[9] was conceived as an exercise in ecopsychological awakening. In addition to cajoling, caressing, insinuating, reasoning, confronting, embracing and tracking, this ecopsychologist at least finds it necessary to construct a mirror whose reflection may be more revealing, more convincing, and more constructive to the task of assailing self-denial. It is also my exercise in deliberate harassing.

Because I am now writing in Switzerland, the character is named Heinz Droz. But "he" could be man or woman, Swiss or Congolese. "He" could be Joe Smith or Juan Robótico or Darth Vadar. "He" stands as the condition of a pervasive, easily recognizable malignant and cancerous psychological deterioration waiting to be accepted or treated by most psychologists, counselors, or psychiatrists.

Meet Heinz Droz: Narration, Biography and Eulogy

Heinz Droz *sub-exists* much like the domesticated animals he keeps in bondage for pleasure or food, not recognizing that he is one of them, also in chains (Shepard, 1982). Therefore, he is incapable of true compassion for himself or for the beasts he tortures because this type of inclusive compassion would require a formidable look from without, from outside his senseless condition. Additionally, and because his bondage does not bother him or he is unaware of it, he fails to recognize political or societal dissent or revolutions in oppressed peoples who have such insight: he penalizes their plight and ridicules their courage. The right to dissent or to revolt, peacefully or with blood, against the cancerous, corporate, gluttonous, materialistic ethos seems to him the exclusive enterprise of the hysterical downtrodden (he is not) or the enterprise of some *dinosauric* historical ancestor, "the patriot". Finally, Droz refuses to take responsibility for his freedom, or to be responsible for anything worthwhile and *Good*. True rebellion, righteous rebellion, is seen, alternatively, as bad form, a vice, or only to be employed as a means to insure that the easy and disposable life he is addicted to continues. An animal zoo, he is anxious about the very idea of a cage's door opening for good. He will bite off the very hand of the liberator! Plenty of food and much diversion are nevertheless accepted.

Like in the movie *Groundhog Day*, Droz wakes up each day to the same surreal and alienated life, parrots the expected script and meaningless text, moves from one thermostatically stable environment to another, pushing buttons, moving levers, and punching cards. He is now thoroughly transformed into a wheeled cyborg, half human—half car, for whom walking itself is seen as a form of rebellion, dissent, or a deviant act he won't tolerate.

In a 24-hour cycle, a 7-day period, month after month, year after year passing through developmentally significant periods, Mr. Droz spends very little time outdoors. For the many Drozes of the world, going "outdoors" signifies *building hopping*, or car-to-bulding-to-bus-to-plane-to-Ipod hopping. He successfully tunes out the rigors of LIFE, the natural tempo of LIFE, the full-fledged atmospherics of LIFE, and the blood of LIFE. He has substituted physical risk with perpetual comfort, or with virtual or menial entertainment, addressing psychological ills with escapism amply provided for by a brainwashing society. Too tired from working in an undesirable workplace, and in Germany or Switzerland, forced to choose his professional future at a young and inexperienced age,[10] unprepared to do anything else, he escapes from one unsavory social condition to another seeking solace in family and destroying the idea of a larger planetary community.

Any morality or sense of duty that he might develop is a commitment to the survival of self or his immediate family or comes from traditional religion (Kohlberg's *Pre-Conventional* and *Conventional* levels, 1981). This restricted sense of duty may not recognize *ecopsychological estrangement* as a result of failing planetary interconnectedness, or if it does, ties it to some formula of eternal salvation that undermines scientific understanding. Without sharing or being an active ecological participant in a better planetary-communal vision for himself and for his family, society and the planet become his enemy. Without communal support, the necessary roots for revolt against the *status quo* are severed. The vision, assuming that he can glimpse it, is more than distant—it is a fantasy. In his case, this vision is seen cynically as science fiction created by some angry ecopsychologist in order to perturb his docile and imploded way of life.

He has substituted moral or righteous indignation with acting-out behavior, violence, passive aggression, incessant complaining, or insufferable whining. In fact, Heinz Droz's speech, no matter what other language he speaks in addition to Swiss French, is punctuated by a tendency, every other sentence, to self-pity and injured ego dramatis. When sober, the crescendo from incessant complaining to insufferable whining extends easily to projection, stereotype, and prejudice. The world is "wrong" because there are too many Turks, too many Italians, or too many Bosnians living and working where he is used to whining about every other thing.

However, there are escapes from these threats. The artificially enhanced, toxic, and distracting complexity of modern life provides ample and necessary opportunities to remain locked-up in its cancerous cocoon. Because modern life is artificially complex or downright meaningless, because it is also manufactured and serviced by others, because social sanctification is politically and economically advantageous to those few who control so much, Heinz is powerless to combat its combined onslaught. The democratic process means simply replacing one set of profit-driven variables and gluttonous representatives with another set of hungrier and more vicious ones, never achieving a revolutionary and medical ecological transformation that can lead to permanent healing. The patient, Heinz Droz, and the entire planet thus slowly bleed. To the extent that profit-driven policies (their economics and heartless bottom lines) and gluttonous representatives control the government machine, Heinz is, all alone, powerless and alienated. Whatever his outward expected behaviors, confident and in control, they are a coping hollow persona-cover of a psychological eunuch or fetal form curled up in a corner of a padded room, because these lack a true ecopsychological grounding.

Fundamentally, and we cannot blame him for this, Heinz lacks an understanding of how his own consciousness is affected by propaganda and ideology: BAD TEXT. He lacks an understanding of how language is crafted by others, of how technical jargons make many important facets of LIFE interruptible and *unintegratable* into a cohesive matrix that could inform in ecological and/or mythical terms. He talks into a cell phone hoping that his alienation will be relieved by a distant voice which is serviced via satellites or booster towers controlled by others—communication and meaning being a costly service. Language itself is fragmented and is the vehicle to talk about the million or so disruptive things that prevent him from integrating the wilder side of LIFE back into his existential equation. When language becomes a distraction, noise, or propaganda, a cost, it is no longer trusted as LOGOS; or even better, it ceases to be a communal function with NATURE and for the intrinsic "reasons" of NATURE.

Singularization as A Restrictive Semiosis

Elsewhere, I have written about the semiotic process I call *singularization* and described it as *funneled-semiosis* (Conesa-Sevilla, 2005). More specifically:

> . . . *singularization* implies a . . . narrowing down, or impoverishment of meaning because the object [natural] being designated no longer exists, or, more importantly, has lost its original *telluric connection,* and because the semiotic triad does not function in its original context [in pristine, natural conditions]. By losing its *telluric connection* I mean that its original denotative and connotative function as part of a hunter-forager and early sustenance agricultural ethos, or, its *hypological* and intra-psychic function[11] is no longer available to conscious mind.

To the extent that I still believe this to be the case, and to the extent that the loss of a *telluric connection* generates a new text that may be referred to as surreal or false, then the more false and surreal a culture is the more it will impact language detrimentally, arriving at not only a state of false consciousness, but at illness. Because the estrangement is away from an original natural dialectics, then ecopsychological well being must be studied semiotically, or biosemiotically as well. At the very least, the ecopsychological therapist or counselor must always be on the alert against using semiotically corrupted text and slipping it in as part of an agreed-upon cure. The ecopsychological therapist or counselor should never say, "Mr. Droz, take a drive to . . ." or "Take this little blue pill thrice a day," or "Get a hair cut and you will feel better."

It was Karl Marx who said, "Language comes into being, like consciousness, from the basic need, from the scantiest intercourse with other humans." Marx was not an ecologist, thus he could not extend his insight to an original and pristine mind in close dialectical exchanges with raw nature or derive from this insight a more encompassing philosophy leading to ecopsychology. Otherwise, Marx fails us, more often than not, like any other thinker who describes human activity anthropocentrically. Authentic language that signifies meaningfully and profoundly, has its origins in direct experiences,[12] and ideally, in experiences chosen by the individual to enhance LIFE and human development. To update Marx, if we can be so presumptuous, we must say that "Language comes into being," or at least it did in the beginning, ". . . like consciousness, from the basic need," *of a full-fledged immersion in a grander natural universe that included entire ecosystems and their mythical description when language, authentically, described an ecologically valid reality.*

Both capitalist and socialist philosophies often disappoint us by ending with a bottom line that excludes the WHOLE PLANET and with descriptions of language that arrive at the humanistic phrase "the needs and the wants of a human." In their exclusion of grander natural processes, in their assumption that humanity sits in a parapet above these processes ready to yield utilitarian bottom lines, both ideologies leave humanity's spirit thirsty and a planet in ruins.

As I said earlier, Mr. Droz's experience with TEXT, semiotically defined, is: *chaotic, fragmented, propagandistic, technically alien, created and served by others, and extant from a genuine dialectics of manual dexterity disciplined by patience, apprenticeship, or true craftsmanship in the service of LIFE.* To the extent that behavior, cognition, and language not only inform one another but are shaped to their mature and life-fulfilling forms by a cultural context, then an artificial and fragmented life leads to an artificial being who is fragile in his psychology and oblivious to LIFE's fundamental realities.

It is a much more complicated and dire problem than when Marx and Engels (1844) singled out *Estranged Labour* or the alienation of labor. My previous paragraph describes an extended and perpetual *being* condition *where the laborer can never escape his sub-existence, even when he is removed from the inhuman conditions of repetitive and meaningless labor. The entire horizon of Droz's existence is dominated by false consciousness created by false TEXT (propaganda), false institutions, false meanings, false ideologies, and a host of materialistic narcotics.* Droz is also provided with a false sense of empowerment, an earned and disposable income (and credit as a new form of usury), that allows him to continue on with his slumber from one purchase to another, from one toy to the next.[13] This restricted sense of freedom, *consumer freedom,* [14] cannot be underestimated by the ecopsychologist because the practice taps into earlier juvenile wish-fulfillment trends assisting a pernicious regression.

Marx did reveal a significant element of an ecopsychological equation when he wrote:

> To say that man's physical and mental life is linked to nature simply means that nature is linked to itself, for man is a part of nature.
>
> Estranged labour not only (1) estranges nature from man and (2) estranges man from himself, from his own function, from his vital activity; because of this, it also estranges man from his species. It turns his species-life into a means for his individual life. Firstly, it estranges species-life and individual life, and, secondly, it turns the latter, in its abstract form, into the purpose of the former, also in its abstract and estranged form.
>
> For in the first place labour, life activity, productive life itself, appears to man only as a means for the satisfaction of a need, the need to preserve physical existence. But productive life is species-life. It is life-producing life. The whole character of a species, its species-character, resides in the nature of its life activity, and free conscious activity constitutes the species-character of man. Life appears only as a means of life.
>
> The animal is immediately one with its life activity. It is not distinct from that activity; it is that activity. Man makes his life activity itself an object of his will and consciousness. He has conscious life activity. It is not a determination with which he directly merges. Conscious life activity directly distinguishes man from animal life activity.

I would argue that the human animal, regardless of the fact that he could make "his life activity an object of his will and consciousness," is equally "immediately one with its life activity" in the same manner and to the same degree that other animals experience this intimacy. If this intimacy were not possible or frequent it would not be reflected, strongly so, in naturalism, animism, Taoism, Shinto, or even Zen Buddhism. If this intimacy did not exist, we could not explain the common feeling of connection obtained while in nature, or after having switched to activities that increase the awareness of new body routines, the feeling that the person is "one with the task," or better, "one with the task of living."

Furthermore, picking up on the last two sentences, and developing Marx's logic a bit further, then one assumes with other ecopsychologist writers that if a human "has conscious life activity" and this awareness originates in a general and fundamental animal ecopsychological intimacy where the non-human animal "is immediately one with its life activity," then that phylogenic connection can be resuscitated. The fact is, according to Marx, that "Man makes his life activity itself an object of his will and consciousness," and thus makes semiotics a significant avenue for this recovery. Understanding and then challenging how language is used and abused against us paves the way for ecopsychological insight. Understanding how language interacts cognitively with the whole of a person and how a person is ecopsychologically changed by it, is an ecosemiotic enterprise. In the drudgery of an ill wanted or hated job, the internal track is definitely not happy. Or this internal text track supposes, rationalizes, and then resolves its *cognitive dissonance* with palatable explanations that never make the task any less poisonous to one's soul. The drudgery of a job that runs counter to Buddhism's "right action" or "right livelihood," could undermine humanity itself where the worker finally becomes the thoughtless and joyless drone.

To reiterate and sum up, to even say that Droz employs a *feral text* is to be kind and generous. The text is thoroughly fictional, thoroughly synthetic, and most of the time, animated by infantile wanting that never ceases and for which a plethora of corporations aim to satisfy it for profit.

Finally, in the semiotic sphere of Mr. Droz there is no *biosemiosis*, no room or time to interpret *natural signs* so that these can inform him of LIFE's processes (Conesa-Sevilla 2005). Imagine that all we know about LIFE came from cartoon TEXT. How could one go from this reality to a reality of public television, A&E docu-dramas, and other quality TV TEXT? Imagine further that ALL TEXT is TV TEXT or TEXT that comes from an artificial and tautologically surreal culture that, more and more, is losing its grip because it is no longer grounded in raw nature. What is the ecosemiotic condition of the lied-to ape? Could this condition lead to illness? If so, what type of illness?

The condition, to amalgamate meanings, is one of: LIFE interrupted and *unintegratable*, funneled-semiosis, lost telluric connections, estranged labour at the very least, continued commodity fetishism, spiritual pauperism, and over-extended juvenile delinquency in the absence of going hunting to feed the group who prays, sings, or plays under the oak tree.

In addition to a mass phenomenon and problem of *false consciousness* we might suppose that the deteriorating text, as George Orwell observed fictionally,[15] is ultimately a problem of the *unconscious* as well:

The stuff that was coming out of him consisted of words, but it was not speech in the true sense: it was a noise uttered in unconsciousness, like the quacking of a duck.

Ecopsychologist Theordore Roszak (2001) places a great deal of confidence in an individual's[16] *ecological unconscious* that could save humankind if only we can tap into its telluric, primal, and authentic source. But if the psychological spring source turns out to be the muck where ducks wallow, then there is no hope for Heinz Droz. Even orthodox psychology admits that some psyches may not be salvageable and that it might be best to form anew an *ecological unconscious* with oncoming generations of receptive youth. No matter, the foes produced by ecopsychological estrangement or alienation are not new or solely produced by insipid suburbia, busy commercialization, or blaring industrialization. In a true ecopsychological sense, the *unsalvageable* are already institutionalized and sequestered away in suburbia and cities and shall remain there until they die another thousand little deaths.

It is not a new illness, and by different names, for at least 9,000 years, it has been treated with *actions*: simplicity, frugality, discipline, clarity, silence, physical activity, walking more, singing more, devouring less, and recognizing idle divertimentos as the soundtrack to a mad piper who takes you to the river, not to appease your thirst, but to drown you.

Heinz Droz Could Rebel

Heinz Droz can rebel without thinking he is rebelling, at least at first. That is, Droz can recognize that some elements of culture, the social situation he finds himself in, are not always conducive to happiness or even healthy. Cultural relativism can no longer be used as a valid excuse for prolonging his insanity. *Normative psychology*, in our case, ecopsychologically testable truths, must be paid attention to. However, he does not have to believe in the cynical or the optimist ecopsychologist before he starts doing something that can immediately address his sense of frustration and forlornness. A more radical approach: Return to the Wild by whatever means necessary, including discarding the ecopsychologist who talked you into embracing wilderness. Short of living "with the red of blood in teeth and claw," there is a large continuum of "back to the wild" scenarios that could fit almost any presently deformed "civilized" living style, that can substitute for it in a long-lasting and meaningful way.

He can walk, bicycle or take a bus. He can try to identify all the birds and plants he sees no matter how small and humble, and learn something about their niche needs. He can walk more often without thinking that walking is a socially deviant action with lewd movements akin to dancing the *Lambada*. He can imagine the benefits of recycling and composting without undue mental effort. He can think seriously about animal bondage and how nutrition, honor, and compassion are diminished or eradicated by it in his own body and soul. If bold, he can hunt to survive or raise "happy, free range chickens" and learn to kill them for communion with compassion and gratitude.

Droz could also resist the easy answers and deals that might buy him some short-lived convenience or "happiness." He decides never to open errant emails with alluring subject lines that pledge "Fuller and harder erections," "Strike it rich," "Guaranteed credit card approval," "One Minute Millionaire," "Free Computers," or "Our store is your cure all." In fact, he pitches all sales pitches and, deliberately, self-imposes frugality by purging consumerism as a way of life.

In terms of his chosen profession, he must think twice or thrice about sacrificing a quality of life for its hypnotic tinsel quanta. He must understand that a collector hoards objects under the guise of a rationalized pretense and that hoarding behavior is not normal. Whether Droz is a capitalistic fellow by nature or by indoctrination, he is on the mend when he accepts Marx's dictum that *a productive life is* "life-producing life."

All of these actions, or any other of Droz's actions that foster the integration of LIFE, have something in common. They are *actions*, not idle, self-defeating, pessimistic thoughts, or empty, wishful or confused text. They are also *deliberate*.

In the ecopsychological awakening phase, Heinz Droz takes his clothes off and looks at an animal body and understands that it is an ANIMAL BODY. He knows that his thoughts were once *correctly and authentically singularized* on only one subject and ensuing text that spoke of a *telluric connection* and of a seamless and *integratable* LIFE. After this insight, he ACTS to correct his descent into madness. He 'walks' the real verbs, he is modified by life-giving adjectives, and begins using an appropriate and complex pronoun: Me-Nature—probably, the only pronoun that counts.

> What do you seek, My Countrymen?
> Do you desire that I build for
> You gorgeous palaces, decorated
> With words of empty meaning, or
> Temples roofed with dreams? Or
> Do you command me to destroy what
> The liars and tyrants have built?

Kahlil Gibran, *My Countrymen, Book Four*, (1951: 135)

Preface References

Conesa-Sevilla, J. (2005). The singularization of reality: Implications of a synnomic evolution of language to semiotics, biosemiotics, and ecopsychology. *GATHERINGS: Journal of the International Community for Ecopsychology.* (http://www.ecopsychology.org/journal/ezine/gatherings.html)

Kehl, R. (2001) Breathing on your own: quotations for independent thinkers. Seattle, WA: Darling & Company

Kohlberg, L. (1981). *Philosophy of Moral Development.* New York: Harper and Row.

Marx, K. (1844). Economic and Philosophic Manuscripts.

Olson, S. (1940-1943) *Interval.* America Out of Doors.

Shepard, P. (1982). *Nature and madness.* San Francisco: Sierra Club.

Stetson, L. (1994). *The wild Muir: twenty-two of John Muir's greatest adventures.* California: Yosemite Association, Yosemite National Park.

Additional Ecopsychological Commentary by John Muir, Sigurd Olson, and Aldo Leopold:

". . . I know that our bodies were made to thrive only in pure air, and the scenes in which pure air is found. If the death exhalations that brood the broad towns in which we so fondly compact ourselves were made visible, we should flee as from a plague. All are more or less sick; there is not a perfectly sane man in San Francisco . . . . Go now and then for fresh life—if most of humanity must go through this town stage of development—just as divers hold their breath and come ever and anon to the surface to breathe . . . Go whether or not you have faith . . . from parties, if you must be social, to go to the snow-flowers in winter, to sun-flowers in summer . . . Anyway, go up and away for life; be fleet! . . . When I first came down to the city from my mountain home, I beagn to wither, and wish instinctively for the vital woods and high sky." [J.M.]

"I had been walking along the Moose Lake road for an hour, an hour of dodging the great logging trucks on the way to the camps south of town. Time and again, I had been forced to walk in the soft snow of the shoulder until at last, I gave up entirely trying to follow the open road itself. Each time a truck roared by, the air was white with snow dust and putrid with the smell of burned gasoline and oil. No sooner had I recovered my equilibrium than another would come hurtling down the highway and I began to despair of knowing a single undisturbed moment or enjoying at all what I had really come to see and hear." [S.F.O]

"A man may not care for golf and still be human, but the man who does not like to see, hunt, photograph, or otherwise outwit birds or animals is hardly normal. He is supercivilized, and I for one do not know how to deal with him. Babes do not tremble when they are shown a golf ball, but I should not like to own the boy whose hair does not lift his hat when he sees his first deer." [A.L.]

Chapter One

Defining Ecopsychology and Semiotic Matrix Theory

Eventually night falls, the eagles disappear and the hedgehog . . . leaves the river and walks up the side of the mountain, as confident in his spines as any warrior with his shield in Sparta or in Corinth; and suddenly he crosses the border, the line that separates the earth and the grass from the new road; with one step he enters your time and mine, and since his dictionary of the universe has not been corrected or updated in the last seven thousand years, he does not recognize the lights of our car, and does not even realize that he is going to die.

—Joseba Irazu Garmendia, a.k.a Bernardo Atxaga, Trikuarena (The Hedgehog)[17]

Early on in the formulation of Semiotic Matrix Theory (SMT)[18] I was, alternatively, making causal bridges and connections to ontology, ecopsychology, and Deep Ecology. When I read back what I wrote in 1998 and what has developed in theory and by empirical efforts to be a *biosemiotic consilience theory*, I am encouraged that all these interlacing threads are twined even tighter under this title. With the clarity of hindsight it is now obvious that this should be the case. The connections were surely influenced by taking classes from Deep Ecologist William Devall in the late 1980's and soon after by reading Paul Shepard.

The unmistakable link, at least in my mind, between a biosemiosis that speaks of an existential connectivity at a fundamental level on the one hand, and the emergence of communicative intelligence that necessitates its natural history and premium telluric strata in order to produce authentic meaning on the other hand, has ceased to be merely an intellectual position to become *authenticated doings* as a way of ecopsychological practice.

But two foci, *biosemiosis as existential connectivity at a fundamental level and the emergence of communicative intelligence predicated in and in need of its natural*

history and premium telluric strata, when disrupted by bad text, tinsel economics,
and unsustainable societies create the Heinz Drozes of the world. Such is our thesis[19].
Garmendia's hedgehog and Droz's new existential condition are similar, if not the
same. It does not matter that the human Droz created the conditions for psychological
and social decontextualization that kills the hedgehog and makes Droz neurotic or
even psychotic. Droz is equally *deslumbrado* (blinded) by the nonsense products of
his false consciousness and text. More than a mere state of confusion prior to feeling
the impending crushing of the bones by fast approaching metal, the condition of
ecopsychological estrangement or *alienation* assumes that the injuries are internal,
psychological, and that they have already been inflicted and are bleeding in fluvial
torrents. Cars kill both humans and hedgehogs without discrimination.

But before we can continue making claims for or against ecopsychology, or for
or against SMT, it behooves us to familiarize ourselves with clear definitions and
descriptions of both. The next section provides a generic definition of Ecopsychology
that, I presume, would please most of its rare and brave practitioners.

Following that, I present excerpts about SMT published or presented elsewhere. Even
when abstract and theoretical, SMT should be thought of as the basic *ontological*
foundation underpinning ecopsychological claims that adhere to natural explanations
of human origins.

Ecopsychology

Ecopsychology is a relatively recent field within psychology[20] that employs empirical,
theoretical, and clinical means in order to understand and treat the rapidly changing
and recent[21] human condition and dysfunction based on a radical and continuing
estrangement from wild and natural spaces.

The degree and speed to which estrangement and alienation from wild and natural
places occurs are both accelerated by the unsustainable practices that reduce the actual
physical extension of the Wild or the Natural or by limiting access to its biosemiosis
(e.g., deforestation, unplanned urbanization, *mega-metropolization*, and, in general,
development that does not consider environmental consequences). In our last psychology,
ecopsychology, one must factor in a negative feedback loop where disappearing pristine
human habitat, sustainable physical space, *causes* mental illness or psychological
instability. That an unsustainable outer environment produces an unsustainable inner
one should not be a surprise to any psychologist. Simply put, *we have become aliens to
the very original matrix of life that gave, and continues to give, rise to our very BEING.*

Thus, ecopsychological endeavors, empirical, academic or clinical, are based on the
premise that a once widespread human-nature intimacy and link has been fragmented,

and in many cases severed (leading possibly to pathology—Paul Shepard, 1982) by decontextualized and meaningless work in commerce or industry, the insensitivity to life in large-scale agrobusiness, and living in chaotic urban existence. Neither modernity, nor progress, nor larger scale agriculture, nor even urban existences are themselves the causes of this estrangement. Rather, it is the thoughtless methods and the alienating culture that these can degenerate into that are responsible for human estrangement, and that Ecopsychology or *Green Psychology*[22] aims to address and/or correct. What begins with estrangement may lead in many cases to alienation and finally to mental illness.

Additionally, the lack of intimation with natural spaces (within or without) is caused also by factors such as rampant consumerism, materialism, lack of authentic human and non-human companionship, or any form of social alienation that is not substituted with a re-energizing, ongoing ecopsychological practice.

Although these are not the only factors that could give rise to a breakage from these primordial relationships (severe physical or mental handicaps are others), these causes are often cited as the main reasons why so many people find themselves in a situation of estrangement from natural spaces. This is a semiotic problem since it means that the wild and natural text is no longer understood (except within all the situations where people still partake of natural settings and are intimate with respect to nature's cycles).

Moreover, Ecopsychology or Green Psychology is more and more understood as a clinical practice where ecologically minded and trained psychologists or counselors employ a variety of traditional as well as non-traditional means (therapies) to sensitize, habituate, educate, as well as bring people toward a reconstruction of their affinity to the wild and the natural.

Main Thesis

I often associate the words *biosemiotics* and *ecopsychology*. In their linking, there is a crucial difference and implication that civilized culture produces *semiosis* and cannot be called ecological or ecopsychological (as K. Lewin, U. Broffenbrenner, and A. Lang did); and that to the extent that civilized culture is significantly *estranged* or even *alienated* from *raw nature* and its processes, *it cannot be called ecological or ecopsychological*. (It should not!) This careless labeling deceives by implying that humans, immersed in the civilized milieu, still have the capacity to interpret natural or biological signs[23] and thus enter into a proto-human *biosemiosis* with pristine surroundings. It is only the human at the fringes of civilized culture, or the one who is fully immersed in raw nature, the one who MUST understand the natural sign, who has an *ecopsychology*. This distinction and relationship might be better understood with an imperfect but nevertheless useful analogy:

semiosis : psychology :: *biosemiosis : ecopsychology*

This shorthand analogy is my main thesis, in many guises, throughout this book and distinguishes, I believe, my *ecopsycological* and *biosemiotic* perspectives from those of others. This analogy says that on its left side belong *synthetic and corruptible text*, on its right our *more ancient telluric origins and original text*. This analogy is imperfect in that its *biosemiotic* and *ecopsychological* side also implies a higher experiential level[24] and *becoming*: transpersonalization into NATURE.

Once this relationship and analogy are understood, both the *biosemiotician* and the *ecopsychologist* can shake hands and recognize that they are doing the same work. On the other hand, the human at the fringes of civilized culture, or the one who is fully immersed in raw nature, need not hear from me about their fundamental intimation.

Aims

With many degrees of personal needs and limitations (the unique circumstance of each individual), time availability, ruling out severe organic disorders, and always considering the variation of personality, the means toward mending this severed (or severing) primordial association (self-recognized or recognized by an ecopsychologist) could be as simple as incorporating life (plants and animals) into an aseptic household environment or taking up gardening on a grander scale. It could also include the necessity of beginning and maintaining a daily practice of "wandering"[25] that gradually brings one into urban park settings and less tame landscapes. This necessity can also extend into frequent visits and retreats into wilderness proper, alone or with others. Finally, for some, this may also mean selecting a new environment where the wild predominates over the cultivated and the civilized.

As in our previous case study, *Heinz Droz*, many of these practices are not strenuous, and incrementally re-edify, intensify, inform, and begin to establish a new vocabulary of relating that could become the ideal, if not simply better biosemiosis. As before, if you and your family live in the woods or are in constant touch with nature and are generally happy, then this book says nothing new to your own realizations and insights. If so, you are entitled to laugh at the expense of this ecopsychologist or orthodox psychology.

Equally important, since Ecopsychology is also a daily mindful practice (William Devall & George Sessions, 1985) and proactive seeking to establish a sense of balance and harmony with nature, ecopsychologists often use meditational, relaxation, hypnotherapeutic, or other concentration means for creating significant cognitive and affective states that promote further ecopsychological exploration. Even though these practices can take vernacular designations such as "reconnecting with nature," "back to the wild," "getting in touch with nature," they may miss the important ecopsychological point and fall into the hands of singularization of reality by diminishing the gravity of a planet in crisis. That is why it is important to reiterate and emphasize the *Deep Ecological* point that these actions must be deliberate, working on the ecopsychological self, and part of a larger strategy and recognition[26] that our very mental stability is predicated on partaking of natural spaces. If this simple claim were not true, vacationing ona deserted island while ditching your cell phone would not be such an attractive proposition or fantasy for most of us. Who goes to Las Vegas for relaxation and meaningful experiences anyway? The historical and still intimate connection between the *Deep Ecology Movement* and Ecopsychology will be explored further in Chapter Seven.

At least one type of psychologist, a renegade at that, has embraced ecopsychology as part of a transpersonal therapy—their trade. Indeed, it is transpersonal psychologists and psycho-synthesis therapists or counselors who have been most impressed by the seamless motifs between their well-honed psychological art and deep ecological values. In all fairness, it is mostly through their work and enthusiasm that ecopsychology is surviving while the patient, the doctor, and society are running around in circles trying to explain the obvious: *we have injured our telluric connections and this has produced nefarious repercussions. We have lost our totemic animal spirits along the way, the mnemonics of our planetary duty, and traded them in for a Porsche or a laptop, a coronary, harder erections, bigger boobs, and other delusions. It is the duty, interest, and calling of transpersonal psychologists to feed ancient archetypes and totem animals until we can return, en mass, to our origins.*

Finally, ecopsychology is sensitive to and always eager to learn from regional and traditional means for achieving this sustainable balance and harmony. Each country, region, city, village, and has its own specialists who continue fostering these connections. In ecological therapy it is highly advisable to seek out and join existing clubs and associations, or create new ones, that form the basis of a support group, thus maximizing the daily practices. In some cases where urban life or industry has pushed away even the vestiges of ancient ways of relating to the local environment, it may be necessary to borrow old ecological wisdom and co-opt its practices and reinterpret them anew or replant them into new soil.

Making The Patient Ill

Adding insult to injury and ignorance to myopic orthodoxy, if the human-nature estrangement becomes dysfunction, its symptoms may mimic or piggyback upon symptomology commonly treated anthropocentrically or polis-centrically as maladaptive to, ironically, the very civilization that is the source of the illness. As other ecopsychologists have pointed out, the orthodox psychologist patches up the bleeding patient and after making them feel even more guilty with respect to their social mal-adaptation (calling it by a variety of symptom names, marital discontent, combative personality, defiant of authority, negativity, etc., rather than by identifying root ecopsychological causes) sends Droz back into the boiling water with the useless mantra: "Be calm, adjust to your boiling water situation." Sadly, I know only a handful of psychologists who stand by the curb way of a hypocritical decaying society and clamor, with ecopsychological confidence, the following:

> If one reads clinical psychology as *normative psychology*, then the orthodox practitioner would want the *nature alienated* patient to swim in the polluted, shark infested waters of society's own perverse making and have him swim in beautiful and well-choreographed strokes. Notwithstanding the fact that this is bad or desperate therapy, the therapist becomes an evil co-dependent and facilitator of the demented status quo. Should that patient or any of us have any respect for the maimed psychologist?

At the end of our caricature of the delinquent and *embedded psychologist*, a pragmatist-reductionist, he/she would say something along the lines, "You see, the little blue pill and my counter conditioning made you into an agreeable extrovert who can fit into society. If it works then it must be true. Therefore, your insurance company will pay me, you can go back to the shark infested pool, and my child can have her I-pod to tune out the evils of the world."

Roszak (1992-2001) criticizes this deficit as one of the greatest failures of mainstream clinical psychology or psychiatry when he says:

> Therapy makes no demand for clean air, the songs of birds, the presence of trees or sea, mountain or stream. The troubled soul locked in a tortured ego will never be coaxed to look out and around at something greater, more lordly, more ennobling: a state of nature that invites the mind to contemplate eternal things. Yet common experience tells us that a solitary walk by the river or ocean, a few calm hours in the woods restore the spirit and may produce more insight into our motives and goals that the best labors of the professional analyst. The quiet contemplation of the night sky before one turns to sleep and dreams might do more to touch the mind with a healing grandeur than weeks, months, years of obsessive autobiographical excavation.

Similarly, Paul Shepard (1982) remarked of the same willingness to remain passive, impotent, or dulled in the face of such a dysfunctional setting when he wrote:

> It is odd, after seventy centuries of city life that we can continue to be uneasy about it and uncertain as to what is wrong. The situation is like those psychological illnesses in which the patient shows a devilish capacity to obscure the real problem from himself. A demon seems to make false leads, so that deliverance requires more of the same, confusing problem and symptom. It is as though traffic, smog, disease, violence, crime, uncaring strangers, dirt, drug addiction, and unemployment collectively provide distraction from something that perhaps cannot be dealt with . . . Let us suppose, with some evidence, that the city is typically a sink of psychological problems. In the individual these are partly caused by city life, but in the longer view they cause the city. Where can the cycle be broken, and what are its processes?

Ecopsychology must address both quoted circumstances: a psychology that has erred in diagnosing and treating *nature estrangement or alienation* in context, and on the other hand, the reluctance of a patient in a social milieu to recognize his/her estrangement or alienation. Both excerpts also underscore the need for some deep structural language that can be used by the patient, the counselor, the philosopher, and society at large, that can transcend the individualism, the professionalism, or the xenophobia of all. If we have a common language, then there is the hope that rhetoric will be employed less as a rationalization scheme and that dialectics will replace contradictory propaganda. Semiotic Matrix Theory (SMT) proposes such a language.

How SMT Fits In

The problem I think we face when arguing for psychology as ecopsychology is that of lacking *a unified ontological structure* to speak with or from, or that of an ontology that can speak for all of us, including all planetary and even exo-planetary organisms. In many ways, the obstacle toward realizing a universal ontology or *pansemiosis* is a legacy of postmodernism and cultural relativism gone astray. Therefore, without such a commensurable noetic platform no psychology or ecopsychology feels confident enough to become a paradigm.

Logically and sadly, without a paradigm no synthesis of psychological fields and converging intellectual efforts is possible. The encompassing paradigm must also have *biosemiotically sensible features* that can be recognized by workers in other fields, particularly those in the biological sciences, so that they too feel as though they can contribute to our common interests.

While settling on a set of principles with the appropriate "biosemiotically sensible features," the paradigm is truly encompassing if it also considers purely semiotic or culturally derived signification in order to assist the work of colleagues in social sciences and the humanities. If all these needs and factors are considered, the end result will have to be a bare-bones ontology that is both falsifiable and elegant. It is premature and presumptuous to qualify SMT as either. All I can say is that this ontology has allowed me to abstract most of what I read across many disciplines and find relevant connections and fruitful bridges that mesh with my ecopsychological ones.

The maxims and text that follow are from an earlier paper presenting its full-fledged thesis[27]. I chose to present SMT in a nutshell version first and then move on to explain specific terms with the intention of facilitating its comprehension. Given that SMT is central to this book, I have let redundancies reiterate its main points in the next ten pages or so, allowing the repeated presentation of its theses.

In a Nutshell . . .

1) Living organisms (and other "things") are matrices.[28] Therefore, in living entities, Energy, Safety, and Possibility need, and functions, and their feedback interactions, are *consubstantial*, giving rise to the emergent dynamics of what I define as matricial activity, or a matrix as an integral entity.

2) As matrices 'we' embody Energy, Safety and Possibility needs and the umwelt provides sensorially and perceptually comprehensible sets of *invariant* information that can then be turned into *affordances* (J. J. Gibson, 1979). *Affordances* can then be interpreted as providing these basic matricial needs. This is why SMT is *a biosemiotic theory because it takes into account that a seamless and pervasive existential complementary exists between the object, the sign, and the interpreter which provides the basic sustenance for all meanings. This existential complement and yoked-in triad permeates and predates all sign systems, and all sign transactions.* The historicity of an organism, partly programmed by its own genome and partly learned, is fundamentally and existentially the *historicity* of Energy, Safety and Possibility needs; however this *historicity* is played out in the diverse attempts to deal with, and to eke out an existence.

3) Organic (*maenadic*-animals and *ensilic*-plants) matrices have evolved countless metabolic, physiological, behavioral, and mental adaptations to express and complement these *matricial* needs by first reacting, responding, identifying or labeling objects in any environment that they encounter as resources to meet these needs. Thus, a biosemiotic structure might be derived from a description, understanding, and prediction of these interactions. I have argued that the topological mathematics of Kurt Lewin's (1936 and 1939) *Life Spaces* could

be a computational first step to learn something about these interactions, if only some Lewinian topological terminology were replaced with matricial functionality and simpler vocabulary.

4) All human knowledge, in all areas of interest, is an attempt to describe, understand, and/or predict how these *matricial* interactions occur. *Incommensurability* across these fields exists only insofar as lower level, technical jargon is used to define (without interdisciplinary effort) their phenomena of interest, a continuum of biosemiosis[29].

5) The summary of this quest and understanding agrees with Systems Theory somewhat in that life transactions are all ecological (systemic). However, there are limitations to Systems Theory addressed by SMT (Conesa 1999; 2001).

6) To understand the 'system' is to have a science that predicts how the system might behave. This understanding must also be semiotic as others intuited, pointed out and corrected (Maturana, Varela, 1980; 1987). In this sense, a good 'life' theory, psychological, biological, economical, etc., describes significant *matricial* events that occur in a system and is able to make predictions about these.

7) Ecological Ethics, or Ecoethics, is an emergent necessity and the backbone describing the manner and nature of these relationships/interactions insofar as development proceeds from one smaller and physiologically restrictive matrix to a larger one, and yet again to a larger one (zygote, womb, mother, family, school, community, nation, planet, etc.). The *passing* from simpler to increasingly complex umwelten, if it is to succeed, must include a see-through universal biosemiotics rooted in more or less easy to interpret, or easy to learn signs that assist the BECOMING of an organism during its ontogenesis (Conesa-Sevilla, 2006—Mead)[30]. To this end, human organisms (and other species) invent "rules" of ecological engagement that allow them to maximize potential within reason, without destroying the delicate balance of these tenuous relations. Sometimes an organism ignores these ethical rules in order to maximize *matricial* procurements (to dysfunctionally, in the sense of ignoring the consequences to its ecological setting, monopolize); it does this at the developmental or *matricial* detriment of others and while causing injury to an ecosystem. Biosemiotics, in the end, has to deal with ethical questions, and specifically, must include a notion of functional limits found in each umwelt lived.[31]

8) Life processes allow an almost infinite number of strategies for achieving organismic potential; but at the root of these endeavors are the *matricial beta elements: Safety, Energy,* and *Possibility.*

9) Semiotic Matrix Theory specifies the way in which biosemiosis can be structured through an empirical program that tests the ecological validity of these interactions that can then be applied to any study that examines systems.

10) Encapsulated physical bodies are 'simply' the phenotypic expression of these *matricial* forces encountering and surviving diverse environments. Moreover, both genomic and phenotypic adaptations and developments are servicing, through simple and complex feedback systems, the achievement of a *matricial homeostasis*. Being that all organic systems are being drafted, consciously or not, toward this end, *matricial integrity*, then the entire enterprise of merely surviving and/or meaningful existence is participating in a common ground of BEING. If so, then surely a *biosemiosis* dominates from the bottom up and anything else we can explain or discover about semiosis is really a *forced relatedness* or a *forced semiosis* and *sociality* that is always *matricial* at its core.

11) The *historicity* of an organism, any system, however complex, colorful or idiosyncratic, makes an explicit or an implicit reference to *matricial* necessities. It is an existential situation, from the bottom up and in reverse, where a pervasive (and/or perverse if you wish) biosemiotic field is, in my opinion, inescapable. In its new formulation, and contrasted to Mead's ideas, I call it a *hermetic biosemiosis*.

The consequences of these formulations bear directly or indirectly on all the ecopsychological issues presented in this book. And these consequences can be compressed in a few lines:

> The existential-biological-psychological integrity of any organism has precedents in the natural world and its processes. The primacy of these ontological precedents cannot be overruled, bypassed, ignored, or overextended, without causing the organism to adapt to unsettling or harmful conditions. It is human arrogance or ignorance that it thinks it can overrule, bypass, ignore or overextend these *sacred parameters* for anthropocentric or cultural reasons and desires and get away with it Scotch free.

It will be my contention, to reiterate, that without this or another encompassing ontology, we cannot have *biosemiosis as existential connectivity at a fundamental level and the emergence of communicative intelligence predicated in and in need of its natural history and premium telluric strata*. Neither can we begin to understand how, *when disrupted by bad text, tinsel economics, and unsustainable societies*, the same corrupted societies *create the Heinz Drozes of the world* and the perpetuation of bad text and ensuing illness.

The biosemiotic bridge is of paramount importance if we seek to discover a *consilient* theory for psychology, biology, ecology, and polis. If not, if our desires are otherwise, then we can go back to blue pills and temporary patches. Obviously, societies are not permanently better by their administering and no fundamental changes are provided for by these "cures." Worse, the ailing patient, the ailing therapist, and their ailing planet, bleed to death in a downward and accelerating spiral leaving psychology in the dark ages and the planet in ruins. That most psychologists do not see this or cannot comprehend it in the context of what they do is more than troubling. When they understand and withhold these principles from patients or their communities but save themselves and their families, that is an intolerable thought.

Defining the Terms

> "Intelligent organisms on another world may not be like us biochemically. They will almost certainly have evolved significantly different adaptations—from enzymes to organ systems—to deal with the different circumstances of their several worlds. But they must still come to grips with the laws of nature."
>
> —Carl Sagan, *The Dragons of Eden*

I consider these ontologies *invariants* of existence and analogous to perceptual invariants and constancies such as rigidity, movement and stationary-ness or figure-ground perception. Their usefulness to understanding existence lies in being able to (through us, organisms) summarize a complex world and realities into noticeable, finite characteristics that, once detected, can be employed in the existential act of survival. By first noticing and understanding these invariants, with the appropriate biological or cultural hardware, we come to build the foundations of a noetic structure that reaches its azimuth in humanity. Human language then, one of the most abstract noetic structures, expresses and recognizes these invariants because it emerges from existential acts that strive to recognize these invariants. Furthermore, Erik Erikson (1968) argued for the primacy of at least one of our ontologies, Safety, when he placed trust-mistrust as a primordial step in the sequence of human social/personality development. According to his proposal the impact of a biological and psychological bipolarity of pleasure and pain is the genesis of further social and individual categorization and evaluation (not to mention mental illness). Abraham Maslow too devises a hierarchy of needs that strives toward self-actualization. His model parallels the existential needs defined below.

Moreover, a distinction needs to be made between matricial *categories*, *elements*, and *being states*. I will only explicitly deal here with two large categorical ontologies: *alpha*, or matrices, and *beta* (Energy, Safety and Possibility). These categories, and others waiting to be defined and characterized, are ***discrete and essential***, thus it is logical to grant them a collective, functional and existential status. For example, the notion of a matrix as an organism, a functional unit, emerges from the interaction of the *beta elements*. Furthermore, each *category* described here is made up of *elements*. These *elements*, such as the *beta* elements, may interact with each other and with *categories* to create new functions and/or ontological/existential descriptions (meanings). *Elements,* in addition to sharing the properties of *discreteness* and *essence* with the above categories, can be defined as the most *irreducible* and basic unit of existence, and can express unique behavioral and mental continua. For example, the *beta* element *Safety* is an irreducible descriptor of a class of a particular type of needs affecting motivation, behavior, and mental states driving adaptation. Finally, *being states* represent the many behavioral, existential, or energetic *gradients* of any *element* or category (alpha, a matrix) as described by biology and psychology in the context of adapting to an external and/or internal world. Not only is it practical to identify a Safety need in general, existentially speaking, but it is also necessary to grade this need for security along a certain continuum that makes real, adaptive sense. One can conceive of a continuum, represented by mental, behavioral states (or not, it could be simply reflexive in nature), where death or the threat of injury are at an extreme end of this continuum and *abandoned liberation* and feelings of invulnerability are at the opposite end. When categories, elements and being states are accounted for, at least the limited set presented here, they give rise to 245 existentially derived, possible states of *being* (seven elements multiplied by 35 states).[32]

I will now review the definitions of a matrix, the *beta* elements (Conesa, 1999). With this basic set of ideas, we can then move on to describe their ecological interactive potential and their use in all other fields of intellectual and labor production, the larger semiotic field. Specifically, they can be used to speak of ecopsychological wellness or lack thereof when its constituents are performing at sub-optimal levels.

What is a Matrix?

Matrices express themselves independently or through other matrices the universe over. Matrices obey the laws of nature or perish. For[33]:

> "A matrix is anything that is perceived to be the source of Safety, Energy and Possibility at the same time . . . you know you have bumped into a matrix if you can hide inside it and protect yourself, suck nourishment from it, and utilize it for further growth and adaptation. Living organisms, being matrices themselves, are genetically and culturally designed to identify and bond with other matrices."

A matrix is an emergent whole, even though a matrix is made up of the *beta* elements (E, S, and P). Matrices are *entities* because they are or are perceived to be discrete and unique systems; they are also essential. This means that their wholeness, an emergent property of the interaction of their *beta* elements, has a reality and an interactive boundary (systemic, mental, or behavioral). Furthermore, these well-defined borders of being are usually recognizable by flesh; words; ideas; scales, feathers or fur; territorial behavior; actual geological regions; and/or signs. In order to have pansemiosis, a *Rosetta Stone* for communication across all fields, it may be useful to distinguish between *maenadic, ensilic, tartanic* and *ideonic* matrices. Respectively, these labels define animals, plants, inorganic matrices such as our planet or our house, and ideas as matrices (e.g., God or Heaven as matrices). The distinction between *maenadic* and *ensilic, tartanic* and *ideonic* matrices is also the existentialist distinction of having "dasein" or being-in-the-world. Therefore, only *maenadic* matrices exhibit *dasein* and *will*, whereas a city-as-an-*entity*, a *tartanic* matrix, does not. ("The possession of *will* allows a matrix proactive exploration of its world and increasing control and recognition of its own beta components needs.") With this distinction of intentionality in place, from a semiotic perspective, we can say that all matrices communicate with an existential language, or are at least modeled after the *beta* existential restrictions, but only *maenadic* (and *ensilic?*) matrices do so with the specific purpose of understanding. On the other hand, *tartanic* and *ideonic* matrices depend on *maenadic* matrices to describe them and to give them their status as *entities*.

The Beta Elements

Energy

Energy is the engine of matrices, and in a real sense, *the origin of matrices*. Energy is the primordial *beta* element without which Safety and Possibility are meaningless. This basic definition of Energy includes physical, bio-chemical and psychical forms of energy. In all its guises, energy is the fuel of life. Its diminution and fluctuation can be sensed and accounted for in every transaction of life. Energy is linked with cycles of nature, with an awareness of where to seek it, when to tap into it, and how much is available. Energy, its diminution and fluctuation, sets the tempo, the rhythm of life. If we could invent a cosmology for all living things we would have to place Energy at the beginning.

We could read this story as follows: In the beginning there was Energy and it became matter and matter explored and unfolded its potential, Possibility. Some of this potential was the emergence of organisms that now guard (store and use) Energy as a precious commodity. It is hard to guard Energy because it oscillates, it waxes and wanes, it is cyclical and changes states. The instability of Energy introduces the need for another ontological constraint, the notion of Safety. The instability of

Energy, its shifty nature, creates a bona fide *existential uncertainty*. Essentially, an organism's raison *d'etre* comes down to the manufacturing, co-opting, preserving and deploying energy resources in order to survive or maximize potential. Even though it is the most basic contributor to the notion of an integrated matrix, we can only define it in terms of its effects. That is, energy is implied as an underlying force behind more complex behaviors and states. For example, energy is explosive and advantageous if it contributes to bursts of growth. On the other hand, explosive energy may be a hindrance during behaviors such as stalking, sleeping, infant care, etc., which require a control and/or diminution of available energy. The absence of energy obviously limits life processes. Within the matricial context, energy also affects the 'psychological' and thus impairs or enhances mental and emotional status. In this continuum the "optimal" level corresponds to homeostasis and allows for the maintenance of routine functions and behaviors necessary to survive.

Safety

It is the scaffold for life, for the exploration of Possibility given enough Energy. Safety is the beta component indicating and underscoring individual and kin stability, health, and preservation. Therefore, it includes the move toward self-preservation regardless of whether an awareness of the need for safety exists. This means that self-preservation can take the form of basic reflexive, instinctual behaviors or mammalian goal-oriented behavior that anticipates safety concerns. Furthermore, Safety in matrices as systems, shares information with Energy and Possibility.

This *beta* element may be the most telling of the type of organization and patterns that organisms assemble in. Next to Energy requirements, and to some extent Possibility, Safety sets in motion the complexity of interactions within these organic systems with telltale indicators of life and/or intelligence (eggs, mounds, nests, dwellings, borders, fortresses, castles and skyscrapers).

In *autopoetic* language (Maturana and Varela, 1980), Energy and Safety are less mutable, more invariant than Possibility, thus when recognized can become tools for evaluating how intelligence expresses itself in structures and patterns of organization. From a communication point of view, both Energy and Safety contribute more to the functional prerequisites of how societies form and develop. That is, they can be used to describe the outward appearance, organizational mode, the culture, the politics, the economics, and the religious aspects of civilization. In this sense, they are at a higher level of explanation than sociological functional needs themselves, since they can specify other "lesser" social prerequisites. The ontological primacy that I suspect Energy and Safety (and to some extent to Possibility) have is more primordial and real than, for example, Levi-Strauss's kinship systems since these ontologies can be physico-biological and can transcend human culture (Levi-Strauss, 1958).

Furthermore, it can be argued that Levi-Strauss's kinship systems are the result of the matricial ontologies and not, as he says, the result of consciousness in an ontological vacuum: "[a kinship system] . . . exists only in human consciousness; it is an arbitrary system of representations." In my view "a kinship system" and its signs acquire a certain existential reality because consciousness and its products cannot ignore the semiotic and real field of matrices. Consciousness is itself a matrix or it "lives" inside (monitors) one. Either way it is not free from the existential wheel of matricial ontologies. *No natural, existential environment produces arbitrary consciousness.*

Furthermore, Levi-Strauss says:

> But what confers upon kinship its socio-cultural character is not what it retains from nature, but, rather, the essential way in which it diverges from nature. A kinship system does not consist in the objective ties of descent or consanguinity between individuals. It exists only in human consciousness.

I agree with the notion of a creative social interpretation of biological ties and subsequent cultural diversity that ensues from that adaptation. But in the Wilsonian era of sociobiology one can only push the purity and independence of cultural behavior so far. Besides, Edward Wilson (1980) makes a more convincing and elegant case of kinship when he identifies the embeddedness of genetico-cultural adaptation. If biological and cognitive adaptation affects the entire genetico-cultural package, why then the arbitrary dismantlement of one component while ignoring the other?

The continuum for Safety moves from death itself to what I called abandoned liberation. This continuum is unusual in that homeostasis dwells between the states of security and injury-threat. Homeostasis for Safety may move within these two levels in very dynamic ways. For example, although an organism may experience security for a while (psychologically it may translate into a sort of confidence or optimism that things are going well), the shifty nature of consciousness and the reality of life is such that this sense of security can be perturbed at any moment by a threat. The highest state level, abandoned liberation, describes the extreme end of the personal, invincible fable, where the organism accepts danger and a real possibility of injury without cares or concern for well-being. Abandoned liberation could exemplify risk taking during courtship, including animals in heat; the sense of discovery, as in experiencing an epiphany; or during the reported religious bliss associated with mystical states. It may be bad form to clump animals in heat and religious conversion into one series of examples, but in my mind both convey the temerity and daring behaviors associated with this highest Safety state. This high state is needed to explain pro-social and altruist behavior in animals, especially the intensity of parents defending their young.

Possibility

Possibility is akin to Abraham Maslow's idea of self-actualization, or a propensity to reach a certain organismic potential (Maslow, 1968). This potential can be realized either by creative means or coerced by biological, environmental forces. When experienced by self-aware organisms, it is a clear and unambiguous sense of what is realizable (from Webster's definition: "The fact or state of being possible."). Experienced as emotion, it is *an immediate insight of what can be achieved accompanied by a sense of awe, promise and elation*. Admittedly, self-actualization is never a finished product but an ever-expanding opportunity horizon: individual excellence always lies ahead in the future. In this sense, Possibility (and Safety) is an organismically perceived (or evolved to) parameter and cannot be a nebulous, *a priori* source in a real, existential philosophy (Sartre, 1956).

Possibility includes sensing, perceiving, and interpreting stimuli as *invariants* or as potential for further growth. Moreover, in intelligent creatures, the interpretation of data as *invariants* or opportunity allows for a bootstrap effect. This means that new environmental landscapes being explored could be seen in novel perspectives. Intelligent creatures see, understand, and create patterns and use this information to move beyond a present state, perhaps to a higher realm of behavior, thinking, and being where the very idea of what is possible itself can change, ca be expanded. New signs may be invented to describe possibility at any level, but Possibility is always a venture whose capital comes from Energy and Safety. That is, both Energy and Safety tend to be sacrificed in the pursuit of the unknown opportunity. With the exploration of what is possible, further erosion of recognizable patterns of the exploring culture occurs. In this light, archeology is the study of the remnants of Safety and Energy: Possibility itself leaves few traces. Even in ancient tombs, which seem at first to point to the idea of transcendental Possibility after death, resurrection, have more to do with a guarantee of Safety—weapons and the actual fortification of the burial site—or the provision of Energy for the ultimate journey in the form of food and sacrificed servants.

Possibility as a strategy for further development is there when embarking on conquests, looking for spice, stealing from your neighbor, and in all journeys of discovery. It is the invisible garment of the gambler, the liar or a promise. It is equally the journey of the hero and the one who slaughters, the peregrine and the one in exodus.

A continuum for possibility encompasses being states from a vegetative or inert state to transcendental: potential with transformation. At the highest state, as in the case of matricial transcendence, an organism could move to a new order of being (e.g., understanding or speaking three or four languages, choosing pacifism over aggression, loving thy neighbor, etc.). This new order of being is generally a slow process in an evolutionary sense when new species are formed. But in humans, the transformation could happen rather quickly with dramatic cultural changes and demands or with the purposeful manipulation of the genome for novel adaptations. However, most of the time, our potential seems rather mundane and static, maintaining a comfortable equilibrium.

Accepting these ontological invariants seems at first to contradict the reality of Uexküll's highly subjective umwelts. However, I believe it is possible to reconcile SMT, Gibson's affordances and a subjective umwelt by assuming that in this final synthesis, SMT acts as a metalanguage above Uexküll's idea of a *functional circle*.

Summary

a) SMT as an ontological origins theory precedes systems and/or self-organization theories including the concept of ecology. It refines and goes beyond proposals such as Autopoeisis in that SMT tries to explain WHY life organizes itself in the patterns that we see and study. To me, it is not enough to say that life self-organizes. There might also be a reason WHY it organizes. I think this question deserves to be explored as well. As an analogy, we may peer into a round pond and say that the water organizes "itself" into roundness without appreciating the fact that real constraints such a beach, a periphery, exist. Neither wings nor fins "self-organize." Air and water are the forces that shape these forms into being. The human brain or a single-celled organism too was made for something. Matricial beta constraints are both ephemeral and real in that, like beaches, these forces shape systems into recognizable matricial patterns and forms.

b) In a sense, SMT, I will concede, can be considered the most basic ecology and/or the reason WHY life organizes in these peculiar but familiar ways. Behind every round pond, fancy wing, or cell there are forces that specify their genesis.

c) SMT speaks about organic ecologies from the origin of a **"fluttering"** energetic universe. The instability of **energy qua energy** gives rise to a universe that "senses" this instability when "sensing" becomes part of an existential doing and function. Thus matter itself is impacted by this fragile state. I called this instability **the first "habit" of the universe**, as we understand it. Organic life itself and its possibility to become, grows embedded in this instability. **Life internalizes this instability as a concern for Safety and the pursuit of Possibility.** Both, in the end, are about the first requirement of life: Energy. Life is obligated in this sense to Energy and must pay attention to the internal "fluttering" of its cycles. To ignore these is to die. To ignore these is never to become: to pursue potential, opportunity, or organismic Possibility. In short, **Energy is a kind of "troubled" first cause**, giving rise to a "paranoid universe": matter inherits the "fluttering" of energy and so do we as organisms, as safety and possibility needs. If energy were stable and abundant, this would be a different universe indeed! Thus the necessity of homeostatic regulation follows, logically, existentially, and functionally from Energy fluctuations, and the need to control these to achive adaptation to a real physical world.

d) **Possibility,** in this real sense, **is a perception within the Umwelt and not a construct in metaphysics.**[34] If there was a god and it created a universe, we might be able to speak of the option of the possible or not. If we were Hindu and we spoke about cosmology we might be able to entertain a metaphysical dilemma where "The One" considers becoming the two and the many. But this is un-testable metaphysics. And it seems to me that all we can prove and research is the real notion that after the Big Bang, **Energy, and only Energy, moved to beget the universe as we see it. We can only "blame" Energy for the instability of the universe.** If this is true, Possibility is the "consideration" (conscious or not) from inside the many umwelts, of how to efficiently proceed within my life space with an inescapable awareness that to become what I must become, what I want to become, I must pay attention to cycles, to spurts, to diminutions, even to the cessation of Energy.

e) SMT is not necessarily anti-metaphysical, but it demands that any metaphysics be potentially testable, that it should be grounded on present-day knowledge of physics. Otherwise we limit our discussions to interminable treatises that revert back to "He said, I like him, therefore it must be true" un-testable arguments. **If biosemiotics is to become scientific, the strength of its proposals ought to be falsifiable.** The ideal of this scientific inquiry demands that we part company with comfortable or known ideas when these can no longer sustain semiotic reality. Biosemiotics may prove to be the experimental medium with which these ideas can be tested.

f) SMT points to processes leading to existential efficiency through a universal noetics. Making BEING matricial makes the question of universal noetics possible. That is, universality in BEING gives rise to a **universal heuristic** about existence that is recognizable and assists the development of any organism. The rules of engagement are matricial at the core of existence. **Only in this sense do I write about a pansemiosis.**

g) The extension and interactions of **alpha** (the matrix), **beta** (energy, safety and possibility) and **gamma** (control, power, and generativity) elements give rise to lexicons, to most words that describe real ecological engagement. Therefore all meaning is traceable to these origins. Our psycholinguistic data suggest that empirical work along these lines may prove to be useful in tracing back these interactions.

h) I agree that SMT is new and that it competes with established orthodoxy. Like any other new theoretical proposal, its validity depends upon future empirical testing and the willingness to pursue/test its claims.

i) I suspect matricial dynamics are already written about in all disciplines, albeit under different guises and mathematical formulas. However, no unified theory ties these approaches together. All these fields of inquiry, from economics to psychology, to the arts, and biology, try to understand mechanisms that are grounded on matricial dynamics. SMT claims that this diverse semiosis may be better understood by a unified semiotic and biosemiotic approach. Unfortunately, systems theory is still at a low explanatory level and metaphysics have obscured rather than elucidated the path of understanding.

Take-Home Message

The story of life with its emergent psychologies is the story of matrices interacting with each other and with their environments (*umwelten*). SMT could serve as shorthand devise to keep track of all this interactive complexity by assigning these interactive functions simple and yet meaningful labels and properties. In ecopsychology, the assumption is that wellness or illness, fulfillment or depression, can now be interpreted biosemiotically, by asking questions of communicative efficiency between matrices, beta, or gamma dynamics. To the extent that these dynamics are improvised by the genomic and phenotypic decontextualizations from nature, the production of false text and consciousness, and the exigencies of bad culture and its propaganda, then we can assume that these deficient interactive functions will exhibit symptoms and that these can be gleaned as biosemiosis gone astray.

Additional Commentary by Aldo Leopold:

"There are two spiritual dangers in not owining a farm. One is the danger of supposing that breakfast comes from the grocery, and the other that heat comes from the furnace. To avoid the first danger, one should plant a garden, preferably where there is no grocer to confuse the issue. To avoid the second, he should lay a split of good oak on the andirons, preferably where there is no furnace, and let it warm his shins while a February blizzard tosses the trees outside. If one has cut, split, hauled, and piled his own good oak, and let his mind work the while, he will remember much about where the heat comes from, and with a wealth of detail denied to those who spend the week end in town astride the radiator."

Chapter Two

The Singularization of Language as Ecopsychological Alienation

> *How does using language as a first approximation of consciousness help us relate feelings to brain mechanisms? This requires another conceptual leap. We defined feelings . . . as conscious experiences having to do with the individual's welfare. We must now translate this statement to read, "linguistic coding having to do with the individual's welfare." But a linguistic coding of what? Here is the leap. Feelings result when language systems receive input from [emotion-driven] limbic areas.*

—Joseph E. LeDoux, The Neurobiology of Emotion

When we first met Heinz Droz in our preface we said that, "*The entire horizon of Droz's existence is dominated by false consciousness created by false TEXT (propaganda), false institutions, false meanings, false ideologies, and a host of materialistic narcotics.*"

In this chapter we will trace this semiotic decay as a probable historical degeneration of the usage of language from telluric, totemic, hunter-forager functions to its proliferation and final cultural saturation during superfluous, mercantile, and anthropocentric functions. Of Droz's text we also said that it was "thoroughly fictional, thoroughly synthetic, and most of the time, animated by infantile wanting that never ceases and for which a plethora of corporations aim to satisfy it for profit." In these uses of language we might begin to see *the breach from an original mind whose linguistic inputs and outputs were mediated and closely self-regulated by a real ecology and its forces and by our emotional ties to its ancient functioning.*

In the following article and pages I have taken one of Jung's insights and elaborated it into my own model for an ecopsychology of language regression from an original *hypological* or intra-psychic function of personal mythology rooted in authentic ecological dealings and causalities to its present-day use as a tool for political and social propaganda, denial, and self-deceit. I have made the case that ecopsychological illness cannot be understood at a fundamental level as "LIFE interrupted and *unintegratable*" without tracking how consciousness, language, and our emotive life synthesize a vision of an authentic self and wellness. Without undergoing this analysis, it is difficult to see how we can revamp linguistic processes in our daily lives or in therapy to deter and prevent the impact of false propaganda. This is an extended use of deconstructing language in order to affiliate ourselves, once again, with an original text that was *Good* for us.

In "Meet Heinz Droz" we already introduced the problem of singularization as forced or funneled semiosis. The following pages present the complete version of these arguments followed by a set of dialectical questions. In short, if language processes are restricting a psychology of self, then we must understand how language is restricted or restrictive and by whom in order to address their impact on my ecopsychological development.

The Singularization of Reality: Implications of a Synnomic Evolution of Language to Semiotics, Biosemiotics, and Ecopsychology[35]

Key terms: *Synnomic evolution of language, abstractification, alienation, propaganda,* "false consciousness"*(falsches Bewusstsein),vectorial space, onomatopoeic, biosemiosis, funneled-semiosis*

Abstract

Carl G. Jung's *synnomic* model of the evolution of human language was expanded here to include Erich Fromm's concept and the consequences of the *abstractification* of language as the instantaneous and mass-shared phenomenology of a meaningless text, the semiotic function and concept presented here as *singularization*. In general, and in conjunction with Jung's synnomic model, Fromm's concepts of *alienation* and *abstractification* are used as diagnostics to understand ecopsychological and biosemiotic *alienation*, both examples of a corrupted and over-culturized text.

It is argued that Jung's model can still be useful to address "reality" problems in semiotics and in biosemiotics and their consequences leading to a destabilizing *ecopsychology*. Specifically, synnomic evolution offers a way to address, once again, the problem of "false consciousness" *(falsches Bewusstsein)* and its principal consequence, the *singularization* of language and reality. As a related problem, the limitations of *city-dwelling vectorial space and transit,* as well as other problems associated with the biosemiotics of territorial trialectics (Conesa, 2001), are treated as additional instances of a *singularization* of a truer biosemiotic way of relating to space itself.

"When one speaks of the 'three-million-dollar bridge,' one is not
primarily concerned with its usefulness or beauty, that is, with its concrete
qualities, but one speaks of it as of a commodity, the main quality of
which is its exchange value, expressed in a quantity, that of money."

Erich Fromm, *The Sane Society*, (1955: 106)

Introduction: The Singularization of the Reality of Language

Stereotypes are cognitive adaptations to complexity, heuristics, and as such are generally useful, and sometimes they are not. They are also an example, in semiosis, of a more pernicious process I have termed *the singularization of reality*, a sick and dying triad.

Erich Fromm's example of and reference to an actual physical object, a bridge, as exclusively possessing monetary singularity, a "three-million-dollar-bridge," is one example of the *singularization* of reality using language originating from, in this case, a limited mind set and capitalistic paradigm. Additionally, and capitalistically-driven as well, phrases such as *I am worth it*, or *How much am I worth in the market*, are paraphrases from Fromm's many other examples of capitalistic *abstractification*.[36] It is Fromm's brilliant psychosemiotic thesis (Fromm, 1955) that links the many examples of singularized impoverished self-definitions as forms of psychic erosion leading to modern neurosis and even psychosis. Because for him the process of linguistic *abstractification* logically leads to social and self-*alienation*.

To paint a larger context, Fromm's concept of abstractification is one of many observations supporting his grander thesis of *normative humanism*—then, and even now, a radical critique of a supposedly inherent relativistic value given by anthropologists to every culture to do its social business and function however it wishes. By taking this radical approach he is opening the door to an examination of universal existential psychic qualities that hold true for every culture, and if violated, lead to mass neurosis or even insanity. Fromm was counter-post-modernist before this movement had been born:

> It is the task of the "science of man" to arrive eventually at the correct description of what deserves to be called human nature. What has often been called "human nature" is but one of its many manifestations—and often a pathological one—and the function of such mistaken definition usually has been to defend a particular type of society as being the necessary outcome of man's mental constitution.

Fromm is very explicit about how perverted cultural semiosis can be created so as to lead to artifactual or idiosyncratic rather than fundamental (universal) expressions of a true human nature when he says:

Just as man transforms the world around him, so he transforms himself in the process of history. He is his own creation, as it were. But just as he can only transform and modify the natural materials around him according to their nature, so he can only transform and modify himself according to his own nature.

However, even though I very much like where Fromm has taken the idea of impoverished, straight-jacketed cultural norms and language and their implications for mass insanity, I will use the term *singularization* instead of his *abstractification,* to designate a semiotic process proper which is further depriving and restricting of an original and true text. Thus, *singularization* can derive from at least: 1) a conscious and manipulative propaganda effort to control what the masses think (Chomsky, 1968); 2) a simplification of the meaning of words given the restrictions of a social milieu and its corresponding ideological paradigm (Mannheim, 1936); 3) the loss of the original meaning and derivation connected to specific words when, in the present, such words are spoken in formulaic, unconscious ways; or 4) the perfectly unconscious and automatic forgetfulness that occurs when a word is used mechanically for its sound characteristics alone, as in the games children play of repeating any word until it sound like gibberish. Later in development, this "gibberish" (Spinoza's *Amanuensis;* Heiddger's *Gerere*) can still be of "value" as in a chanted, meaningless mantra (e.g., "We are the world, we are the people.") that the masses repeat incessantly until they are hypnotized and herded away.

I also prefer the use of the term *singularization* to Fromm's *abstractification* because, in addition to the accepted linguistic assumption inherent in Fromm's term that language abstracts, *singularization* implies a semiotic aspect to *abstractification*—the absence, a narrowing down, or impoverishment of meaning because the object being designated no longer exists, or more importantly has lost its original *telluric connection,* and because the semiotic triad does not function in its original context. By losing its *telluric connection* I mean that its original denotative and connotative function as part of a hunter-forager and early sustenance agricultural ethos, or its *hypological* and intra-psychic function, is no longer available to conscious mind (see Table I). Simply put then, *singularization* is funneled and decontextualized semiosis.

True enough, human language has evolved to reflect these cognitive biases, *abstractification* and *singularization,* insofar as single words are allowed to stand for complex processes. *Abstractification* and *singularization* are perfectly harmless processes (and sometimes very useful forms of shorthand-thinking) as long as we remain conscious that they function in a simplified modality, as limited metaphors and poor substitutes of the objects designated in culture or nature. Obviously, the general *abstractification* properties of the human language are a great advantage in summarizing a complex universe, but when language "just happens" without an ongoing metalinguistic or metasemiotic examination of the *historicity* of these cognitive processes, then language is not only stereotyped but can be used for derogation, forming the basis for prejudice. Taken together, these processes are also examples of a further evolutionary deviation from an original and *telluric* paleo-text and ways of relating, biosemiotically, with natural spaces.

Anticipating the next section, and in brief, in its *onomatopoeic* and *sound symbolic* usage origins, the human language was perhaps more biosemiotic than semiotic (more saurian or mammalian than Saussurian[37])—an ecopsychologicaly-attuned language of natural imitation, and was perhaps a language, totemic at its core, of literal-natural triadic relations. Or, in quoting Lévi-Strauss, Paul Shepard (1973) speaks of this original semiotic totemic relation as hunters culturizing "a false nature truly," and of farmers (historically placed in this writing at the beginning of the singularization process) naturalizing "a true culture falsely." In addition to its *onomatopoeic* and *sound symbolic* usage, words as symbols, even if arbitrary, had a more intense and pervasive natural-semantic ground. They spoke of intimate, life-and-death relations with *wildness*, unimaginable to most individuals today, that were also inescapable.[38]

In other words, supposedly this primal communication was a language of personal identification with the natural, to a greater degree than most urbanites could ever achieve, and this personal and direct natural engagement, more or less directly, kept the biosemiotic authenticity of this communication in check. To illustrate, the lethal consequences of bear behavior from the perspective of three culturally different hunter-forager tribes was identical. Supposedly, three languages describing bear behavior, no matter how creative and imaginative, would have arrived as the natural consequences of dealing with bears *sui generis*. This immediate, authentic experience and semiosis could be contrasted with present-day romanticized ideas of bears, a *singularization* and insult to both men and bears, as Coca-Cola cuddly polar bears, responsible fire fighters Smokey Bears (and its Teddy Bear icon), and Jungle Book Baloo dancing bears. We even over regularize these "cuddly" bears to the point of forcing marsupials to become "koala *bears*." Anyone who has been near a real koala can testify to the fact that they can be quite dangerous, they smell rather bad, and that they make awful grunting noises that pass for vocalization. They are also magnificent animals with the amazing digestive ability to neutralize menthol and camphor.

I will argue here, as I have argued elsewhere (Conesa, 2004; and Conesa, 2005), that this ancient and more authentic communication (if one agrees, generally speaking, with Nietzsche [1909/1986], Freud [1900/1996], Mannheim [1936], Fromm [1955] and Shepard [1972] that human nature and its semiosis can be corrupted by overwhelming social complexity, deviant politics and economics, ideology, or religious dogma) was telluric and, more importantly, *self-correcting* back to *Telos*, for a number of reasons.

One of the reasons for the text having built-in *self-correcting* properties had to do with the reality of hunting real bears as opposed to merely cuddling fake stuffed animals. When masses of ontogenetically arrested adults continue to be further infantilized by needless toys, not only do the collections of stuffed animals swell in closets, but the rationalization of these toys as "investment opportunities" swells into neurosis that infantilized psychologists, themselves toy collectors, cannot cure (Roszak, 1992-2001). This is a revisiting of the problem of "false consciousness" (*falsches Bewusstsein*) when it is causally derived from a text that has ceased to be culturally or evolutionarily meaningful. The I-Pod holding, Volvo driving, mild-tempered, sweet talking psychologist is as much to blame for the propping up of *falsches Bewusstsein* as any nefarious industrialist tycoon. They are equally part of the unconsciously driven consuming herd.

In opposition to collecting stuff animals, in the totemic reality of hunter-forager life, the bear, carved as a family emblem and summary of desired clan values, is respected for all, inclusively, lethal and real natural historic characteristics. *Singularization* is thus funneled and false semiosis in the sense of Lévi-Strauss' description of the authenticity of totemic relations as contrasted to the later extraction and forgetfulness of these relations at the beginning of agricultural life. But even when one argues that a nascent soil-bound agricultural way of life generated in turn a true semiosis, this semiosis and its text is many times removed and even incomprehensible in industrialized society.[39]

The original text was (is) also *self-correcting* to the extent that the *synnomic* progressions related to us by Jung may have a cyclical, historical and social component which identifies the failure of artificial semiosis as propaganda and brings in a "barbaric" or telluric correction (see Tables I and II).

To recap, *singularization* as funneled-semiosis is either perfectly naive and unintentional, or perfectly diabolical and intentional. However, the effects of *singularization* are the same insofar as these result in a myopic approach to the study of anything, from self to the human-other, to bears as non-human otherness (Shepard, 1973). It also produces unstable societies and mental illness since absurd realities and absurd texts multiply and no common telluric ground is remembered, or if remembered is not trusted.

On this note, it needs to be said that the process of *singularization* is not an exclusively linguistic erosion of the meaning of words and their departure from an original, real text, but is also represented in other socio-semiotic processes. These two features of *singularization* are complementary aspects of the same *telluric* alienation. For example, *singularization* as ideology and utopia is observed in Karl Mannheim's

(1936) socio—historical analysis of the origin of thought. In tracing the origins of and finally arriving at a definition of ideology, Mannheim (1936, pp. 61) says:

> The distrust and suspicion which men everywhere evidence towards their adversaries, at all stages of historical development, may be regarded as the immediate precursor of the notion of ideology . . . The particular conception of ideology therefore signifies a phenomenon intermediate between a simple lie at one pole, and an error, which is the result of a distorted and faulty conceptual apparatus, at the other. It refers to a sphere of errors, psychological in nature, which, unlike deliberate deception, are not intentional, but follow inevitably and unwittingly from certain causal determinants.

If ideology is an incomplete rendition of reality and a distortion of hard facts (consciously or unconsciously) for the purpose of associating with a particular group that espouses this ideology, then a reduction of meaning and an encapsulating of formulaic language in the form of propaganda can be seen as aspects of *singularization*. In this sense, the thesis can be proposed and tested that hunter-forager peoples have no ideology (or utopia). More precisely, it can be ventured that hunters-foragers cannot afford an ideology without risking their lives and the lives of the members of their clan.

In tracing the "causal determinants" of this faulty reasoning, Mannheim thinks that ideology is born when the object "out there" ceases to be "real" or at least when its epistemological value is in doubt. In our ecopsychological case, this means when the psychological "inward" becomes more credible than a complex matrix of interrelatedness and LIFE out there. Furthermore, ideology can never be *self-correcting* because it is biased toward and born from synthetic culture that is itself reactionary toward another ideology or point of view. All views are relative to each other and no epistemological natural ground can be counted on or trusted (because a sensitivity, connection, and bonding with a telluric ground has ceased to exist). If biosemiotic, authentic communication was telluric and totemic, the clans whose animals were displayed as a psychological mnemonic were never in ideological competition with each other but were instead complementary aspects of a grander ecological semiosis where each member "spirit" and corresponding set of behaviors added to the whole. Arguing from the logic of Mannheim's thesis, utopias are also inconceivable (or at least are useless) for the hunter-forager mind because these are also based on limited knowledge of what is probable or real.

Biosemiotician Kalevi Kull (1998) hinted at a biosemiotic process of *singularization* when he wrote:

> Although living nature is itself largely linguistic and discrete, human signs cannot copy all the details of non-human signs, and thus, the

reconstructed and constructed natures always simplify and restrict some
of the relationships in nature itself.

To use his idea then, hunter-foragers were in different relationships with respect to
Zero, First, Second, and Third natures;[40] that is, their engagement with all these
aspects of "nature" were based on totemic-mythical and sustainable relations. If so,
then their relationship with their material interpretation and use of natural resources
was minimal when compared to present-day agricultural and industrialized abuses
and transgressions. Kull, in anticipating a semiotic (ecosemiotic) understanding
of the repercussions of bad, overculturized text, said, "Therefore, the examples of
balanced ecosystems can serve as examples of balanced sign systems." Certainly, the
four types of nature engagement are altered when an isolated hunter-forager band
meets another. Infusions of ideas and of words are to be expected which have the
potential of changing a previously held, and fairly stable, relational Umwelt. But this
alteration, provided all hunter-forager groups maintain similar perspectives about
nature, does not challenge the core, pristine, and authentic ecopsychological ethos,
and it might well reinforce it. This meeting-of-semioses situation is much different
than a missionary group encountering an isolate band and proceeding to "culturise
the savage." This is the beginning of the end of good text.

Moving on to a further deteriorating text and habit in the sciences, psychology, which
should have known better, still *singularized the complexity* of intelligence, naming it
with a capital "I", for most of the twentieth century. The capital "I" changed as new
theories came and went. Whereas in totemic culture an intelligent individual would
never confuse a real bear with a Coca-Cola polar bear, an intelligence test will give
high marks for recognizing this culture-bound linguistic insult as something real
and significant and worth testing. When intelligence tests are based on Coca-Cola
polar bears and not on polar bear behavior and ecology, are these intelligent at all?
What does it say about the psychologists who make them?

But even my general use of the word "psychology" is an example of this *singularization-
as-oversimplification* to the extent that I really don't mean all psychology or all
psychologists. I only mean those psychologists who singularized intelligence by
stuffing us with perverse ideas. Furthermore, "love" was and is singularized too as the
romantic or the sexy, until it was operationalized as different types of love variables
(Sternberg, 1988).

"Science" is singularized by the popular media to mean just about everything and
usually little because hardly ever is it referred to as The Scientific Method. The
terms Americans, Arabs, Europeans, and Latinos are also linguistic singularizations
and in this process they become convenient stereotypes. These terms exclude the
complexities and diversities of an entire continent of Americans, diverse Arab groups,
diverse Europeans, and a plethora of Latinos. I know I am preaching to the converted,

but sometimes, even among the converted, I find that each person makes singularistic allowances for their favorite semiotic funnel: the concept of "god" for example.

The problem is not with ideas such as COCA-COLA BEARS, GOD, LOVE, PSYCHOLOGY, or SCIENCE but rather with semiotic ignorance and/or mischief. To be fair, the alienation from an ancient telluric source did not begin with human civilization, or with capitalist and communist propaganda. It could be argued that the process began when some form of ape acquired a full-fledged self-aware status and acquired, to boot, a sequential verbal machine that transcribed thoughts into audible and peculiar signs. These are burdens in and of themselves. But when the ape forgets that it is part of nature and comes to believe that it is the very words it uses, then social chaos and mental illness are not far behind.

A Synnomic Progression of Language

We semioticians owe too much. We are, really, antiquarians. We are always in obligation to the copious foundational ideas of too many writers. Thus, maintaining an original stance and perspective in semiotic writing is as difficult as being a creative historian without the risk of changing history itself. Depending on what we happen to be writing about on a given day, semiotic writing is an interminable and intense labor of annotations, historical references, legends and antiquities.[41] But two semioticians, whether they knew themselves as such or not, who need to be showcased more often outside the semiotics of psychology are Sigmund Freud and Carl G. Jung.[42] Their footnotes need to be larger than they are today.

I will concentrate on the contributions of C. G. Jung in this section—his *synnomic* model. From Jung we have the same problem of deciding what to borrow, change, critique, and save as enduring and relevant to semiotics. In his *Symbols of Transformation* (1944) Jung begins the first chapter, appropriately enough, with a theory of language, speech and thought. In fact I read the entire book as a semiotic treatise aimed at tracking the mythical origins of thought in contrast to "directed thinking" or thinking with language. In this sense, this entire text is relevant to semiotics. This much is obvious to several semioticians who have discovered, talked about, and continue to expand this connection. Here I do not want to critique Jung,[43] but my aims are to employ his linguistic structural model "off the shelf," so to speak, in as simple a way as I can, in order to make the ecopsychological points that will be brought up later in this text.

Jung himself is caught in the act of semiotic discovery through referencing by selecting voices and ideas congruent with his notions of the mythical and of dreaming as the source of the MYTHICAL. Thus, we cannot give all the credit to Jung for these linguistic dichotomies and distinctions, but we can applaud his intense scholarship in gathering the materials for our use and reflection. For the purposes of simplicity and summary, I refer the reader to Jung's book.

The model he presents is summarized in Tables I and II. These tables have been modified by me and also include additional and modern terms so that the semiotic and biosemiotic scholar can bridge the classical and the contemporary terminology, conveniently, in a single image. Table I tracks in four columns what I have generically labeled *a synnomic progression*.[44] The first column of Table I labels this synnomic progression with terminology used by Jung and found in his references. I have also included and emphasized the *synnomic* progression in ecopsychological terms. The second column, which was not in Jung's original, comes via Heidegger and Paul Shepard (1967). Its aim is to track an ecopsychological-to-nature-alienated progression. The third column tracks a theorized *aim* of this intellectual historical perspective of language function. These aims are personal, political and/or communal. The fourth and last column tracks the *synnomic* progression proper of language with respect to its *function relations*—its biosemiotic function.

Table I: A Synnomic Evolution of Language
Historical Unfolding of Language and its Semiotic Functions
From Natural, to Mythical to Logical Thinking

Stages	Nature-Thought Affiliation	Aim	Synnomic Function
I. Supra-Linguistic (or *Hypological*) Language: **Intra-psychic** Personal Mythology	**Telos** A high degree of *consiliency* between thought, action, words, and natural existence. *Dream Thinking*	*Onomatopoeic (& sound symbolism)* Natural imitation and literal relation; personal identification with the natural	*More Intra-relational than Inter-relational, but Inter-relational with nature* and the natural; subjective and personal
II. Ancient-Linguistic Language: **Inter-psychic** Shared Mythology	**Logos** Partial meaning knowledge of quanta of word meanings. The beginning of formulaic (esoteric) and non-democratic language and meanings.	*Scholastic* Philosophy and religion as science. Everyday living is more and more dependant on priestly rituals	*Decontextualized signs but still mythical* Increasing borrowing and infiltration of foreign terms and beginning of separation from *telluric* sources
III. Hyper-linguistic (or *Hyperglossal and Hyperlogical*) Language: **Exo-psychic** Instantaneous and Mass-shared phenomenology. The end of MYTH and the proliferation of ideologies.	**Gerere*** Speaking fluency, for fluency's sake and the amassing or accumulation of quantities of knowledge *without synthesis*. Erich Fromm's *Abstractification*	*Polis* Political and Technical sciences separate *Logos* and *Telos*	*Abstract arbitrary sign*, technical languages, propaganda, singularization of complexity and experience. *Inter-relational in large scales* with diminishing meaning impact.

* Heiddeger

Table II: A Synnomic Evolution of Language
Historical Unfolding of Language Proxies and Their Semiotic Functions
From Natural, to Mythical to Logical Thinking

Phase	Where	Proxies	Synnomic Function
Phase 1: **Shamanic**	Between Stages I and II	The *Shaman as* a valid *Proxy* for the natural or the supernatural.	Spiritual specialist and *mediator* between social, natural, and spiritual realm.
Phase 2: **Rhetorical**	Between Stages II and III	The *Storyteller, Poet, or Orator as* a collective memory. *Aesthetics as Proxy for nature*	A *repository* of stories, language, proper uses of language, and *encyclopedic function*.
Phase 3: **Transcendental** (& deconstructive)	During the deconstruction of, and Beyond Stage III	The *Mystic-Scientist.* Ecology and ecopsychology as consilient forces. New Interrelatedness. The realization that *the dogmatic "proxy" is itself an alienating force.* Reevaluation of personal and Communal responsibilities	Natural laws and habits prove more difficult to describe in scientific categories. A move toward the *ecumenical. Statistical know-how* forces a move toward *interdisciplinary dialogue*

Stage I or...

To this table we need to add three transitional phases in order to further summarize and accommodate other treatises that propose linguistic origins or track the development and function of speech. These transitional phases are the *Shamanic*, the *Rhetorical*, and the *Transcendental* as seen in Table II. The columns follow the same orientation as in Table I, except that this progression tracks the "proxy" of language, or the linguistic mediator and midwife of semiotic processes (respectively, historically speaking, the shaman, the storyteller-poet-orator, and the mythical scientist).

Before we proceed to highlight, deconstruct, or apply this synthesis let's pause for a moment and read from Jung the following: "The secret of cultural development is the mobility and disposability of psychic energy. Directed thinking, as we know it today, is a more or less modern acquisition which earlier ages lacked."[45]

And furthermore:

> It would be a ridiculous and unwarranted presumption on our part if we imagined that we [modern mind, and people] were more energetic or more intelligent than the men of the past—our material knowledge has increased, but not our intelligence. This means that we are just as bigoted in regard to new ideas, and just as impervious to them, as people were in the darkest days of antiquity. The centre of gravity of our interest has switched over to the materialistic side, whereas the ancients preferred a mode of thought nearer the fantastic type. To the classical mind everything was still saturated with mythology, even though classical philosophy and the beginnings of natural science undeniably prepared the way for the work of enlightenment.[46]

It is clear from these and other passages that Jung (1952, and also Freud, 1900/1996) believes in a connection, via dream experiences at least, to an ancestral mind. In Jung's analysis there is no such thing as a "primitive" mind, if by that we mean lower thought capacity. Therefore, the only difference is one of *synnomic function*, or a difference in the mode, function, and aim of language. To elaborate, a *synchretic* or "primitive" thought-language mode is compact and *existentially intimate* as compared to the *synnomic* uses of language in increasingly larger social groups. If we believe with Jung that:

> Language was originally a system of emotive and imitative sounds—sounds which express terror, fear, anger, love, etc., and sounds which imitate the noises of the elements: the rushing and gurgling of water, the rolling thunder, the roaring of the wind, the cries of the animal world, and so on; and lastly, those which represent a combination of the sound perceived and the emotional reaction to it. A large number of onomatopoetic vestiges remain even in the more modern languages; note, for instance, the sounds for running water: *rauschen, rieseln, ruschen, rinnen, rennen, rush, river, ruscello, ruisseau, Rhein*. And note *Wasser, wissen, wissern, pissen, piscis, Fisch*. (Jung, 1956:12)

Then not only are many of these words still present in modern languages, but more importantly, speakers accept no substitutes even when many of these terms, it can be argued, are remnants of proto languages now extinct, such as Proto-Indo-European.

Equally noteworthy, if this ancestral mind and its communicative functions belong to what ecopsychologist Theodore Roszak (2001) calls the "ecological unconscious," then this unconscious functions in the temporal present and it may continue to invent new onomatopoetic terms to express a burgeoning material and informational world. For example, it is interesting to me that the name for an unthinkably large number, a google,[47] was invented by a child, still synchretic in his thinking, and has the sonorous quality of unquantifiable masses of water. It is even more interesting, and very relevant to Jung's selection of onomatopoetic water terms, that the term *Google* is used to describe a company and web informational portal where people "surf" the web. This is not only an apt and ecopsychologically expected term but it elegantly expresses the new informatics and experience of managing copious amounts of information and "skipping" the philosopher's stone from hypertext to hypertext. Even if we were to argue that only sonorous sources of stimuli lend themselves to *onomatopoesis*, this sense predominates in speech and may be the best indicator of archaic linguistic connections or functions.[48]

However, with increasing social complexity, a discrete or objective language modality is needed and becomes more prevalent simply because it makes social transactions more efficient and because the increased affiliation toward the more material and incremental *polis* (a proliferation of technology and of objects being manufactured; living in closed quarters; and complex political and religious relations) demands a direct and oversimplified approach of communication. For example, onomatopoetically speaking, the sound of a car engine (e.g., a Ford Model T) has changed considerably in one hundred years. Even when kids and adults from three generations have made onomatopoetic sounds after engines, nevertheless, these are different and no one can assume that kids will be making the same sounds two hundred years into the future.

Also, and particularly a symptom of contemporary consumerism and materialistic life, purchasable goods and objects proliferate in fashion waves so rapidly and in such a disposable manner (in their existence and value) that the labels we assign to these products are quickly rendered (semiotically) obsolete. The labels are rendered obsolete precisely because our relational Umwelts with these objects were superficial to begin with. In short, the synnomic function of language is increasingly more about logistics and keeping longer and longer inventories than about keeping track of a handful of real, close-up affiliations.

In this additional sense, one can appreciate why dreams may be more "real" than these linguistic and material goods. This is a paradox for Jung and others, that dreaming may be more authentic and real than the products we consume or the fat-girth that increasingly surrounds our bodies. The reason they will give us, I think, is that dreaming is still rooted in and connected to and will always be about Stage I (Conesa, 2004). Roszak goes further in his belief that this telluric connection precedes even homo species and recedes farther back into the very origins of life.[49]

Therefore, dream interpretation methodology in psychoanalysis is truly the only avenue left to investigate how this primal mind is doing in the midst of an over-civilized and unnatural world. The natural or primal mind, *Telos*, has a greater difficulty for confabulation because a wilder and more lethal world exacts immediate consequences. Or if it lies, it is not personal or ideological.[50] Rationalization and confabulation, not just mere intentional deceit, belong to the realm of civilization, to *Logos* and to *Polis*.

The transitional phases that I have included can also be an empirical test of Jung's model (and my interpretation-addition) since one could determine if a group of humans, using their own language, needs a mythico-existential *proxy* in order to relate to nature OUT THERE. If they do and the proxy is a nature-wise family member or a shaman, we can still describe these humans as maintaining a credible *intra-psychic* connection with nature. But if the shaman begins to substitute the real with the idiosyncratic and personal, then reality may also change for his/her trusting customers.

The model also predicts a breakdown in the quality of semiosis, a degeneration of both inter- and intra-psychic relations that the scholars within a given stage or phase may or may not be aware of. That is, the primacy of language *per se*, within a purely anthropocentric milieu that excludes nature at large, may be seen as an indication that the human SIGN reigns supreme and absolute. This is a perspective that, if not recognized, excludes biosemiotics,[51] once again assuming that by biosemiotics we also mean an original human-nature semiosis giving rise to our present-day cognitive and consciousness apparatus. This later morbidity and exclusive view of the SIGN is problematic in psychological practice because it renders both the patient and the clinician blind to their respective telluric alienation. Roszak (1992/2001) criticizes this deficit as one of the greatest failures of mainstream clinical psychology or psychiatry when he says:

> Therapy makes no demand for clean air, the songs of birds, the presence of trees or sea, mountain or stream. The troubled soul locked in a tortured ego will never be coaxed to look out and around at something greater, more lordly, more ennobling: a state of nature that invites the mind to contemplate eternal things. Yet common experience tells us that a solitary walk by the river or ocean, a few calm hours in the woods restore the spirit and may produce more insight into our motives and goals than the best labors of the professional analyst. The quiet contemplation of the night sky before one turns to sleep and dreams might do more to touch the mind with a healing grandeur than weeks, months, years of obsessive autobiographical excavation.

Continuing on, Phase III could be an ideal, if it is thoroughly transforming and encompassing in its ecology and enough "mythic-scientists"[52] exist, with enough political power, to enable and sustain a social and cultural deconstruction facilitated by empirical-statistical knowledge. Thus, when encountered, it could seem to be a chaotic patchwork of voices and criticisms (ideological cacophonies) and might therefore be limited in its ability to transform a diverse and competing global community so that anti-ecological and selfish trends are effectively curtailed. Semiotically speaking, at least three forms of discourse are competing with each other, and/or occurring simultaneously. Empirical-statistical knowledge, espoused by the mythic-scientist, challenges political or ideological rhetoric and pseudo-shamanism in a social arena where the audience is not interested, nor trained, and frankly, ecopsychologically too ill to get up from its hospital bed. The strange and turbulent times of Phase III make for strange bedfellows. That is, biologists and environmentalists alike meet up and form alliances with *true shamans* everywhere, and with remaining first-nation peoples in order to maximize *noetic* efficiency and for survival's sake.

The hypothetical and global realization of Phase III supposes a breakdown (not necessarily peacefully or harmoniously) and complete reorganization and cooperation from nations that are today anachronistic and antagonistic to one another. For example, upcoming third world "have-nots" such as India, enjoying rising levels of growth and economic prosperity, refuse to embrace ecological science and logic so it can finally enjoy the wealth and prosperity industrialized nations have had. Understandingly, some Indian politicians view with suspicion well-intended ecological occidental ethos as an impediment to this growth. They believe they have a right to the same affluence that the West has enjoyed. So, it is not only the material complexity of a single *polis* or the materialistic attitudes of its citizens that prevent the implementation of ecological integration and ideals. In short, Phase III is further challenged and impeded by how wide spread and well-integrated the new psychological outlook is, a return to Phase I, across the myriad of conflicting interests, most of which run counter to this conversion and deconstruction. It may also take two or three generations of consistent telluric gains to achieve some degree of stability—no small task.

The separation from *Telos* implied in Stages II and III readily invites a *barbaric societal correction* with possible *transcendental* solutions. That is, it is their initial or outright alienation from *Telos*, exacerbated by the *stranger proxies*, that opens the door for an infusion of the barbaric as a correcting force both in language and in existence. The "barbaric" stands for a return to the dignity and truth of self-reliance and to a renewed intimacy with natural existence even though it may not achieve this ideal. More importantly, with the implosion of closed sign systems and the encountering of natural laws and habits that contradict a cherished *Logos* that cohabits with materialistic trends, the same hyper-linguistic forces seek *transcendence* and liberation and conspire with the incoming barbarian to "shake things up a bit." The flower power and sexual revolution in the 1960's is an example of this "treason" within. The ecological unconscious was unleashed once again.

Given what Jung believes about the purity and the wellness-holism of the ancestral mind, then we must remind ourselves that the barbaric as a force representing or fighting for *Telos* can never be called "infantile." The barbarians can be said to be naive or innocent with respect to the artificiality of *Logos* but never infantile because this derogation implies a misbehaving from a superior developmental platform, which as we have seen, cannot be found in successive stages. Only in the biosemiotic chaos of Stage III, as we exist today, can behavior be called infantile. It is not surprising then that the anthropological literature conveys ample examples and narratives of natural peoples' commentary about us: we are backward, we are childlike, we spoil the world, we trash our own house, we don't even speak with a language that signifies deep enough, that describes accurately.

The remarks of Albert White Hat, Sr., a Lakota language instructor, in reference to how the Lakota language was misused and misinterpreted by both missionaries and anthropologists, are neither infantile nor unsophisticated. In particular he makes reference to the unidimensionality and *singularization* by both groups of a complex Lakota concept embodied in a single word, *wakan*, which traditionally meant "energy," both positive and negative:

> Young people need to understand that language contains the power to give life or to take it away and that it therefore must be used with respect . . . For example, *wakan*, used as a noun, means "energy." It teaches that all creation has the power to give life or to take it away. Christians understood this word to mean "something sacred." Anthropologists translated *wakan* as "mystery." In such ways traditional Lakota meanings get corrupted and, eventually, lost.

That Christian missionaries missed the dichotomizing opportunities of the original meaning or that anthropologists were uncreative, not sagacious enough with their science, to explain what the "mystery" was, is unimportant to the fact that a telluric connection that existed, and still exists, between *wakan* and some Lakota speakers was not lost in translation. If it were not for people like Mr. Albert White Hat, Sr. and countless others who are reviving these telluric connections in other endangered languages, the cosmological insight of first-nation peoples would be lost to history altogether. Anyone who speaks of language as having "the power to give life or to take it away and that it therefore must be used with respect" deserves our respect and counts as a semiotician or linguist of note.

In the next section I will continue sharing some of the general implications that I see, if my expansion of Jung's model is adequate, in the emerging field of ecopsychology as a deconstruction of mainstream and politicized psychology, and the opportunity of utilizing semiotics and biosemiotics as analysis.

General Implications of a Synnomic Model of Language: Self-Correcting Biosemiosis and The Cyclical Nature of Semiosis

Earlier I made the claim that my expanded version of Jung's Synnomic language-thought model describes a breakdown of human semiosis from natural and grounded to the hyper-logical or the ultra artificial. Another way of saying this is that synnomic evolution moves from biosemiotics to anthropocentric semiotics, or worse, as Spinoza suspected, to the condition of an *Amanuensis*, to civilization using a groundless language as a parrot philosopher reproducing extant and exotic useless texts of which the individual has no knowledge.

I have also qualified semiosis as "perverted" insofar as the scholastic gains made in Stage II are continued into *Stage III* and result in the study of and perhaps obsession with sign systems *sui generis* without considering their telluric aspects (biosemiosis) and origins. For example, the illusion of a supremacy of sign discoveries and developments in mathematics and logic soon run into trouble when someone points out that we are really speaking about closed sign systems that might have simplistically under-represented natural laws or habits: our minds, our languages, and their origins.

Specifically, it is rather odd to speak of mathematics as if it were *the* language of nature or *god's* language. Mathematics is neither; it is a human invention. We do not know whether beings in other worlds utilize mathematics as part of their *noetic* system. Some SETI[53] astronomers seem to think so. But, it is equally conceivable that the sensory-perceptual-cognitive systems of conscious beings on other planets bring them closer, via immediate and intuitive access, to natural laws or habits, thus eliminating the need for mediating sign systems to comprehend these realities. Equally true, let's not forget that the visual artist and the musician also make similar claims about pictures or music being nature's or god's language. Either some of these occurring and "supreme" semioses are arbitrary, or god is a multi-signing phenomenon.

Stages I through III, with intervening phases I through III, reflect this disintegration: an obsession with the sign or a particular sign system (usually one's favorite language) and becoming conveniently forgetful about our common telluric origins of communication, with predictable psychic and societal consequences. If language no longer stands for a real telluric connection, then it can be easily abstracted to the point that Earth and its natural processes are inconsequential abstractions to humankind and therefore can be singularized into merely utilitarian commodities, with other consequences such as moving down the slippery road toward dehumanization, alienation, or modern brutality in order to feel that something is "natural." Too much has already been lost when people, bridges, and our planet can be described exclusively in monetary terms.

Additionally, I am proposing that there are reasons to believe that this synnomic evolution is also cyclical. I do not have to look farther than the history of the European continent—with civilized proper and barbaric pauper many times over; to Roman and Celtic or Germanic conflicts; Middle Ages and Enlightenment into Rousseau; to decapitations and Hitler and superman ideals; to a cold war and flower people again; to more Tarzan Disney movies and novo-druid worship—to make this point. This contrapuntal dance is both a horrific and fascinating cycle of yin yang epochs, of alternating back-to-nature and basics to *Logos* and *Polis*, back and forth. Additionally, we can look to Mayan, Easter Island and Egyptian societies and their synnomic dances to find similar analogies. The Mayans, ironically, may have been very keen to celestial cycles, but in the end, their Stage I or II civilization reverted back to shamanism and small-scale interpersonal dynamics, magic mushrooms and marginal jungle subsistence, that is, to Stage I. If we believe the archeological data this "correction" might have occurred in the aftermath of a Phase II that included environmental degradation, political coups, and the dismantling of a priestly caste.

North Americans (and Europeans as well) have incorporated the "barbaric" into the puritan languages and strict religions of England and Spain. Tomatoes, tobacco, chilies, and chocolate did some spicing, but native languages, telluric philosophies and manners of thought did so too. As a consequence of this relatively recent brush with the barbarian, the Old World, stereotypically, treats these Americans as unrefined newcomers, as juvenile and abrupt. And at the same time, Western-themed movies were and are adored as a symbol of embeddedness in nature. More in vogue nowadays is the practice of making a trip to South America to recapture ancient ways, or to feel a renewed sense of humanity. The exported American (North or South) "culture" is always embraced by co-conspirators, internally, by "treason-within" despite the protest of old continental puritans. And if one is not into *cowboys, vaqueros,* or *gauchos,* then one can travel even farther yet and bask in the Australian stereotype of camels, kangaroo meat, wild Snowy-River horses, koalas, and didgeridoos. We seek the exotic because we have lost it or because it reminds us of an authentic telluric biosemiosis.

As if these examples were not enough, for all these alternating epochs one can find avatars, prophets, heroes of all kinds, priests, etc., all recognizable individuals with their deeds amply recorded, who function as the three types of proxies named in the three synnomic phases. No semiotician can observe so much historical bloodshed and energy and deduce that countless humans have been in the habit of killing, defending, changing, challenging, and transcending, without language being implicated in these transitions, and impacted as well, cyclically and with a recognizable direction to and from linguistic synnomic poles.

I am, on the other hand, making a bolder claim that language (through dream semiosis as Freud and Jung maintained—Conesa, 2004) "remembers" a telluric past and forces civilized semiotics back to its origins. How could this be the case? Why should scholastic, refined beyond recognition from an autochthonous meaning, boring semiosis be self-correcting toward the telluric and biosemiotic origin? What is the gain in semiotic regression? Language will always do so, regress to the its telluric base, if we accept that an ecological unconscious (Roszak, 1992/2001), as both Freud and Jung observed,[54] is already embedded in ancestral modes that exist always in an eternal present tense in the unconscious (Freud, 1900/1996 and 1949/1989). If the first and original ground of experience (which is being maintained by countless individuals and communities even to this day, through their daily actions and ecological mind sets) is to be found in intimate relations with a real and authentic world (natural), why then wouldn't a still present function of this original MIND, language, want to do the same? Move the synnomic needle too much toward *Logos* and *Polis* and the human mind and its organically based language with onomatopoeic origins "feel" marginalized, accused, accosted, barraged, insulted, and tricked—a stranger in a strange synthetic land. Then, language cannot stand it anymore and rebels with rock-and-roll, poetry, or tango!

We must not accept the above arguments from authority. We shall instead simply look around and see the emergence of other "tangos"—at the raw poetics of rap music, the noisy grunge, the multiple piercing and tattooing of youth and the middle aged alike, at novo-tribal ecstasy and didgeridoo playing, at extreme sports, and the "barbaric" among us—all clearly visible and even understandable as an inoculation against *tinsel economics*, and as a return to the telluric. Even Freud passionately enjoyed the most *telluric* of enterprises, mushroom hunting, as a balance to his academic pursuits. This was an intriguing and fitting hobby for someone whose career was spent understanding the larger mycelium of the Id in order to better understand and even heal the mushroom fruiting body of the Ego. According to Ernest Jones' biography of Freud (1961:364):

> The most characteristic feature of Freud's holiday pursuits was his passion for mushrooms, especially for finding them . . . One of his daughters told me there were three things her father was especially desirous of teaching his children: a knowledge of wild flowers, the art of finding mushrooms, and the technique of the card game tarock. And he was completely successful in all of them.

To add nuance to the complexity of great minds, and equally relevant to our discussion, the anthropologist and semiotician Lévi-Strauss almost ends his famous *Tristes Tropiques* with a curious chapter entitled, "A Little Glass of Rum." I will let the reader find the footnote that explains this title as an additional pun to our synnomic story. In this chapter he writes:

> In Martinique, I had visited rustic and neglected rum-distilleries where the equipment and the methods used had not changed since the eighteenth century. In Puerto Rico, on the other hand, in the factories of the company that enjoys a virtual monopoly over the whole of the sugar production, I was faced by a display of white enamel tanks and chromium piping. Yet the various kinds of Martinique rum, as I tasted them in front of ancient wooden vats thickly encrusted with waste matter, were mellow and scented, whereas those of Puerto Rico are coarse and harsh. We may suppose then, that the subtlety of the Martinique rums is dependent on impurities the continuance of which is encouraged by the archaic method of production.

Even though Lévi-Strauss intuits something I am not ready to deal with here, *synnomic balance*,[55] this passage can function as an analogy to the synnomic evolution and perversion we have been talking about. Namely, Telos as the Martinique rum, because it is grounded in the organic and the natural, tastes better than the "civilized" and hyper-technological *Logos* or *Polis* rum. His example also speaks to the diversity of methods in the many refineries and tastes connected with the traditional production techniques. That is, with civilization also comes the loss of individuality and multiplicity of expression and the prevention of synnomic inter-psychic relations. If language was like rum, then we could say that a language rooted in Telos is multifaceted and signifies expansively in contrast to the monopoly of distilled purism and singular views.

Telos is rum from Martinique and we long to taste its exotic origins because we instinctively know it is better for us, more authentic. *Polis* (and *Logos*) is Puerto Rican rum, and other than the inexperienced teenager who is just beginning to drink, who drinks that white and insipid stuff anyway?

In agreeing with Shepard's theses that our original semiosis with nature was more biosemiotic than semiotic,[56] I am the first to admit that I am taking a rather extreme position. For example, in an important qualitative sense (an ecologist would argue quantitative as well), I would disagree with Kull (1998) when he said, "A human community with nature, even at its best, cannot be a community with wilderness. Living with nature ultimately means changing nature. Ninety percent of trees growing in England are not of indigenous species . . ." Neither Lévi-Strauss, nor Kull, nor

I, because of our respective novo-anthropocentric and "civilized" biases, can begin to imagine how present-day Yanomamos, *still living* in pristine Amazonian forests, relate to wilderness or how *First nature* "uses" them. I can only observe the obvious: that their way of relating to nature has not caused so much mayhem, but our way has. Or we can say that their singularizations of First nature are better than ours. By better I mean sustainable and non-destructive in a catastrophic sort of way.

Their text is, in this sense, more biosemiotic and less semiotic.[57]

Practical Consequences of a Synnomic Progression: Specific problems and limitations of *city-dwelling vectorial space and transit*

It was the ethological work of Uexkull's colleague, Martha Muchow (Crain, 2000), who demonstrated how children's view of space was, unlike the forced mobility imposed by urban settings, *non-vectorial*[58] and that their transit through space exhibited a richer and more diverse motoric deployment and general involvement with their surroundings than adult mobility. In a manner of study similar to Uexkul's study and understanding of the *Umwelt* of a fly (Werner, 1948; Crain, 2000), Muchow showed how German children in a dock in Hamburg, unlike the adults who followed a prescribed fenced downhill path, played and engaged with the different elements (fence, hill, path) in ways that might have tested the patience and propriety of any adult. Who has not waited in line, obediently glued to an invisible spot, and admired the boldness of a child who hangs from the queue cord, cutting across several more of these imaginary adult-made boundaries, disobeying all adult-made fictional barriers while embracing the perceptual freedom of his/her own wide-open horizon?

City dwelling demands the *vectorization* of three-dimensional space into, semiotically speaking, the *singularization* of streets, roads, car lines, vertical space, and human queues. Movement along vectors is common in natural spaces, such as when animals utilize preferred trails, paths, and directions for foraging or other uses. Humans who traverse natural spaces also show vectorial preferences, and this word, preference, is important, for certain routes or trails. Usually, these routes are suggested (never dictated) by the safest and most efficient vector between and along two points and, given the theoretical assumptions of Semiotic Matrix Theory (SMT), these constraints may be *panbiosemiotical* and prevalent across diverse species (Conesa, 2001).

The unimpeded exploratory mobility in hunting or foraging or of the type seen in children, knows no trails. And it is partly due to this freedom of movement and perceptual monitoring that humans were able to acquire the *noological*[59] and consciousness apparatus that is now being funneled, cajoled, and directed toward consumer items, that is beaten into submission by visual or auditory regulatory symbols, and by the annoying and territorially offensive bumping into a sea of human bodies. The *singularization* of space in urban settings is propaganda at its best, of this or that other competing ideology. *More fundamentally, the ideology is that of the anthropocentric ape who is distracted from natural telluric contemplation by the illusion that in tight vertical space lays the culmination of his superior mental faculties and feels a perverse need to advertise it in such a prolific manner.*

What is not seen in human hunter-forager mobility is the ever-present (even relentless) semiotically perverse obligation to unidirectionality, then the reiteration of this command by a plethora of symbols and signs which bombard and confuse the senses, then being herded by the hurrying masses into unwanted directions, and finally, the additional threat of negative consequences for disobeying this imposed mobility. I can remember receiving a fine ($20.00)[60] when I first arrived in Los Angeles for jay walking, a common behavior in Venezuela, and being thoroughly confused by what somebody was defining as a transgression. For in Venezuela, as in other "barbaric" countries, cars seem as bulls that can be averted with grace and skill even if a cape is not handy.

"Jay walking" may be more dangerous and messier than zebra crossings, but it is also more efficient in any traffic environment when the person is swift enough. But this is not the first time that *tellurically* adaptive behavior has been penalized or misunderstood.

Even cognitive psychologists[61] may miss or singularize an earlier adaptation bias to forming and relying on mental maps as an inferior heuristic to their favorite theoretical bias. Such is the case when subjects show reliance for *route-road* knowledge (physically experienced traversed routes) while estimating the distance between two cities, over actual map information (survey knowledge). That is, the actual traversable territory, with its limitations and vectorial singularizations, is given preference to a map representing distances ("truer and shorter") that, true enough, even a crow can fly over faster (McNamara, Ratcliff, and McKoon, 1984). If an Australian aborigine were participating in such an experiment he would protest by observing that it does not matter that the *kookaburra* is able to fly over Ayer's rock. A person must walk around the big rock, therefore any points along that route are real distances counted in calluses, not flying-meters. Additionally, the Australian aborigine might mutter something like "the map is not the territory, especially if you bring *Dreamtime* into this reckoning."

Moreover, recent data suggest that indeed humans are reckoning distances and traveling through unknown territories logically and naturally by relying on landmarks first, then by examining the space between the landmarks, and finally, by incorporating this information into configurational knowledge (Hunt & Walter, 1999).

The impoverished semiosis of city space is more insidious when even a compass becomes obsolete in city navigation (one needs a compass while traveling in the Venezuelan open savannahs). If one is driving a rental car through an unknown city it is useless to know that one has to travel north or south of one's present position when one-way traffic is impatiently pushing one's vehicle in the opposite direction. It does not help that all types of traffic symbols and signs are rapidly passing us by while we are simultaneously bombarded by the rest of the billboarded city and more useless text. Anyone who thinks that this kind of text extraction is normal or that it is conducive to deep and meaningful relations or understanding must surely think me odd. I readily admit that I belong to another epoch, one with horses and chariots or dazzling whizzing gazelles.

While moving in natural spaces—deserts, savannahs, water, forests, or mountains— these restrictions and pressures are either non-existent or apparent only as an acceptable or logically insurmountable geological obstacle that the mind and the senses can accommodate. Once again, there is more than an analogy here between the *singularization* of space in city dwelling and Coca-Cola polar bears. Both are the result of five or six thousand years of degrading biosemiosis into a culturally accepted madness we call civilized life or normal semiosis. Synomically speaking, we have also reached the ecological "pay up" moment when fallacious and adorned text cannot fix ozone holes, resuscitate countless species from extinction, or think up clever things to say to patients who really long for, whether they realize it or not, clear water, fresh breezes, physical activity, and unimpeded vistas of horizontal complexity.

The consequences of city life, rationalized or not, and of its detrimental effects on physical, mental, and textual health are not a new topic of discussion. What is remarkable is that "civilized" and semiotically scrutinized life has been around for such a long time with but a handful of humans protesting it, much less clamoring for its transformation and the cessation of its nefarious psychological influences. Paul Shepard (1982) remarked of the same willingness to remain passive, impotent, or dulled in the face of such a dysfunctional setting when he wrote:

> It is odd, after seventy centuries of city life, that we can continue to be uneasy about it and uncertain as to what is wrong. The situation is like those psychological illnesses in which the patient shows a devilish capacity to obscure the real problem from himself. A demon seems to make false leads, so that deliverance requires more of the same, confusing problem and symptom. It is as though traffic, smog, disease, violence, crime, uncaring strangers, dirt, drug addiction, and unemployment collectively provide distraction from something that perhaps cannot be dealt with . . . Let us suppose, with some evidence, that the city is typically a sink of

psychological problems. In the individual these are partly caused by city life, but in the longer view they cause the city. Where can the cycle be broken, and what are its processes?

Conclusion

It is an open question, and an ongoing semiotic experiment, to affirm that humans are adaptable enough to survive (or even learn to enjoy?) chaotic and meaningless semioses of the types described above and believe them to be superior (the progress of a triumphantly marching forward creative and "clever" text) to a moment of solitude and contemplation in an alpine meadow. And even if a minority of humans can adapt to such a chaotic environment and accompanying semiosis, what would they be like? Like most of us today?

It may not be an accident that both types of singularization, linguistic and space-vectorial, co-exist synomically in time and place. To the extent that urban life and the cult of the city are signs of an alienating trend away from natural spaces and their original and authentic biosemiosis, the city also becomes the citadel and fortification where nature cannot reach us (Roszak, 1992-2001). Consequently, city dwelling exacts a semiotic tribute that is none other than a perverse forced semiosis, with a password of "progress," an artificial and corrupted text—all human minds and bodies "kindly" form a straight line.

The resulting logico-existential sequence is simple even when combining all of our ecopsychological and biosemiotic analyses presented thus far: *banal, unnecessary and counter-ecological artificiality produces banal, unnecessary and counter-ecological text, which in turn produces neurosis. Neurosis leads to a further degradation of reality and text and to an exaggerated reaction, usually in the form of further illness (both physical and mental), with accompanying depression and violence.*

It may give some semioticians and psychiatrists alike a sense of job security that the new oversemiotized ape is so confused and disturbed. But both professionals will run out of customers, and/or their academic pursuits will seem at least cruel or misdirected when the sick ape, its dying text, and the alienating vertical space it has constructed for itself all disappear in the chaos and aftermath of yet another telluric revolution. Didgeridoo players who sport totemic tattoos won't necessarily like the academic types[62] nor have any need of psychiatric handholding in the aftermath of the next telluric revolution. They won't like the jibing accented man who smokes a pipe and says to them, "Hey, hey, that is faulty language . . . and your mother was a whore." The didgeridoo players who sport totemic tattoos will carve an *Ommis Korecta* (Bragg, 2003:183) tattoo on some body part of the pipe smoking accented man and send him piping elsewhere.

Chapter Two References

Bragg, M. (2003) *The adventure of English: the biography of a language*. London, Hodder and Stoughton.

Chomsky, N. (1968) *Language and mind*. New York, Harcourt Brace.

Conesa-Sevilla, J. (2001) Topo-existential equilibrium: Constraints of Energy, Safety, and Possibility on 2-D and 3-D terrestrial foraging, predation and defense of city and fossorial systems (Application of Semiotic Matrix Theory to the Biosemiotics of Territorial Dialectics). *Paper sent to Gatherings in Biosemiotics 1*, May 24-27, 2001, Copenhagen, Denmark—. Abstract in: http://www.zbi.ee/uexkull/**biosemiotics/conesa**.rtf

Conesa-Sevilla, J. (2003) Sleep Paralysis Signaling (SPS) as a natural cueing method for the generation and maintenance of lucid dreaming. *Presented at The 83rd Annual Convention of the Western Psychological Association*, May 1-4, 2003 in Vancouver, BC, Canada.

Conesa-Sevilla, J. (2004) *Wrestling with ghosts: a personal and scientific account of sleep paralysis*. Pennsylvania, Random House-Xlibris

Conesa-Sevilla, J. (2005) The realm of continued emergence: the semiotics of George Herbert Mead and its implications to biosemiotics, Semiotics Matrix Theory, and ecological ethics. *Sign System Studies*,

Crain, W. (2000) *Theories of development: concepts and applications (4th ed.)*. New Jersey, Prentice Hall.

Freud, S. (1949 & 1989) *An Outline of Psychoanalysis*. (Translated by James Strachey) New York, Norton & Company.

Freud, S. (1900 & 1996) *The Interpretation of dreams*. Translated by A. A. Brill. New York, Random House Value Publishing Inc. (Gracemercy Books).

Fromm, Erich 1955. *The Sane Society*. New York: Holt, Rinehart, & Winston Printing.

Jones, E. (1961) *The life and work of Sigmund Freud*. New York, Basic Books, Inc.

Jung, C. G. (1956 & 1976) *Symbols of transformation: an analysis of the prelude to a case of schizophrenia*. (Translated by R.F.C. Hull) Princeton, N.J., Princeton University press

Jung, Carl G. (ed.) (1964) *Man and his symbols*. New York, Dell Publishing Co. Inc.

Hoffmeyer, J. (1996) *Signs of meaning in the universe*. Bloomington, Indiana University Press.

Hunt, I., and Walter, D. (1999) Orienting and wayfinding: a review. *ONR Technical report*, N00014-96-03801. Arlington VA: Office of Naval Research.

Kull, K. (1998) Semiotic ecology: different natures in the semiosphere. *Sign System Studies*, 26: 344-371.

Lévi-Strauss, C. (1977) *Tristes tropiques*. (Unabridged translation by John and Doreen Weightman.) New York, Pocket Books

Mannheim, K. (1936) *Ideology and utopia: an introduction to the sociology of knowledge.* New York, A Harvest Book.

McNamara, T. P., Ratcliff, R., and McKoon, G. (1984) The mental representation of knowledge acquired from maps. *Journal of Experimental Psychology: Learning, Memory, and Cognition,* 10(4), 444-453.

Nash, R. (1982) *Wilderness and the American mind, 3rd Ed.* New Haven, Connecticut, Yale University Press.

Nietzche, F.W. (1909) *Human, all too human.* (Translated by Helen Zimmern and Paul Cohn) and published in London was Jung's reference found in a different format in Nietzche, F.W. (1986) Human, all too human: a book for free spirits. *In:*(Translated by. R. J. Hollingdale from *Menschlich, Allzumenschliches*: Erste Band, 1878.). Cambridge, Cambridge University Press.

Shepard, P. (1973) *The tender carnivore and the sacred game.* New York, Scribners.

Sternberg, Robert. J. (1988) Triangulating love. *In:* R. Sternberg and M. L. Barnes (eds) *The psychology of love.* New Haven, CT., Yale University Press. p.119-138.

Shepard, P. (1982) *Nature and madness.* San Francisco, Sierra Club.

Roszak, T. (1992 & 2001) *The voice of the earth.* New York, Simon & Schuster.

Werner, H. (1948) *Comparative psychology of mental development (2nd ed.).* New York, Science Editions.

White Hat, Albert Sr. (1996) Lakota language. *In:* F. E. Hoxie (ed) *Encyclopedia of North American Indians.* Boston, Houghton Mifflin Company. p.328-329.

Additional Commentary: The biosemiosis of Sigurd Olson:

"It suddenly came to me last night that what I might write is a description of the sort of enjoyment all of us get: the joy in the moonlight between the islands, the flickering of the northern lights, the smooth dip and flow of the canoe beating before the waves, the smell of cedar, the sharp sweet smell of Sweet Gale as it was bruised by the canoe, 'a thousand million open pores spilling out the fragrance'."

—Sigurd F. Olson, idea for the book *The Singing Wilderness,* July 6, 1952

Chapter Three

Cognitive "Movement" From One Frame of Reference to Another

In the quest to relate the self to society, we contemplate how we want to relate to others, what place we wish to occupy in the social world, and what societal roles are available to us.

—J. Reeve, Understanding Motivation and Emotion

In an ecopsychology of self, and in addition to understanding how language contributes to its edification or erosion, it pays to understand the many mansions and self functions that transcend social transactions and restrictions, or at least, that incorporate a significant relational aspect to the wild. After all, this relational aspect to the wild was a central component or force in socialization for a much longer period during our history and pre-history than present-day constructs and models which have, for all practical purposes, excised any natural influence in the construction of our selves. Since they have so excised nature out of Self studies, this ecopsychologist, at least, takes this to mean that nature estrangement and nature alienation are more pervasive and widespread than previously thought, influencing (putting blinders on) the very development of scientific thought.

The above quote by Reeve depicts a typical anthropocentric and contemporary view of self relations where the self as an agent is myopically instructed to examine his existential horizon *solely in the realm of the humanly manufactured*. Very rarely in psychological works (except perhaps from psycho-anthropology) do we obtain self-relational models that are immediately committed to explanations of self-relating to non-human animals, an ecosystem, and the biosphere. Without this exo-human-societal ability it is difficult to see how humans feel morally obligated to (ought to be) the welfare of animals, identify with animal intelligence and behavior, or place themselves in the perspective of the animals they study in order to understand their natural history.

Furthermore, while reading from Self psychology[63] one gets the impression that humans existed, have existed since our species' origin, in a civilized vacuum where only certain types of societal structures express themselves and that only these can influence our psyche. To refer to this grand omission as being anthropocentric is being generous. That such a gigantic blind spot endures in topics such as personality indicates that these psychologists are so influenced by this hyper-humanistic view that they cannot see the forest for the trees.

One significant exception, accepting his emphasis of that social milieu and approach as well[64], is found in the work of George Herbert Mead, considered the father of American sociology. Mead accepts socialization as the main process through which we acquire our sense of self, consciousness, and language. In that acceptance, and while ignoring human-nature relations he is open to the same ecopsychological deconstructive criticism as any other thinker, more so because his writings have influenced so much of psychology and sociology. However, a lot of Mead is salvageable or transmutable to a reconstruction of self-psychology that maintains human-nature relations as the central story. More specifically, Mead himself is very generous in his *semiosis* in that he allows for, now and then, an open-ended interpretation of his thoughts to be consistent with an ecopsychology of the self.

In almost one perfect philosophical sweep Mead conjoins the concepts of *Sociality*, *Consciousness*, and *Communication* into a coherent explanation of multiple referentiality, a theory of mind, and the concept of *passing* from one frame of reference to another. It is these three concepts that I will address next with an emphasis on explaining Mead's idea of *passing* so that it becomes useful in problems of ecopsychology and biosemiosis.

At least that is my argument in the next few pages which highlight what I described earlier as the more complex or taxing article presented in this book. But its main questions are, at first glance, simple: How do you or I "flex" our *selves* in order to accommodate so many social and natural situations? What mechanisms exist that allow such flexibility? Are there limits to this flexibility?[65] *More specifically, if we know that some constructions of Self are textually false, can we, through some form of ecotherapy, reconstruct it so that it conforms to more natural phylogenic boundaries?*

As we shall see, Mead opens the door to the discussion of these questions and the article may just give us a few answers. One of the answers is that SMT may provide a basic set of ontological parameters, or if you will, sign posts, to ensure this passage from self-situation to self-situation while preserving Self integrity.

The realm of continued emergence: The semiotics of George Herbert Mead and its implications to biosemiotics, semiotic matrix theory, and ecological ethics

(Originally published in *Sign Systems Studies*, vol. 33,
Tartu University, Estonia[66])

Abstract

This examination of the often-inaccessible work and semiotics of George Herbert Mead focuses first on his pivotal ideas of *Sociality, Consciousness*, and *Communication*. Mead's insight of *sociality* as forced relatedness, or forced semiosis, appearing early in evolution, or appearing in simple systems, guarantees him a foundational place among biosemioticians. These ideas are Mead's exemplar description of *multiple referentiality* afforded to social organisms (connected to his idea of the *generalized other*), thus enabling *passing* from one umwelt to another, with relative ease. Although Mead's comprehensive semiosis is basically sound, and in concordance with modern and contemporary semiotics (and biosemiotics), it nevertheless lacks a satisfactory explanation of how conscious organisms achieve *passing* into new frames of reference. Semiotic Matrix Theory (SMT), its *pansemiosis*, describes falsifiable existential and cognitive heuristics of recognizing Energy requirements, Safety concerns and Possibility or Opportunity as "passing" functions. Finally, another type of emergence, ecoethics, is an embedded constant in biosemiosis. Not all semiosis is good semiosis, not all text is good text. Because our species is moving away from ancient biosemiosis and interrelatedness, this *historicity*, even ductile enough to invent synthetic semiosis or capricious umwelten, is facing the ecological reality and consequences of an overly anthropocentric text.

> "*Tarantula*: an insect whose bite is only cured by musick."[sic][67]
> —Melvyn Bragg's (2003:213) entry and selection from
> *Johnson's Dictionary* (1755)

Introduction

It is an understatement to write that Mead's idea of *sociality*, and the mechanism of *passing* from umwelt to umwelt, are underused and understudied in biosemiotics today. With notable interpretations and exceptions to his contributions in general (see Wiley 1994; Harries-Jones 1995; Kilpinen 2002), a neglected obligation to his crucial ideas is due partly to the intractability of Mead's text, often promising to continue in development where some of his ideas seem to walk a step further but no more, or suddenly stopping altogether, his freedom to produce additional text restricted due to his multiple academic and administrative responsibilities.[68] The antiquated and modern term *sociality*, perhaps an unfortunate choice and label today, seems also so biased toward purely human semiosis, thus turning off potential biosemiotic readers in search of a biological synthesis.

Without deciphering what Mead meant by this term and, in general, with the apparent lack of relevance of Mead to biosemiotics, judging by the smaller ratio of his name in references to the names of other turn-of-the-20th-century semioticians, in my opinion, has forced many contemporary writers to almost reinvent the "Mead Wheel". Specifically, if *sociality* is understood as he meant it, forced and pervasive, even inescapable, relatedness or *semiosis*, it provides an additional historical foundation for understanding biosemiotics proper, from endosemiosis to the human text. This is clearly illustrated when Arthur Murphy, a better interpreter of Mead than I, while trying to summarize Mead's communicative processes, says, "[. . .] the appearance of mind is only the culmination of that *sociality* which is found throughout the universe".[69] From endosemiotical-hormonal to human communication, Mead's concept of *sociality*, in tandem with his ideas and definitions of *consciousness* and *communication*, leaves little doubt that he was thinking of a grander biosemiosis while finally being canonized by history as the father of American sociology.

These words are obviously a tease of a more complex and synergetic semiosis that must explain all three concepts to present-day biosemioticians. It may be difficult to do justice, in this short examination, to all of Mead's writings, in which, in fragmentary manner, these concepts are used as the foundations of other elemental ideas. So I have opted instead to focus on *The Philosophy of the Present* (Mead 1930, 1932) as the most cited source and text for further analysis and discussion, yet other references and works will be cited. In the next section, I will try to illustrate in broad strokes, how *sociality*, *consciousness*, and *communication* are intimately connected, thus, once again, anticipating the writings of present day non semiotician, semiotician, and biosemiotician scholars alike. Section Three will connect all three concepts of *sociality*, *consciousness*, and of *communication*, if not in a logical system, at least into a coherent definition and semiosis that exemplifies what evolved semiosis could look like.

Living with more or less consciousness: When is a 'thing' really a part of its Umwelt?

"Always," might answer Mead, with the rest of biosemiotics, at least since the moment it became an organism. But there are differences and degrees of differences of existential embeddedness and the ability to extract meaning from different umwelten. Depending on the organism's evolution of consciousness and the ability to communicate with gestures or signs whose meanings are constantly derived from existential doings; depending on the degree of embeddedness and the ease with which an organsim *passes* from umwelt to umwelt; then its mind can reach a certain threshold referred to earlier as multiple referentiality, on in Mead's term, the capacity for *continued emergence.*

These abilities, which Mead (1932) traces in evolutionary and relativity theory terms, as he understood them, finally place the very construction and manipulation of a SELF within and as part of all the objects found in the umwelt. That is, when an organism is capable of referring to itself as an object among other objects, utilizes the sensations and experiences in reference to its umwelten, and is able to communicate the meanings of all these interactions to itself as well as to others, then that organism has acquired *consciousness* in Mead's (Mead 1932: 82) interpretation of this concept: ". . . the organism responds to itself as affected by a tree and at the same time to the tree as the field of possible interactions".

The interpretative participation of the SELF emerging from and always embedded in a social universe dominates Mead's semiotics. The earlier allusion of the Batesonian phrase describing, in a pithy phrase we have all made into a slogan, the condition of interpretation, 'a difference which makes a difference' (Bateson 1979), would mean for Mead the following:

> Signification has . . . two references, one to the thing indicated, and the other to the response, to the instance and to the meaning of the idea. It denotes and connotes. When the symbol is used for the one, it is a name. When it is used for the other, it is a concept. But it neither denotes nor connotes except, when in form at least, denotation and connotation are addressed both to a self and to others, when it is in a universe of discourse that is oriented with reference to a self. If the gesture simply indicates the object to another, it has no meaning to the individual who makes it, nor does the response which the other individual carries out become a meaning to him [. . .] (Mead 1922: 246)

In short, the "difference" that would make a difference for Mead is that of a social entity that has internalized its social umwelt entirely, knows itself as a SELF, and within the province of this self, assumes universal interpretation of its broadcasted sign. This is the beginning of multiple referentiality, or the beginning of a theory of mind (Premack, Woodruff 1978).

In achieving multiple referentiality, and while addressing the human condition specifically, social beings are able to internalize the roles of others into a meta-schema that Mead made famous: *The Generalized Other.* Many books and articles written across different disciplines have elaborated upon, co-opted and attempted to deconstruct Mead's concept of the *generalized other.* Mead's concept anticipates or stands side by side with Piaget's (1932, 1972; or Vygotsky's beginning of social 'otherness thought,' 1934), depending how one interprets history, emphasis on intelligence being predicated on the ability to take on the perspective of *the other*, tracing its development of scheme from reflexes to circular reactions to egocentrism, and beyond, to formal operations.

'Theory of Mind' researchers and theorists (Premack, Woodruff 1978; Woodruff, Premack 1979; Dennett 1983; Whiten, Byrne 1988; Byrne, Whiten 1988; Dennett 1991; Byrne, Tomasello 1995; Whiten 1996—as well as detractors—see Heyes 1993; 1998) must always pay tribute to Mead in some fashion or another, and the *generalized other*, by any other pseudonym or novel coinage, whether apes do it, rats do it, or human children after the age of four do it, establishes intelligence as that capacity to somehow internalize the thinking of *the other* for any number of social and personal uses from deceit to altruistic empathy. Speaking of altruism, and extending Piaget's and Mead's ideas into the realm of moral reasoning, Kohlberg (1981) seeks and is able to demonstrate with empirical confirmation to Piaget's (1932) and his original intuitions that the abilities in perspective-taking and higher social consciousness set the stage for higher rational ethical thought.

More recently, with the increased focus on Emotional Intelligence (Goleman 1995), the idea of the *generalized other* can be placed on a practical and even empirically testable continuum that even Mead might approve of, beginning with the total neglect of *the other* as being significant to one's own selfish survival, proceeding further in development to familiarity with someone, continuing perhaps into tolerance for someone, graduating into sympathy and finally having empathy for others. Even within our own species, the higher end of this ethical continuum, as the many mansions and umwelten of possibilities of relatedness, is not achieved universally or consistently as Kohlberg's later data show (Colby *et al.* 1987).

A more important reason for revisiting Mead's triple conception of *sociality*, *consciousness* and *communication*, in addition to paying tribute to his foundational ideas, is that in his thinking there is in a solid base and independent confirmation that a mind that evolves in rich social contexts is nicely suited to: (1) extending the range of relatedness to such a fine point where it becomes *the other*; (2) that this now social mind is obligated to communicate the meanings derived from perceiving itself and using the capacity to be *the other* embedded in ever changing umwelten; and (3) that this mind so embedded in a social (objectively external and/or internalized) realm and exposed to a myriad of interactive opportunities has the potential to grow consciousness so as to integrate, no devour, umwelten that are truly extant to other less embedded organisms, as Piaget suggested (1972).[70]

Consciousness and sociality

For Mead the journey of a mind on the way to acquiring consciousness ends up being a communicative and thus semiotic odyssey. He speaks of a first prerequisite of consciousness as an organism *selects* a new umwelt *at will* based on its own organismic needs and sensitivities and amalgamates this ability of selection with the new environment, resulting in further interaction possibilities in the newly forming umwelt. Of this process he writes:

> [...] its first characteristic [the characteristics of a mind acquiring consciousness] is consciousness, that emergent which arises when the animal passes from the system in which it formerly existed to an environment that arises through the selectiveness of its own sensitivity, and thus to a new system within which parts of its own organism and its reactions to these parts become parts of its environment. (Mead 1932: 84)

The intimacy and degree of subjective participation in Mead's rendition of a functional circle marks him as a biosemiotic thinker of note[71] when he underlies the importance of this embeddedness:

> [...] the systems to which I have referred are in all cases interrelations between the organism and the world that reveal itself in an environment, determined by its relationship to the organism. Any essential change in the organism brings with it a corresponding change in the environment. (Mead 1932: 84)

The next step in minds acquiring consciousness is due both to sensorial and cognitive peculiarities that place the interpreter in a Peircian triad (Peirce 1916/1966) in a situation of *mental reflection*. In Mead's own words, "this next step is reached with the dominance of the distance senses and the delayed responses to these".[72] In contemporary terms, a 300 millisecond delay between processing a distal stimulus and its final cognitive recognition, plus additional computation time in higher order, intermodal associative cortex, in communicative animals, offers or enforces a reflective capacity that I believe Mead finds to be crucial for the emergence of consciousness.

The final step in the acquisition of consciousness occurs when, "the characters of the environment constitute the stuff out of which values and meanings later arise when these characters can be isolated though gestures in communication". Therefore, Mead links consciousness itself with valuative communicative processes. Another way to encapsulate this process, as I understand Mead, is to say that *consciousness* is a semiosis on a grander scale, of meaningful and mediated (through communicative exercises) existential responses with a sense of *historicity*.[73] This final leap, according to Mead, opens the door for an appreciation of universals, a signature of evolved consciousness.

Furthermore, it is important to highlight the fact that Mead is perfectly aware of the distinction between consciousness and Self-consciousness, and I believe the final step he refers to in the acquisition of consciousness is really the possession of Self-consciousness. This is clear to me, when, for example, we read him in *Mind, Self, and Society* making this distinction:

> It is the social process of influencing others in a social act and then taking the attitude of the others aroused by the stimulus, and then reacting in turn to this response, which constitutes a self. Our bodies are parts of our environment; and it is possible for the individual to experience and be conscious of his body, and of bodily sensations, without being conscious or aware of himself. (Mead 1934: 171)

This interpretation and read of Mead may leave some biosemioticians with a blank stare and perhaps even disappointed. So, to the extent that Mead's *consciousness* is so dispatched and made to be the unique property of certain types of creatures who do valuative communicative processes, it may rub the wrong way and upset biosemioticians and other students of consciousness who have described consciousness as ubiquitous in the animal kingdom (from the inorganic realm to the plant kingdom and beyond), present from the beginning in the origin of our universe, albeit in some minor quality form, or teleologically evolving toward a certain type of universal presence-consciousness, thus opening the door for moralizing or simply imagining the random adaptation of species as guided development toward a god-like state (Davis 1999).

But Mead "saves the day," in a manner of speaking, because he makes his concept of *sociality* the genesis and integral component of his biosemiotics, if we can begin to be comfortable describing his semiotics as such. Since *sociality* is, simply put, forced relatedness, or forced semiosis, which appears early in evolution, and is present at the lowest levels of organismic interaction[74], he is admitting to the primacy of semiosis, from the beginning, while pointing out that we must be mindful of the obvious qualitative differences that arise when different types of creatures achieve different possibilities of relatedness with their respective umwelten. The highest degree of relatedness that humans understand and can empirically test in nature is the *sociality* he terms, *The Realm of Continued Emergence*. Only creatures like we who can meaningfully evaluate our actions in the face of a changing environment and ask ourselves, in our own minds, the question, "What are my acts in relation to a changing environment?" or "What could these acts mean in possible X or Y environments?", can achieve this sort of specialized consciousness.

Finally, and perhaps more importantly, Mead is naming and describing this particular set of ideas with the intention of determining what the real existential moment is for any creature. Does existence lie in the past? Does it lie ahead in the future? Mead's answer is nay, relatedness with an umwelt is always in the present, even though *historicity*, in the way of habits and learned responses, predisposes a certain biased attitude with respect to accommodating a new umwelt. As Arthur Murphy (1932) interprets Mead, "The present is the locus of reality." But humans, who supposedly live in *The Realm of Continued Emergence*, are ductile in their accomodability to novel situations and in their possibility/opportunity to derive, constantly, new meanings from most changing environments, and to re-apply them. Not only do we inhabit this singularity of the present, but also, according to Mead's own read and interpretation of relativity theory, we could inhabit several umwelten at the same time. In order to explain how this comes about he employs the functionality of *passing* as the mechanism allowing this multiple referentiality.

I will turn next to Mead's idea of *passing*, the mechanism through which an organism moves from umwelt to umwelt while preserving the integrity of crucial aspects of its *historicity*, and at the same time, adapting its *historicity* to new experiential realms.

Passing

It may be easier to summarize the interpretative and organizational function of *passing* using a simple organism and example. A simpler organism such as a cicada (or, e.g., Uexküll's example of relatedness in 'flowers and girls', see Uexküll 1992; 1926; 1982), or any other similar creature is forced to relate semiotically with a (finite) set of umwelten and could organize each new circumstance by means of *habits* (which I have replaced here with a new sense of *historicity* to include both learned behaviors and instinctual repertoires of responses, and conscious-voluntary and unconscious-involuntary responses—a probability value of the likely actions we expect to see displayed given the sum total, or the appropriate dispending, of one or more of these factors), by somehow recognizing and reacting to a new *circumstance*, and finally by accommodating the new umwelt of experience.

Assuming that the cicada has a sense of the limits of its own body-shell, of self-enclosure or any sense of being an entity with a certain set of constant peculiarities and functions (it feeds, it flies, it fights, it mates), then it can adapt to the new forced semioses with *historicity*. *Historicity* itself facilitates the *passing* from umwelt to umwelt although *historicity* itself does not guarantee that a cicada (or any other organism) will be able to accommodate a new situation in a manner that maximizes survival. If the cicada was a more complex organism, an organism with a mind, it might even be able to also *select* and *organize* the new umwelt so its *historicity* acquires new meaning in the novel circumstance. But alas, the mostly *ergodic* cicada is enslaved to play only limited sets of expected roles. *Passing*, according to Mead, from umwelt to umwelt, includes all of these functions and it allows an organism a higher probability of not only interpreting the new scenario appropriately, but also of deriving new meanings that can then be *transferable*, to use a behaviorist and cognitive concept, into new environments-umwelten-circumstances.

From previous sections then, it follows logically that conscious beings who possess multiple referentiality, due to their social expertise and the ability to simulate *the other* many times over within their own minds, are able to transmute *historicity* into practically anything they need to in order to manage the new circumstance. To them is bestowed the greatest prize of all: to privately, in their own minds, think up umwelten *ad infinitum*, or *ad nauseam* if you prefer, and relate to these even when these worlds do not materially exist. For example, imaginary umwelten could conceivably extend into complex dreaming life, particularly into a semiotics of *lucid dreaming*, when consciousness reappears and can be manipulated at will while exploring uncanny dreamscape semiosis (Conesa 2003; 2004).

For now, let us accept the idea that multiple referentiality, to some degree or another, is achievable by most members of a given species endowed with consciousness and that this is generally a good thing. This is a big assumption, but if true, then Mead asserts that we are now in the position to inhabit multiple frames of references at once and that only conscious organisms that exist in *The Realm of Continued Emergence* can do so.

That is, a human being, and only a human being, can imagine being a passenger inside an imaginary rocket ship traveling at the speed of light AND, simultaneously, a stationary person who remains on the face of the earth watching the rocket rise and then disappear. The fact that we can inhabit both perspectives (umwelten) is shown by the fact that many individuals of our species, for example Einstein, are (were) able to imagine such a dual perspective or circumstance at the same time. Mead did not say this, but if he could, he would say that relativity theory can only be a product of a *conscious* mind, and that in *passing* from one frame of reference to another, this mind is also able to maintain or retain so much *historicity* as to be able to make both realities part of their real present.

Mead also uses examples more mundane than the one given above, including the meaning of a dollar to several individuals. He cites, for example, that even though the first two individuals may be seeing the value of a dollar in a restricted sense, and each from their own unique perspective, a third individual can incorporate both perspectives and synthesize, to boot, a novel perception that gives him the monetary or investment advantage. Suffice it to say, for the purposes of this examination, that maintaining multiple referentiality while *passing* from umwelt to umwelt confers upon the conscious organism a tremendous advantage and opens the door to unimaginable possibilities, that even though removed from the utility of the present, allows semiosis to overreach and, if lucky, make possible umwelten that previously did not exist. By the way, his position is also an argument against absolute *incommensurability*, within a conscious species' *passsing* (Kuhn 1983; Feyerabend 1987), since no probable umwelt is truly extant from this sort of advanced consciousness.

Despite Mead's convincing and interesting elaboration (realistically speaking, only a smaller number of individuals belonging to a conscious species might be able to experience full-blown multiple referentiality as in the case of Einstein's insight[75]) of the real experience of inhabiting several perceptual spaces, simultaneously, this idea does not explain *passing* itself, at least not without first determining what bridges are (can be) built between probable umwelten that renders null the idea of two truly *incommensurable* environments. In the next section, I will try to show how the *transferability* of these elements, as explained by Mead, is not sufficient to track the successful *passing* from umwelt to umwelt and that SMT already has a vocabulary that handles these passings. In short, *passing* as explained by Mead seems to be dependant mostly on whatever cognitive or general talents are available to an organism thus lessening the potentiality, in the electrical sense, of a sort of impossible existential relativism that would prohibit movement and adaptation to a novel umwelt.

The elemental currency of "passing":
A pansemiosis or heuristics of matricial doings

The reader is referred to a more complete treatment of the original version of SMT (Conesa 1999). The following basic positions presented in the previous chapter are reintroduced here to address the Mead discussion presented thus far. These propositions, were as follows:

1) Living organisms (and other "things") are matrices[76]. Therefore, in living entities, Energy, Safety, and Possibility need and functions, and their feedback interactions, are *consubstantial* giving rise to the emergent dynamics of what I define as matricial activity, or a matrix as an integral entity.

2) As matrices 'we' embody Energy, Safety and Possibility needs and the umwelt provides sensorially and perceptually comprehensible sets of *invariant* information that can then be turn into *affordances* (Gibson, 1979). *Affordances* can then be interpreted as providing these basic matricial needs. This is why

SMT is *a biosemiotic theory, because it takes into account that a seamless and pervasive existential complementary exists between the object, the sign, and the interpreter which provides the basic sustenance for all meanings. This existential complement and yoked-in triad permeates and predates all sign systems, and all sign transactions.* The *historicity* of an organism, partly programmed by its own genome and partly learned, is fundamentally and existentially the *historicity* of Energy, Safety and Possibility needs however this *historicity* is played out in the diverse attempts to deal, and to eke out an existence.

3) Organic (*maenadic*-animals and *ensilic*-plants matrices) matrices have evolved countless metabolic, physiological, behavioral, and mental adaptations to express and complement these *matricial* needs by first reacting, responding, identifying or labeling objects in any environment that they encounter as resources to meet these needs. Thus, a biosemiotic structure might be derived from a description, understanding, and prediction of these interactions. I have argued that the topological mathematics of Kurt Lewin's (1936 and 1939) *Life Spaces* may be a computational first step to learn something about these interactions, if only Lewinian terms are replaced with matricial functionality and jargon.

4) All human knowledge, in all areas of interest, is an attempt to describe, understand, and/or predict how these *matricial* interactions occur. *Incommensurability* across these fields exists only insofar as lower level, technical jargon is used to define (without interdisciplinary effort) their phenomena of interest, a continua of biosemiosis[77].

5) The summary of this quest and understanding agrees with Systems Theory somewhat in that life transactions are all ecological (systemic). However, there are limitations to Systems Theory addressed by SMT (Conesa 1999; 2001).

6) To understand the 'system' is to have a science that predicts how the system might behave. This understanding must also be semiotic as others intuited, pointed out and corrected (Maturana, Varela, 1980; 1987). In this sense, a good 'life' theory, psychological, biological, economical, etc., describes significant *matricial* events that occur in a system and is able to make predictions about these.

7) Ecological Ethics, or Ecoethics, is an emergent necessity and the backbone describing the manner and nature of these relationships/interactions insofar as development proceeds from one smaller and physiologically restrictive matrix, to a larger one, and yet to a larger one (zygote, womb, mother, family, school, community, nation, planet, etc.). The *passing* from simpler to increasingly complex umwelten, if it is to succeed, must include a see-through universal biosemiotics rooted in more or less easy to interpret, or easy to learn signs that assists the BECOMING of an organism during its ontogenesis. To this end, human organisms (and other species) invent "rules" of ecological engagement

that allow them to maximize potential within reason, without destroying the delicate balance of these tenuous relations. Sometimes an organism ignores these ethical rules in order to maximize *matricial* procurements (to dysfunctionally, in the sense of ignoring the consequences to its ecological setting, monopolize) it does this at the developmental or *matricial* detriment of others and while causing injury to an ecosystem. Biosemiotics, in the end, has to deal with ethical questions, and Mead's *passing*, specifically, must include a notion of functional limits found in each umwelt lived.[78]

8) Life processes allow an almost infinite number of strategies for achieving organismic potential; but at the root of these endeavors are the *matricial beta elements*: *Safety, Energy, and Possibility.*

9) Semiotic Matrix Theory specifies the way in which biosemiosis can be structured through an empirical program that tests the ecological validity of these interactions that then can be applied to any study that examines systems.

10) Encapsulated physical bodies are 'simply' the phenotypic expression of these *matricial* forces encountering and surviving diverse environments. Moreover, both genomic and phenotypic adaptations and developments are servicing, through simple and complex feedback systems, the achievement of a *matricial homeostasis*. Being that all organic systems are being drafted, consciously or not, toward this end, *matricial integrity*, then the entire enterprise of merely surviving and/or meaningful existence is participating in a common ground of BEING. If so, then surely a *biosemiosis* dominates from the bottom up and anything else we can explain or discover about semiosis is really a *forced relatedness* or a *forced semiosis* and *sociality* that it is always *matricial* at its core.

11) The *historicity* of an organism, any system, however complex, colorful or idiosyncratic, makes an explicit or an implicit reference to *matricial* necessities. It is an existential situation, from the bottom up and in reverse, where a pervasive (and/or perverse if you wish) biosemiotic field is, in my opinion, inescapable. In its new formulation, and contrasted to Mead's ideas, I call it a *hermetic biosemiosis*.

If the above points can be accepted at face value, at least for the purposes of this aim, namely, to elucidate the problem[79] of *passing* from one frame of reference to another while maintaining a principal and primordial existential objective, then the following might make more sense. The cicada, an organism with limited 'mind' and thus with limited frames of references, as well as a human being, an organism who inhabits the multi-referential realm of continued emergence, in moving from one existential circumstance to another, must both maintain a common denominator and heuristic that transcends the 'many flavors' of speciation, the exuberant display of multiplicity of signs, and the many opportunities for passage from umwelt to umwelt. In addition to all transferable commodities that assist the *passage* from one frame of reference to another (including: instinctual responses; acquired cognitive skills; cultural and genetic adaptations; the grandiose SELF; short-term or long-term learning; or any other bodily or mental propensities that one may wish to even remotely associate with my term transferable commodity) and give life, purpose, and meaning to their expression is an *ontological semiosis* that reads a universal matricial manual before commencing to select, organize and then get cozy in a new frame of reference. This thoroughly enveloping *ontosemiotic baseline*, at least a facilitator of *passing*, is even more crucial for organisms who are mentally ductile in multiple referentiality, because they have an even greater need for an ontological compass, given that some automaticity of responding can now be supplemented or taken over altogether by the 'little voice inside the head,' and given that the little voice may be sometimes wrong.

When the 'little voice in the head' is wrong, along with the rest of the little voices inside the heads of the society from which individual Self-consciousness emerges, then we might be partaking of dysfunctional semiosis. As Erich Fromm (1955) said, "That millions of people share in the same forms of mental pathology does not make those people sane." The next section presents the position that deep ecological and green psychological movements put forth, namely the necessity of re-establishing an authentic and long neglected biosemiosis, at the cultural level, absence which is the cause of individual unhappiness and illness, as well as a societal disintegration.

Mead, SMT, and ecological ethics

The apparent existential freedom of continued emergence also comes with a social and psychological price to pay (Fromm 1955) and a duty to ecological ethics (an ecological morality). That is, to deep ecologists (Naess 1973; Shepard 1973; Naess 1979; Shepard 1982; Devall, Sessions 1985) and green psychologists[80] (Roszak 1979; 1992; Metzner 1971; 1999) who see BEING, and in particular healthy BEING, as predicated in the natural and specifically in the wild, such creative semiosis could turn out to be a dysfunctional semiosis, precisely because it may deviate and stray into purely fictional and aberrant semiosis (culturally driven or subjectively creative, both types could be delusional in the sense that Erich Fromm stated in an earlier passage) from an original *telluric* and biosemiosic ground (Shepard 1973; 1982). As Paul Shepard brilliantly demonstrated (an idea that continues to be debated), "the tender carnivore" has been domesticated by an agricultural and deviant text and semiosis and therefore has long ceased to be in harmony with ancient patterns and is no longer socially or mentally sound. But the above criticism is not new, and even before many were blaming *modernism* as another non-inclusive 'ism' that lacked this or that, or that was not addressing the needs of this or that group, a modernist voice and philosopher, George Santayana, recognized in a speech that was later to be printed (Santayana, 1926), that something was wrong with European philosophy with respect to ecological ideas when he said:

> A Californian whom I had recently the pleasure of meeting observed that if the philosophers had lived among your mountains [California mountains], their systems would have been different from what they are. Certainly very different from what those systems are which the European genteel tradition has handed down since Socrates; for these systems are egotistical; directly or indirectly they are anthropocentric, and inspired by the conceit notion that man, or human reason, or the human distinction between good and evil, is the center and pivot of the universe. That is what the mountains and the woods should make you at least ashamed to assert. (Devall 1985: 46)

It is not certain whether the "Californian" Santayana was referring to was none other than the Scott naturalist and founder of The Sierra Club, John Muir. But William Devall (1985) certainly thought that this modernist voice was the beginning of a new era when he writes, "[the speech at The University of California at Berkeley] . . . was a historical turning point in the development of the contemporary search for an alternative worldview and an environmental ethic that would not be subjectivist, anthropocentric, and essentially materialistic." Devall's statement is also an example of and recognition that contrary to stereotypical descriptions of a particular age, each epoch conveniently invents derogatory as well as admiring terms for other epochs while rewriting their own history, and in so doing, highlights or ignores *text* when this text is either beneficial or contradictory of their stated positions, respectively. Thus every epoch is more or less modern or more or less dark in comparison to another. Santayana's text speaks of a sentiment that was not really completely lost in European thought (Nash, 1982; and Devall & Sessions, 1985). After all, John Muir, a Scott, who migrated to North America, hiked and fell in love with this wilderness and pushed "American" politics and psyche from the romantic ideal of nature toward the observation of its intrinsic right to be sustained and thus protected.

Interestingly, both William Devall (1985) and Erich Fromm (1955) go further into history to bring back another voice, Spinoza's, who can validate their shared thesis that a particular collection of dysfunctional meme-texts can be admitted as normal by a given culture or at least tolerated to a certain degree. Erich Fromm (1955: 24) quotes a passage from Spinoza's *Ethics (IV)* that it is worth examining,

> Many people are seized by one and the same affect with great consistency. All his senses are so strongly affected by one object that he believes this

> object to be present even when it is not. If this happens while the person
> is awake, the person is believed to be insane . . . But if the greedy person
> thinks only of money and possessions, the ambitious one only of fame, one
> does not think of them as being insane, but only as annoying; generally
> one has contempt for them. But factually greediness, ambition, and so
> forth are forms of insanity, although usually one does not think of them
> as illness. (Spinoza: 44)

I share the above passage to suggest that any predisposed or learned behavioral singularity that it is not ecologically edifying, a *fetish*, is a form of illness. There is at least a logical implication in Mead's yoking of SELF with SOCIETY (Mead 1932), or the social, that allows the conclusion that the ethical clarification within the self of what is right or wrong (even sane or not in Fromm, 1955) emerges from the semiosis between Self and society:

> Since society has endowed us with self-consciousness, we can enter
> personally into the largest undertakings which the intercourse of rational
> selves extends before us. And because we can live with ourselves as well as
> with others, we can criticize ourselves, and make our own values in which
> we are involved through those undertakings in which the community of
> all rational beings is engaged. (Mead: 90)

If so, it is equally probable that: *a SELF, originating within the social realm as it does, while intuiting, apprehending and utilizing its universal meme-text, is capable of realizing that his polis, the cultural semiotic world that gave origin to the 'little voice' inside his head, is thoroughly corrupted and so is the text inside his head.* This is the beginning of healing for the above-mentioned deep ecologists and green psychologists.

If we are creatures of *continued emergence* that can grasp universals, above and beyond the very social matrix that gave us the power to so do, then we can also fix the corrupted meme-text. In attempting to do so there is, first, a need to describe, biosemiotically, how this dysfunctional, industrialized or agricultural, text might be looping into nonsense or even illness, looping into perversion and narcissism, and moving faster and farther from a true concept of community, and intimation with each other as umwelten and with wild nature as the most authentic backdrop for these intimations. As hinted at earlier, any of these are dysfunctional social loops, or *fetishes*, because they deny identification with a larger ecology hyper selecting, thus reducing, a larger potential field of biosemiosis. For example, who would argue with the thesis that mass, ravenous consumerism, an inclination toward the artificial, and a reduced ability to tolerate the inclemency's of bad weather make for a stronger self or a more factual biosemiosis? Deep ecologists as well as green psychologists are awaiting a more earnest effort and dogged contribution from our lot. Without our concerted ensemble contribution dictionary entries such as the one I shared at the beginning of this text, "*Tarantula*: an insect whose bite is only cured by musick, [sic]" in another form (such as the still prevalent bad habit of avoiding using the word 'animal' to designate humans) will continue as examples of *fetish*, or anthropocentric semiosis.

To conclude this section, it is fair to say that the biosemiotic intellectual paradigm, with the assistance of other ecological (deep and shallow) disciplines, if it chooses to lead in that direction, could actively be involved in these deep ecological discussions and build a more inclusive semiotics where biosemiosis is not limited to the sign-in-nature, but more broadly puts forward an authentic effort in examining the consequences of the absence of the *original sign* in the present human text. Even though there are already noteworthy successes of this kind of extended a more inclusive biology within biosemiotic writings (Emmeche, Hoffmeyer 2001; Kull 1997), the deep ecological sentiment in biosemiotics is not well covered. Also, a recent review of theories of emergence (life, consciousness, biosemiotics) did not list Mead as a reference. I only mention this because, at least to me, it seems important and even logically necessary to connect theories of emergence, biosemiosis with those of ecological ethics.

Discussion

Thus far, I have argued that in phylogenic and ontogenetic forms of BECOMING, and while passing from umwelt to umwelt, matricial truth and aims are reiterated. Ecological ethics are also obligated if we agree with Joseph Chilton Pearce's developmental model (Pearce, 1977). This fractal iteration of BEING grounded on matricial necessities, or another *biopansemiosis*[81] that could replace it, is falsifiable at face value, if we consider the following, as George Santayana (1955) would say, *brute facts*. As negative examples, if an existential biopansemiosis did not exist, of the sort described by SMT, then any sufficiently distinct frame of reference would be truly *incommensurable, thus intraversable and impassable, within (and without) the spaces of self and cultural semiosis. Passing* would be, if not impossible, extremely difficult, reducing the range of semiosis we observe in the life (and *historicity*) of this planet to indescribable and unthinkable senseless events. Logically, speciation would not be possible, assuming that we describe speciation semiotically, as *passing* from a vanishing set of existential accommodations to another emerging set of significantly different existential accommodations, in varying degrees of difference and success.

Moreover, if *passing* is also understood as intra-species accommodation, interpretation or deployment of instinctual behaviors, and some biosemiotic mechanism did not facilitate the functions, then every organism would go hungry and starve to death for no apparent reason. Copulation, as an example of primal forced relatedness or forced semiosis would be a bizarre undertaking, or would not take place at all. Equally, without a biosemiotic set of guidelines there would be no need for nests, burrows, or houses with thermostats and fences, or the distinction between enemy and friend. Bluntly put, there would be NOTHING instead of BEING.

To conclude, focusing on the sign, myopically; on human culture and semiosis, myopically; on the little sounds we make with moving lips, myopically; on the little sounds that birds make when they sing, myopically; on poetry, myopically; we risk missing a grander biosemiotic phenomenon: *everything does the same things except a little bit differently.*[82]

It is quite probable, as Mead intuited and defended, that only social organisms who also achieve multiple referentiality are in a position to maintain so many points of view at once as to begin to apprehend universals. This capacity may sometimes be simply a wishful subjective projection rather than the discovery or intimation of an actual and bona fide universal or natural habit. Sometimes this capacity simply produces mental aberrations and illness. But sometimes this capacity pays off, substantially, and produces an explanation that incorporates extant frames of reference. However, depending on how extant the new frame of reference is, it may or may not be thoroughly incorporated into human culture as a semiosis of mental associations and meanings. Most people, I would venture, do not understand basic principles in physics, psychology, chemistry or biology even though the technologies and ideas that spun from these fields are routinely employed by all of us. This lack of in depth understanding does not mean that these fields are *incommensurable* from each other, or that the average person cannot grasp the essential insights found in all of these fields. But, practically speaking, the average person simply does not have the time to be so comprehensive or inclusive, or he/she simply chooses to specialize in one field at the exclusion of other fields.

Thus, an existential drive can be summed up by the following questions: Can I make a LIVING today? If so, then: What basic elements gathered from raw reality do I employ to even begin to make a LIVING? And, how many of these elements are, biosemiotically speaking, significantly foundational and enduring so that I can continue making a living tomorrow? If a given organism can achieve the Realm of Continued Emergence as an added bonus, then life may seem either more pleasant and interesting or twice as horrifying, depending on one's myopic frame of reference. But through happy dreams or through nightmares, one can be certain that *everything does the same things, except a little bit differently. Sociality* as *forced relatedness,* or *forced semiosis,* and, *sociality* as the driver and engine for semiosis, does so: it makes sure we tug the same ontology along, always matricial at its core.

Chapter Three References

Bateson, Gregory 1979. *Mind and Nature: A Necessary Unity*. New York: Bentam Books.

Bragg, Melvyn 2003. *The Adventure of English: The Biography of a Language*. London: Hodder and Stoughton.

Byrne, Richard W.; Whiten, Andrew (eds.), 1988. *Machiavellian Intelligence*. Oxford: University Press.

Byrne, Richard W.; Tomasello, Michael. 1995. Do rats ape? *Animal Behaviour* 50: 1417-1420.

Colby, Anne; Kohlberg, Lawrence; Kauffman, K. 1987. Theoretical introduction to the measurement of moral judgment. In: Colby A. and Kohlberg L., *The Measurement of Moral Judgement (Vol. 1)*. Cambridge: Cambridge University Press.

Conesa, Jorge 1999. *Ecological Outcome Psychological Theory: Application of Human Developmental Theories to Other Scientific Fields*. New York: Forbes-Thomson Learning Publishing.

—2001. A Semiotic Metalanguage Based on Existential Ontologies. *Presented at the International Summer Institute for Semiotic and Structural Studies in Imatra, Finland*. (June 10-15, 2001.)

—2003. Sleep Paralysis Signaling (SPS) As A Natural Cueing Method for the Generation and Maintenance of Lucid Dreaming. *Presented at The 83rd Annual Convention of the Western Psychological Association*, May 1-4, 2003 in Vancouver, BC, Canada.

Conesa-Sevilla, Jorge 2004. *Wrestling With Ghosts: A Personal and Scientific Account of Sleep Paralysis*. Pennsylvania: Random House-Xlibris

Davies, Paul. 1999. *The Search for the Origin and Meaning of Life*. New York: Simon and Schuster.

Dennett, Daniel C. 1983. Intentional systems in cognitive ethology: The "Panglossian paradigm" defended. *Behavioral and Brain Sciences* 6: 343-390.

—1991. *Consciousness Explained*. Boston: Little and Brown.

Devall, William; Sessions, George 1985. *Deep Ecology: Living as if Nature Mattered*. Layton: Peregrine Smith Book.

Emmeche, Claus; Hoffmeyer, Jesper 1991. From language to nature: the semiotic metaphor in biology. *Semiotica* 84(1/2): 1-42.

Feyerabend, Paul K. 1987. *Putnam on Incommensurability*. London: Verso.

Fromm, Erich 1955. *The Sane Society*. New York: Holt, Rinehart & Winston Printing.

Gibson, James J. 1979. *The Ecological Approach to Visual Perception*. Boston: Houghton-Mifflin.

Goleman, Daniel 1995. *Emotional Intelligence: Why Can it Matter More than IQ?* New York: Bantam Books.

Hoffmeyer, Jesper 1996. *Signs of Meaning in the Universe*. Bloomington: Indiana University Press.

Harries-Jones, Peter 1995. *A Recursive Vision: Ecological Understanding and Gregory Bateson*. Toronto: University of Toronto Press.

Heyes, Cecilia M. (1993) Anecdotes, training, trapping, and triangulating: Do animals attribute mental states? *Animal Behaviour* 46, 177-188.

—(1998). Theory of mind in nonhuman primates. *Behavioral and Brain Sciences* 21(1): 101-134.

Kilpinen, Erkki 2002. A neglected classic vindicated: the place of George Herbert Mead in the general tradition of semiotics. *Semiotica* 142: 1-4

Kohlberg, Lawrence 1981. *Philosophy of Moral Development*. New York: Harper and Row.

Kropotkin, Peter 1914. *Mutual Aid*. New York: Knopf.

Kull, Kalevi 1998. On semiosis, Umwelt, and semiosphere. *Semiotica* 120(3/4): 299-310.

Kuhn, Thomas S. 1983. Commensurability, Comparability, Communicability. In: P.D. Asquith and T. Nickels (eds.), *PSA 1982: Proceedings of the 1982 Biennial Meeting of the Philosophy of Science Association*, Vol. 2. East Lansing: Philosophy of Science Association.

Lewin, Kurt 1935. *A Dynamic Theory of Personality*. New York: McGraw-Hill.

—1936. *Principles of Topological Psychology*. New York: McGraw-Hill.

—1939. Field theory and experiment in social psychology: concepts and methods. *American Journal of Sociology* 44: 868-897.

—1951. *Field Theory and Social Science*. New York: Harper.

Maturana, Humberto R.; Varela, Francisco J. 1980. *Autopoiesis and Cognition: The Realization of the Living*. Dordrecht: D. Reidel.

Maturana, Humberto R.; Varela, Francisco J. 1987. *The Tree of Knowledge*. Boston: Shambhala.

Mead, George H. 1934. *The Philosophy of the Present*. A. E. Murphy (ed.). Chicago: The University of Chicago Press.

—1934. *Mind, Self, and Society: From the Standpoint of a Social Behaviorist*. C. H. Morris (ed.). Chicago: The University of Chicago Press.

—1964 [1908]. The philosophical basic of ethics. In: A. J. Reck (Ed.), *Selected writings: George Herbert Mead*. Chicago: The University of Chicago Press.

Metzner, Ralph 1971. *Maps of Consciousness*. New York: Collier-Macmillan.

—1999. *Green Psychology: Transforming Our Relationship to the Earth*. Rochester: Park Street Press.

Naess, Arne 1973. The shallow and the deep, long-range ecology movements: A summary. *Inquiry* 16: 95-100.

—1979. Self-realization in mixed communities of humans, bears, sheeps, and wolves. *Inquiry* 22: 231-241.

Nash, Roderick 1982. *Wilderness and the American Mind, 3rd Ed.* New Haven: Yale University Press.

Pearce, Joseph C. 1971. *The Crack in the Cosmic Egg: Challenging Constructs of Mind and Reality.* New York: Pockets Books.

Pearce, Joseph C. 1977. *Magical Child.* New York: Bantam Books, Inc.

Peirce, Charles S. 1966. *Selected Writings.* New York: Dover

Piaget, Jean 1932. *The Moral Judgment of the Child.* New York: Harcourt Brace Jovanovich.

—1972. Intellectual evolution from adolescent into adulthood. *Human Development* 15: 1-12.

Premack, David 1983. Animal cognition. *Annual Review of Psychology* 34(Jan.): 351-362.

Premack, David; Woodruff, Guy. 1978. Does the chimpanzee have a theory of mind? *Behavioural and Brain Sciences* 7: 515-526.

Roszak, Theodore 1979. *Person-Planet.* New York: Anchor Press.

—1992-2001. *The Voice of the Earth.* New York: Simon & Schuster.

Santayana, George 1955. *Skepticism and Animal Faith.* New York: Dover.

Saussure, Ferdinand de 1983 [1916]. *Course in General Linguistics.* (Translation: Roy Harris.) London: Duckworth.

Schachtel, Ernest G. 1959. *Metamorphosis.* New York: Basic Books.

Shepard, Paul 1973. *The Tender Carnivore and the Sacred Game.* New York: Scribners.

—1982. *Nature and Madness.* San Francisco: Sierra Club.

Uexküll, Jakob von 1926. *Theoretical Biology.* New York: Harcourt, Brace & Company.

—1982. The theory of meaning. *Semiotica* 42(1): 25-82

—1992 [1934]. A stroll through the woods of animals and men: a picture book of invisible worlds. *Semiotica* 89(4): 319-391.

Vygotsky, Lev S. 1934. *Thought and Language* (Translation: A. Kozulin.) Cambridge: MIT Press.

Werner, Heinz 1978 [1934]. The unity of the senses. In: Barten S. S.; Franklin, M. B. (eds.), *Developmental Processes: Heinz Werner's Selected Writings* (Vol. 1). New York: International Universities Press.

Werner, Heinz; Kaplan, Bernard 1963. *Symbol Formation.* New York: John Wiley.

Wiley, Norbert 1994. *The Semiotic Self.* Chicago: University of Chicago Press.

Whiten, Andrew. 1996. When does smart behaviour-reading become mind-reading? In: Carruthers, P.; Smith, P. K. (eds.), *Theories of Theories of Mind.* Cambridge: Cambridge University Press.

Whiten, Andrew; Byrne, Richard W. 1988. Tactical deception in primates. *Behavioral and Brain Sciences* 11: 233-273.

Wiener, Norbert. 1965. *Cybernetics or Control and Communication in the Animal and the Machine.* Massachusetts: The MIT Press.

Wilson, Edward O. 1984. *Biophilia: The Human Bond with Other Species*. Cambridge: Harvard University Press.

—1998. *Consilience: The Unity of Knowledge*. New York: Random House.

Woodruff, Guy; Premack, David 1979. Intentional communication in the chimpanzee: The development of deception. *Cognition* 7: 333-362.

Chapter Four

Meet Heinz Droz, Again! Wolf Religion vs. Chihuahua Religion

In the garden I plant my hands—I know I shall grow, I know, I know—
swallows will lay their eggs in the nest of my ink stained fingers.

—Forugh Farrokhzad

"Meet Heinz Droz" was the five-cent tour of a longer article I had previously written. In *Biophilia Versus Lebensneid*, the article that follows, I attempted to synthesize much of what we had read thus far (chapters one through three) but with an eye toward the clinical side of ecopsychology.

More importantly, in this article, I decided to address the role that religion plays in ecopsychological unfolding and therapy (also presented in Chapter Ten). This was an important exploration to address human ecopsychological spirituality[83] in its own right, and also to the extent that transpersonal psychologists delve deeply into spiritual matters usually in tandem with what can be referred to as *Nature spirituality*. The distinction or continuum between a *wolf religion* versus a *Chihuahua religion* was not meant to disrespect the important and sometimes central role that religious life plays in *ecopsychological unfolding*. But in this distinction and continuum the reader is invited to inquire whether some religious practices are sometimes at odds with ecopsychological well being or becoming, or even, whether they can be one and the same *spirit enterprise*.

I was recently reassured that religion might always be an important catalyst in environmental activism, if not ecopsychological unfolding, by the news that a group of evangelicals broke ranks with orthodoxy to support environmental policies that would help address the reduction of green house causing gases. In the paper, I refer to these actions as *good religion* from ecopsychological and environmental perspectives.

The paper also deals with the beginnings of an ecopsychological study of personality that looks at the possibility of identifying a health continuum from eco-alienated to eco-immersed personalities. Even though this experiment was not academically rigorous, it nevertheless may prove to be useful as an idea of the type of empirical enterprises that the student and scientist of ecopsychology could undertake. The fact that it was not fully developed in *Biophilia Versus Lebensneid* does not mean that it is any less important.

Finally, the paper also attempts to address from social, political, environmental, and psychological perspectives the following questions that have become central to ecopsychological and Deep Ecological practice: *Why is most of humanity accepting living with less, rather than much more, wildness? and What impedes the embracing of seemingly healthy, productive, and sustainable deep interactions with wilderness and each other?*

My own answers followed closely at times the many answers provided by environmentalists, Deep Ecologists, and ecopsychologists. This overlap provides the reader with a summary of these views from other writers as well. Additionally, I reinterpreted some of these questions from a biosemiotic perspective.

Biophilia Versus *Lebensneid*: Seeking Ecopsychological Balance

Abstract

The ideas presented here are a continuation, and Part Three, of a three-installment presentation connecting ecopsycology with semiotics and biosemiotics (Conesa-Sevilla, 2005a; and Conesa-Sevilla, 2005b). This third installment of the series (Conesa-Sevilla, 2005a; and Conesa-Sevilla, 2005b), suggests ways in which we can begin to deal with and even repair an obsolete text.

The solutions are presented around previously asked questions: *Why is most of humanity accepting living with less, rather than much more, wildness? and What impedes the embracing of seemingly healthy, productive, and sustainable deep interactions with wilderness and each other?*

In the answers to these questions several ecopsychological positions are taken, some new and others revised (Conesa, 1999). One, that most adults living in industrialized nations, ontologically speaking, cannot simply undo, overnight, a dysfunctional bonding with a consumer-driven material society; that the alienation from *wildness* might be permanent. Two, that various degrees of re-affiliation with wilderness, and with a more authentic biosemiosis, are possible given individual differences, health limitations, and various degrees of commitment. This partial re-affiliation is in itself important because it may impact *wellness* in positive and long-lasting ways. Three, even the partial and collective re-affiliation of great numbers of alienated adults can tip the balance favorably and contribute to a new hope and a reinterpreted semiosis that can benefit the next generations substantially. Four, that only future generations can make, if they wish, a total re-connection with wildness, albeit first taught by imperfect, even dysfunctional but well-intending ecologically non-affiliated adults and their societies. Five, that if this re-connection were to be complete, then a global, *ecopsychological* balance might be achieved once again.

> "Everything was green, so green it went into him."
> —Gary Paulsen, *Hatchet*, (1987: 39)

> "The smell of vegetation was extraordinarily strong. As for the greenness, it was so fresh and soothing that strength and comfort seemed to be physically pouring into my system through my eyes."
> —Yann Martel, *Life of Pi*, (2003: 347)

Introduction

In her book *Self-analysis*, Karen Horney (1942/1994) borrows a term coined by Nietzsche, *Lebensneid*,[84] that she translates as "a resentment toward life, a deep resentment of being left out." This selection and its consequences are found in the last chapter of the same book under the title, The Limitations of Self-analysis. I sought out and rejected several terms to encapsulate the intent of this paper before embracing Horney's own selection, namely, to answer the two questions other ecologists and ecopsychologists have asked and I summarize here: *Why is most of humanity accepting living with less, rather than much more, wildness?* and *What impedes the embracing of seemingly healthy, productive, and sustainable deep interactions with wilderness and each other?* Or a combination of the two into one important query: *That is, if LIFE can be said to be archetypically, ideally, naturally represented by wildness*[85], *why then do we reject it?* All three are psychological questions when their investigation and consequences lead to issues of mental wellness or the lack of thereof. More precisely, they are questions within the domain of Ecopsychology. Of course, inherent in these questions are complex psychological, social, political, semiotic, and economical issues making an attempt to answer their full import a very challenging task. Thus, this presentation will fail to do justice to this entire horizon of ideas. However, a distillation of their consequences and of their semiotic contributions can be ascertained in order to seek the remedies needed to deal with the dying parts of our over-civilized text and self.

I have already offered some tentative answers to the above questions (Conesa, 1999; Conesa-Sevilla, 2005a; and Conesa-Sevilla, 2005b) and these, in part, have been influenced by deep ecologists (Naess, 1973; Naes, 1979; and Devall & Sessions, 1985), philosophers of ecopsycology (Shepard, 1973; and Shepard, 1982), and by ecopsychologists (Roszak, 1992; and Metzner, 1999). But my initial explorations did not completely address the answers that semiotics and biosemiotics may provide to such questions. Also, my partial attempt at a synthesis of biosemiosis and ecopsychology (Conesa-Sevilla, 2005b) left me without having proposed a path for recovery to the *wild* that was satisfactory to this ecopsychologist. For example, I initially left out the role of religion or of religious rituals in ecopsychological becoming because others have covered it so well (Devall & Sessions; 1985; Roszak, 1992; and Metzner, 1999).

Nevertheless, here I focus on my own previously un-addressed questions about religion and add my own perspective and ecopsychological practices. In short, the assumption in all three questions, and in other writings, is that collusive madness and collective neurosis (Fromm, 1955; Shepard, 1973; and Shepard, 1982) are ontogenetically formed to create an alienated industrialized and urban human population: a *biophagocitic*[86] rather than *biophilic* (Wilson, 1984) self in its relation to nature.

If as Horney says, "Any severe neurosis is like a tight armor . . . ," then, additionally, the armor also uses a perverse linguistic semiosis and/or more systemic or evolutionary biosemiosis in order to forge its impregnability. It has been my claim that with an understanding of semiosis and biosemiosis the ecopsychologist might fully grasp the predicament of the overculturized psyche and its unstable structure. I would like to take up the challenge here of devising ways of denting this armature, at least, or of finally breaking through its thin metal by using something analogous to a crossbow: the potential energy that has accumulated in the armored-psyche from depriving itself of its telluric source (Conesa-Sevilla, 2005a; and Conesa-Sevilla, 2005b)—our individual and collective *Steppenwolf* (Hesse, 1929). This challenge is only possible insofar as we agree that words and their meanings can be used to rationalize and obscure one own's *biophagocitic* tendencies and to explain away our present *Lebensneid* neurosis. This challenge is only possible if we agree further that ideology and its propaganda delivers a persuasive (and often conflicting or contradictory) text early on in human development and continuing throughout ontogeny, succeeding in the formation an alienated psyche (Chomsky, 1968; and Mannheim, 1936).

Anticipating later portions of this presentation, to the extent that using language leaves a psycholinguistic and therefore cognitive track, then these "sound-mind-tracks" may be edifying or self-deprecating, inclusive of natural process or exclusive of life-giving systems, and may be ideologically blinding or semiotically expansive. If so, then the study of text and its consequences to a developing mind is of utmost importance in understanding ecopsychological wellness or lack thereof. Clinically speaking, methods such as Neurolinguistic programming (deprogramming) NLP, in conjunction with other ecopsychological and hypnotic methods, may be useful in breaching the dysfunctional armor and text. On the academic and literary realms, deconstructive semiotics plays a similar role. But more generally, my assault of this armor will begin by trying to argue around and from the following thesis:

I agree with Paul Shepard (1973, 1982) that many generations, populations, and nations (mine included, myself included) will never be able to achieve a complete and authentically original telluric psychological ground. Ecopsychologically speaking, all that most of us can hope for is a greater degree of relatedness, intimacy and enjoyment, with varying degrees of success and constancy, while partaking of wild spaces, as well as some noticeable ecopsychological incremental change that ensures mental stability. That achievement alone would be a great gift. The magnitude of these changes, toward what Paul Shepard describes as a hunter-forager, cynegetic way of life and mindset, will depend on each person's Umwelt situation, including psychological (innate or ontogenically derived) tools; the availability and accessibility of natural spaces and wild nature; the strength of the prevailing social propaganda and ideology which devalues such immersion as a priority for health or as a better measure of a "high standard of living;" and the availability of credible information (medical, psychological, environmental, ecological, ecopsychological) that leads to healing and guides and recreates a possible cynegetic transformation. However, collective or individual small changes in these areas can help turn the tide away from individual and collective madness (and collusion). Nevertheless, now, only the very young, with the tutelage of cynegetically-ecopsychologically "inferior" adults can ever achieve full-blown cynegetic mentality and health. Each committed generation after that, improving on the learning of the previous one, can build up an authentic cynegetic existential base.

The above and important thesis and caveat must be made even more salient regarding other cynegetic arguments that relate to psychological wellness that follow. That is, in my own thinking, I do my best not to romanticize primal psychological existence, or any type of existence, while ignoring important shortfalls or difficulties, sometimes unknown by social scientists, that these primal psychologies encountered when surviving in wild and pristine conditions[87]. Nor can an ecopsycologist single handedly wash away present-day lifetimes of personal bad habits and cumbersome sociocultural complexity in order to instantly re-create these ancient ways and pristine clear minds. Additionally, and *to play the devil's advocate, for example, primal psychological existence might have given rise, consistently so, to thoroughly unhappy individuals who just happened to live in sustainable ways and lacked the imagination to develop superior technologies or invent the idea of a vacation.* I have also learned not to glamorize by singularizing (Conesa-Sevilla, 2005b) Yanomamos, Swiss people, Fijians, or Paleo-hunters. Specifically, primal peoples, even when I use them as psychological standard for wellness, lacked crucial types and quantities[88] of information, the lack of which made it possible for some of them to abuse and exterminate many species (see Barry Lopez's *Artic Dreams*, 1986).

From an ecopsychological point of view, however, it is necessary to understand whether their embeddedness in natural settings (with respect to the lesser or different relatedness found in the average modern urbanite), increase the probability that they will experience moments of ecological clarity, psychological transcendence, and emotional quietude, all leading to overall wellness, and more importantly, to individuation. I define wellness not only as being physically healthy, but also "healthy" in a psychological sense, as an overall certainty of high quality organismic accomplishment of the quality of living, dealing with LIFE and dealing with DEATH. To borrow and then modify from a mathematician (Steen, 2003), *ecopsychological balance means to enjoy life while authentically interacting, with body and mind, with naturally wild spaces so that the meaning extracted from those exchanges is, semiotically speaking, a "mile deep and miles wide" as opposed to the mostly superficial and "tinsel relatedness" that our modern world forces us into which are only "an inch deep and a mile wide".*

But there is no question that, coupled and synergetic with present-day medical and psychological knowledge, these ancient ways of being-in-the-world may prove to be fundamentally indispensable if modern societies are to evolve into population and knowledge dynamics that are pro-nature, for ecological reality, and existing in sustainable environments.

Wolf Religion vs. Chihuahua Religion

> "It lasted only a few seconds, but it was so intense that it seemed to become part of him. Nothing."
>
> —Gary Paulsen, *Hatchet*, (1987: 51)

A prelude, if not to cynegism, then toward increased ecopsychological wellness and natural spirituality, has been taught by diverse faiths throughout the ages. More often nowadays, I am physically impacted by the fact that the arbitrarily moral human world begins the second after rising from wordless, meditative contemplation in nature. I assume that this form of contemplation was then, long, long ago, and for many thousands of years, a nameless exercise unclaimed by any religious sect or ritual. That is, it was not an institutionalized practice, but was rather as natural and ubiquitous as drinking water or flies, respectively. *Before moralizing commences the body that sits in silence atop a rock in a high alpine meadow or on a sandy beach is holy, innocent, and immersed in timelessness.* (See Appendix C at the end of this chapter.) Two minutes after, a list of random concerns begins. Am I trespassing on this pastureland? Isn't putting bells on cows a form of torture? What is the name of this tiny plant that I am now destroying with the weight of my body? What time is it? What is TIME? Shall I get into trouble if I remain? Am I late for supper? Who are those folks coming uphill? Should I acknowledge them? What are their intentions toward me? Will my nakedness offend? Should I hide? A paranoid swarm of humanly created Do's and Don'ts invade my awareness and pollute an otherwise crystal clear mind that minutes before merged seamlessly with cows, bells, grass, sky, and wind, all belonging together. The previous seamless realization is as tangible and near as my own body or my fears[89]. That is the point: I have a choice—fear or innocence. As an analogy on a grander scale, religious cosmological stories of origin tell us of different gods existing in such timeless void before human history or even life history began. Out of loneliness, or for reasons that continue to mystify us mortals, these lonesome-in-perfect-voids gods create female and male principles. The dynamics of these two forces (in endless semiotic and triadic relations to the original, usually patriarchal, form) lead to oppositional, complementary, and harmonizing solutions that inevitably write a plethora of morality rules.

Furthermore, the same visceral and seamless sensation leads me to the rational thought that *moralizing IS separateness.* As an intellectual factoid this is not an earth shattering revelation. However, as a complete awareness that permeates the totality of "I," the second after contemplative practice in nature, this is a new wisdom for me. Many of you will immediately identify with this wisdom. My newly acquired wisdom, one that moves from the necessity of ecopsychological wellness, itself derived from this natural connection, means that to be immersed in nature is to increase the probability that these feelings will continue and endure. Choice! To participate consciously in nature, with nature, while in contemplation or during "impractical wandering," increases the probability of *primal innocence.* It is not an accident that monasteries and abbeys from different religions have built their hallowed places and sought and continue to seek a spiritual connection in nature. *Time spent here, time in timelessness, is a key finding if we are to bring the combined moral weight of all religions to save this planet and ourselves.*

Deep Ecology poets and writers such as Gary Snyder and William Devall, respectively, have emphasized the historical role that religion, in particular Zen Buddhism and Taoism, has played in sustaining an ecopsychological balance and health and the consequences of lacking their ecolophilosophical ethos. It is their thesis that Zen Buddhism and ecopsychological wellness overlap in immensely significant areas. In probing deeper the question of why many religions are either able to sustain a longer-term (in historical time and relative terms) cynegetic connection, and others rediscover this link in ebb and flow cycles, I thought that much of what I had read and understood in sociology of religion or anthropology of religion could be analogized along the line of the subtitle for this section, that is, a difference between what I refer to as "wolf" and "Chihuahua" religions.[90] My summary will not however, tiptoe along politically correct dotted lines, but aims at a fundamental understanding of the multiplicity and diversity of religious expression as a genetic tree of thought-meme where an ancient, which I term "wolf," hunter-forager attitude of relating to natural processes and to his/her own role in that web of life, has been preserved or not, in various forms, exaggerations, de-emphases, and distortions, as the religions we see today. As semiotic analogy within another analogy, I recommend the novel *Ella Minnow Pea,* by Mark Dunn, who, humorously and in actions that resemble historical fact, tracks the deterioration and manipulation of the written word-text (and its subsequent psychological and communal consequences) in the fictional place of *Nollopton*. Guided by opportunistic and nefarious city fathers and mothers, an original alphabet consisting of 26 letters is reduced incrementally, supernaturally they claim, and hence all the words that can be used, to only five (l, m, n, o, p). If this analogy works, then a once richer genetic soup of Wolf adaptations have been reduced to a few decontextualized and limited breeds. Or, original, personal, and GRAND spirituality too can be reduced to a simplistic "LMNOP" dogma.

The genetic analogy employs a real study of dog breeds all originating in an ancestral wolf-like animal. That is, for the purposes of utility, companionship, aesthetics, alimentation, or human fancy, the many dog appearances, from Chihuahuas, to Pit-bulls, or malamutes, are examples of a humanly chosen group of traits and characteristics from a larger set of phenotypical and behavioral characteristics that are, prototypically, all incorporated and tightly bound in a wolf ancestor.

Furthermore, to make this analogy work, I am thinking under the assumption that an intimate and totally encompassing relationship with nature, including all the physical, mental and cognitive skills (a hunter-forager spirituality of stealth, frugality, gratitude, resourcefulness, strength, ritual, fidelity, courage, patience, perseverance) necessary to survive under pristine pre-historical conditions was more wolf-like than Chihuahuan or Pitbullish. These skills, mental predispositions, and attentionally-here-and-now attitudes are not in themselves necessarily religious, but as an ensemble and as part of a real ancestral context (the struggle for survival with minimum cultural baggage), their combined synergy could become the moral foundation for the birthing of all religions. *That is, a hunter-forager spirituality of stealth, frugality, gratitude, resourcefulness, strength, seasonally meaningful rituals, fidelity, courage, patience, perseverance, are alchemically transformed into genuine pride, other values and virtues and then into the concept of morality. If morality emerges from these basic attitudes, then the individual must be moral, naturally moral.*

It is important to pause and clarify here that I am making a distinction between a real human psychobiological capacity to have a spiritual moment of intimacy and awe, and a belief in the supernatural. I imagine that once the spiritual emotion is felt the latter could be made easier by the former. But this section is not about a belief in the supernatural. Rather, I am trying to figure out for myself why ecopsychological wellness is sometimes equated with *this* or *that* religion, or even with *this* or *that* particular religious ritual and practice. To illustrate with rhetorical questions, why is it necessary for humans to invent cathedrals with high ceilings, colorful glass work, polished rare metals, and decorate the space further with intricate and ornate displays, all this in the same space where a chanting (shamanic?) drone or a spiritual song is accompanying the act of sitting meditatively? Why numerous so-called religious practices seem to be an attempt to replicate an attentional moment of *thereness in nature, in a fabricated nature*? And if golf is akin to religion, why do these sensible adults spend their days in fabricated African Savannahs sharpening their aim and strength while "hunting" small balls that seem to move on their own accord on windy days or on rolling lawns?[91] Why not golf anywhere else?

Buddhism, Taoism, Shintoism,[92] in my comparison are more like malamute or husky dogs and closer to an ancestral wolf cognitive-spiritual relatedness than other religions that pit nature against humanity, the cultivated against the wild, or the baroque and ornate art against the complex interlacing of green vines and purple flowers. *Other religions may be referred to as Chihuahuan if the complexity of an ancestral mind and ecopsychological wellness, their original purpose, has become a set of dead rituals exaggerating the ingestion of diminutive amounts of wildness. Other interpretations of religion may be Pitbullish, if their objectives make use of the bellicose, the paranoid, and revenge as a means to achieve a certain morality and morbid ecstasy.* Self-flagellation too makes sense as a masochistic act, but also, if the hunter has long ago stopped feeling the bushes brushing his skin as he readies for an arrow shot and this loss looms large in the believer's unconscious. *Institutionalizing guilt and/or punishment in the face of the real learning necessity and probability of committing countless errors or misdemeanors in a world plagued with relativistic or dogmatic rules may be a neurotic de-evolution of a total mindfulness that understood that mistakes lead to death, not deals, and that the list of potential errors was no longer than your bow.*

To close this section, *Full-fledged human intelligence, the intelligence that triumphs under the demands of an interesting and full-fledged natural world, becomes morbid or desperate to find the religious sentiment anywhere, however bizarre, once removed from its original paradise. This sentiment is then corrupted and replaced by anything that transfixes the senses and perception into a wasted hypnotic or emotionally over-charged "doing".* What I define later in Section 4g (and in Appendix A) as "bad religion" can be seen as a de-evolution of natural mentality who, wolf-like, embraced ALL, and saw ALL. Only a Chihuahuan-type religion sacrifices human life for no naturally good reason to gods who appeal to human vanity or folly. The hunter saves everything, uses everything, SILENCE above all.

Five Cynegetic Trait-Clusters

In addition to formulating and practicing a spirituality of naturalness, and before returning to answering my opening three fundamental questions, we might continue the preliminary task of understanding what obstacles block the path of even a mediocre improvement, individually or collectively, toward ecopsychological stability. Although it may not always be fair to diagnose each trait-clusters that follows as a form of natural-wild-environmental alienation (as a *Lebensneid* existential situation, as "a resentment toward life, a deep resentment of being left out"), this exercise, nevertheless, may be useful as a simplification of a large range of human mal-adaptations and alienation. But with caricatures and by other means, clinicians must try first to unveil the protective layers laid down by the person himself/herself and/or by societal indoctrination in order to seek a cure. These could indeed be "tight armors." *On the other hand, if people come in for therapy, and the clinician knows they live in small apartments; in a big noisy city; they lack exercise; they are smokers, they heat up and consume easy pre-prepared foods; they don't remember the last time they dug their hands into fertile soil; they can only identify a few of the local wild plants or animals; then the therapy will have to include, irrespective of other syndromes and treatments, the exact opposite of this overall pattern of pseudo-existing.*

The five typologies below are provided for illustrative purposes only. It might be technically incorrect to describe the following behaviors as personality "traits." I have qualified them by naming them *trait-clusters* to insinuate that these can be interpreted as social, rather than psychological traits, itself an oddity. *That is, and consistent with Paul Shepard's ontological thesis, cynegism, a way of life and resulting psychological profile emerging from close-knit relations with wilderness, is environmentally, not genetically derived.* To the extent that cynegetic regression, while interacting with psychological traits proper, can match these illustrations, then they are somewhat valid. Equally important, nor can the reader infer that these are in any order, in degrees of dysfunction, *away from First Order* cynegism. In other words, the numerical progression does not imply increased ecopsychological degeneration.

Moreover, the mixing of and continuum between these convenient caricatures of ecopsychological cluster-traits (II through V), more or less alienated from and improperly bonded with wildness, might compose other kinds of ecological affiliations in your own minds. Mixing can also occur, I imagine, in the upper realms of cynegenism, from the unattainable, for most of us, true hunter-forager-horticulturalist, to the comparably speaking, easier existence of individuals who now live in harmonious and sustainable relations in, if not true wild spaces, at least natural spaces that demand genuine ecopsychological changes leading to wellness and physical vitality.

For example, in Scott O'Dell's Island of The Blue Dolphins, based on a true story, an already cynegetic girl, Karana, must break tribal taboos against women making weapons, in order to survive alone on an island.

The five cynegetic descriptions that follow are literary excerpts themselves of their more complete coverage in Appendix A. The reader may want to look up these descriptions first before settling for the more cryptic entries below. But in short, the following excerpts, except the **Trait-Cluster I: First Order** cynegism, or authentic hunter-forager-horticulturalist mentality, reflect various degrees of semiotic relation and different degrees of human-nature estrangement. **Trait-Cluster II** cynegism, for example, refers to modern-day seasonal, *part-time* hunters and/or individuals who by unfortunate circumstances, find themselves lost in the wild but have every intention of returning to civilization. With respect to the part-time hunters, many of the comforts of civilization are always nearby or can be easily obtained. *Trait-Cluster III* cynegism is *wild behavior* that is simply pointless, rude, disrespectful, and pretends to pass for a real and noble wildness within. *Trait-Cluster IV* cynegism is represented mostly by the easy and predictable middle class or bourgeois life and includes an additional neurotic and anxious component that further isolates itself from wildness. Finally, *Trait-Cluster V, or Improbable/rare* cynegism, is a description of thoroughly fictional characters, who although representing true cynegism, are not real. This last trait-cluster does have, however, the power to influence the thinking of any of the psychological dimensions described and to act as a desired model, albeit romanticized and improbable, of cynegetic life.

Trait-Cluster I: First Order Cynegism

"But perhaps, more than his body was the change in his mind, or in the way he was-was becoming. I am not the same, he thought. I see, I hear differently. He did not know when the change started but it was there; when a sound came to him now he didn't just hear it but would know the sound. He would swing and look at it-a breaking twig, a movement of air-and know the sound as if he somehow could move his mind back down the wave of sound to the source."—Gary Paulsen, *Hatchet*, (1987)

Trait-Cluster II

"My life is monotonous [the fox talking to The Little Prince]. I hunt chickens and men hunt me. All chickens are alike and all men are alike. Men have no more time to understand anything. They buy ready-made things in the shops. But since there are no shops where you can buy friends, men no longer have any friends."
                    —Antoine De Saint—Exupéry, *The Little Prince*, (1995)

"As I took leave of the island I carried on board some special souvenirs of my long stay, including a goatskin cap I had made, my umbrella, Poll my parrot, and the money I had taken from the wrecked ships."
                    —Daniel Defoe, *Robinson Crusoe*, (1995)

Trait-Cluster III

"But the habits and practices of, say, scholars and critics are not deemed fandom, and are not considered to be potentially deviant or dangerous. Why? My conclusion claims that the characterization of fandom as pathology is based in, supports, and justifies elitist and disrespectful beliefs about our common life."
                    —Joli Jenson, *Fandom as Pathology: The Consequences of Characterization*, (1992)

Trait-Cluster *IV*

"A man cannot live intensely except at the cost of the self. Now the bourgeois treasures nothing more highly than the self (rudimentary as it may be). And so at the cost of intensity he achieves his own preservation and security. His harvest is a quiet mind which he prefers to being possessed by God, as he does comfort to pleasure, convenience to liberty, and the pleasant temperature to that deathly inner consuming fire. The bourgeois is consequently by nature a creature of weak impulses, anxious, fearful of giving himself away and easy to rule. Therefore, he has substituted majority for power, law for force, and the polling booth for responsibility."
—Hermann Hesse, *Steppenwolf*, (1929/1969)

Trait-Cluster V. Improbable/rare cynegism

"He could drop twenty feet at a stretch from limb to limb in rapid descent to the ground, or he could gain the utmost pinnacle of the loftiest tropical giant with the ease and swiftness of a squirrel. Though but ten years old he was fully as strong as the average man of thirty . . ."
—Edgar Rice Burroughs, *Tarzan of The Apes*, (1914)

Admittedly, the above literary excerpts are scanty, even mysteriously frustrating. Many more trait-clusters of cynegism may come to the reader's mind than I am able to include here. And there is no question that the causes for the origin of above psychological dimensions are complex and demand an extensive reading across many social scientific disciplines. These causes, however complex, might be environmentally linked to the earlier trilogy of inquires: *Why is most of humanity accepting living with less, rather than much more, wildness; What impedes the embracing of seemingly healthy, meaningful, and sustainably deep interactions with wilderness and each other;? And If LIFE can be said to be archetypically, ideally, naturally represented by wildness, why then do we reject it?*

Having begun this work with the promise that the ecopsychologically null condition I termed *Lebensneid* might be corrected by a renewed sense of spirituality, itself rooted in a respect for nature, then continuing this task by characterizing the groups and trait-clusters of individuals in need (or not) of these therapies, I now devote the rest of this text to trying to answer the initial trilogy of questions.

Why is most of humanity accepting living with less, rather than much more, wildness?

To answer the first question simply: we are psychologically deprived (some of us see, in hindsight), institutionally condemned, and forced or conditioned to think along dysfunctional psycholinguistic paths. These reasons, and more, are reflected in an incredibly large body of sensible, robust, and/or confirmed social scientific and human environmental data amassed from the 1930's until this year[93]. To ease the task of summarizing these findings and of reading them here, I have, again, taken the complete text of the subtitles in this section and "posted them" under Appendix B. Unlike my previous recommendation, this time I would encourage the reader to begin with the italicized bare-bones descriptions first, and then move to Appendix B for clarification. But some of answers to the above question are as follows:

Practical, self-esteem, and existential necessity

Many of the principal social/urban easy-to-access and convenient services and our interactions with more official social/urban infrastructures (e.g., mostly their human bureaucracies) are themselves the origins of our self-worth and self-esteem, and to the extent that their values are distorted and their services conditional on our servitude and automatic deference, so are the interpretations of our self-image. You are what you eat.

Natural resources are depleted, abused, and ecological systems are misunderstood

The desire, hunger, and cost of maintaining a relative "high standard of living," civilization, "progress," and the affluence that allows increased comforts and temporary psychological patches, are fed by natural "things," systems, and systems and "things" in precarious biological balances. Either dominant cultures (capitalist or communist) have abused and ransacked other "lesser developed" societies and plundered their territories in pursuit of these natural resources with impunity, or many overpopulated territories and a bursting-with-people planet have used up their "free" natural-resources ride, never free to begin with. There aren't enough "things" and "goods," resources, for all people on Earth to maintain the above levels of gluttonous and capricious prosperity, and/or to survive. For the most part, ecological science depends on statistical and laborious know-how that the average person does not possess or mistrusts.

Ideological propaganda that utilizes empty meanings or oversimplifies complex issues

"Citizens of many nations accept, unquestioned, without proper educational training, intangible labels and poorly understood concepts sold by the dominant ideology, influential politicians, family members, and even misguided scientists. Bad text is accepted at face value. These intangible labels seem to acquire a certain meaning in the lips of and behind the charisma of leaders who are equally in the dark or simply nefarious and greedy." We are what we read. We are judged by the company we keep. All things being equal, one random hour of public broadcasting has more truth than a week's worth of selected "extreme" or "vindictive" news.

Dysfunctional ontological bonding with all the wrong things

"*The transformation from juvenile patterns of consumption and materialistic and empty-hedonistic fixations can be long and arduous enough, even without a well-defined ecopsychological wellness goal, judging by mainstream clinical standards. The transformation will have to include recognition of complex behavioral and cognitive patterns, a dysfunctional semiosis and biosemiosis, that will interfere with and impede a trajectory toward wellness.*" Only children play with toys. Adults, on the other hand, change the world with GOOD ideas and deeds, and always, always, make the world a better place for children to play with toys and then, as adults, with ideas. Adults leave clean air, water, and food sources for their children.

Individual and/or collective limitations

"*In cases of extreme and incurable psychological dysfunction, the total depletion of ecosystems to unsustainable conditions, or even physiological and genetic impediments, it may be impossible for an individual to achieve prosperity of spirit of any kind, capitalistic or otherwise. For all the other reasons stated up to this point, individually or collectively, we may find more opposition than support, more discouragement than solutions, more ignorance than credible and practical information to begin the transformation.*" We might all be, individually, blind men and women. Collectively, however, we can build a Gaussian noetic structure that is rooted in natural wisdom that can protects us all.

The inability to relate to wildness (mistrusting or fearing "Mother Earth")

"*This has always been the dilemma and the continuing challenge of the cynegetically immersed individual: how to interpret the role and function, real or projected-animistic, of the mother "out there" in the daily, yearly, and generational actions and functions of survival. The solution to this challenge is rather simple in my understanding. Life should be as challenging as learning how to walk; thus exciting, liberating, and fraught with the RIGHT type of danger toward a desired outcome: freedom on two feet or racing with the wind at full gallop. That is because only such a life provides our complex cognitive and physical systems with the necessary alimentation for normal development that can eventually be cashed-in as courage and wholeness. This self-initiated and courageous excitement and sense of liberation, with the additional and mature understanding that all natural things have their hallowed place and are indispensable to an ideal developmental process, is the only assurance that the child or we, on our way to transforming our sickly psyches into cynegetically nimble constitutions, can ever hope for.*" WALK, then RUN.

Religious traditional dogmatic stances about human nature being a special case—anthropocentrism—and separate from telos

"*Religion has played and can play a valuable role in bonding the individual and societies to telluric origins. This is good religion[94]. Indeed, many first-nation peoples have/had such religions and their doctrines, mores and taboos act/acted as a self-correcting (Conesa-Sevilla, 2005b), thoroughly tested, and built-in ecopsychological set of principles that almost guarantees normal cynegetic development and thus an authentic affiliation with telos. A bad religion, on the other hand, is anti-nature; anti-wildness; propaganda and ideology supplanting respect for and worship of the organic origins of the human mind and spirit with illusions of grandeur and impossible transcendence. If the spirit emerges from a balanced communion with telos, if ecoethics emerge as a natural consequence of acting "justly," "mindfully" with regard to the entire complexity of life, then this spirit must be GOOD."* "Father" Coyote does not eat the red berries destined for the children of the future, nor does he condone humans who do.

In short, if we are not up to the challenges of the wild, the challenge of regaining our humanity and well being, because we are not prepared to stand its rigors, we will not partake of its deeper lessons either. If we accept the "easy way out" and a life of ignorance, if we accept it because no viable alternative exists, then we will be unhappy and unfulfilled, and maybe even sick. If we prefer the "easy way out" and the easy life, it is because we have missed many important developmental phases and opportunities for learning how to relate with wilderness and have not bonded properly with a complex planet. And yet, despite of all the challenges, it is our duty to face up to these realities.

But still, there are no promises. Old Oogruk (in Gary Paulsen's *Dogsong*, 1995) himself, the last member of an authentic cynegetic dynasty, makes no promises to initiate Russel. "You are here to learn. And I will try. I will try. But I do not know it all and there will be things I miss. Still, we will do what we can." The consciousness divide that we must all traverse toward cynegism, to be healthy again, is gigantic and even incomprehensible. It is a divide of completely extant *Bewusstsein* that no new age toothpick structures can bridge. Oogruk, as a consummate ecopsychologist, understands very well this challenge when he says:

> We lived so differently, so far back and different that it almost cannot be understood now. Now they use guns and make noise, back then we were quiet and the animals felt differently about dying. But that's just one thing, one little thing, that was different.

What impedes the embracing of seemingly healthy, meaningful, and sustainably deep interactions with wilderness and each other?

Ontogenetically speaking, growing in a milieu of the cultural artificiality of plastic plants and pink rubber flamingoes, mindless consumption, banal entertainment, limited physical activity, and always surrounded by masses of infantalized adults, logically produces arrested development, and perpetuates the above fixations and infantile patterns (4d). All of the above points (4a-4g) combine and conspire and culminate in collusive madness to create tinsel realities that are accepted as the real thing. These are some of the impediments to cynegism. Adding insult to injury "health providers" and psychologists contribute to these infantilized patterns to the extent that they themselves are the products of an infantalized reality. As I wrote in the prequel to this paper:

> The I-Pod holding, Volvo driving, mild-tempered, sweet talking psychologist is as much to blame for the propping up of *falsches Bewusstsein* [false consciousness] as any nefarious industrialist tycoon. They are equally part of the unconsciously driven consuming herd.

All this leads to the very scary situation that we don't know what primal-healthy is anymore, partly because mainstream psychologists and psychiatrists are playing with the same toys and playing the same unnatural game. Nor are we allowed to discover for ourselves, by stumbling or luck, what this primal-healthy is, to the extent that the influence of the present tinsel society is so powerfully felt that it makes our actions seem, if not impertinent and deviant, at least out of step with "sane society". We have lost the Nature dictionary and cannot understand what we are supposed to do in NATURE. Specifically, hunter-forager-horticultural knowledge has been lost, degraded into pseudo new age religion, or is being lost at a rapid pace leaving no school-of-nature left, no authentic guides to help us go back. Furthermore, and semiotically speaking, the popular media and techno-materialistic languages (mostly the "G-8" culture) overwhelm the quiet and simpler syntax and semantics of ancient languages. *These languages are themselves being lost, their ecological metaphors are but dreams of rapidly disappearing and aging populations who are themselves discarded as an obstacle to obtaining more western toy products by upcoming and forgetful generations of first-nation peoples.*

The modern folk who still have a chance rightly perceive their uncynegetic existence in neurotic and pathological terms, as feeling isolated, alienated, confused, barraged by contradictory texts, and in such a situation, existential paralysis can set in. In the absence of real answers, and in order to feel alive again, we purchase more toys and partake of all sorts of escapism entertainment on credit. Religion for some (at least some forms of it) may be a valid vehicle to regenerate a spiritual sentiment and salvage an ailing psychology. But then again, if you go with that medicine, without full awareness of the natural causes for the malady, you might be indoctrinated deeper into hyper anthropocentric or hyper humanistic thinking, thus moving farther away from embracing the totality of your being which includes your genetic past and its requirements. In short, *biophagocitic* tendencies, no matter who sells them, rather than a *biophilic* attitude, lurk everywhere and disguise themselves as the panacea YOU need to be whole again.

Finally, fear is the ultimate impediment toward embracing a cynegetic psychology. It is akin to the fear of a domesticated high rise apartment cat that is suddenly placed outdoors without any accommodation time. It is the fear of being physically hurt by something or other. It includes the fear of being lost in the woods, fear of the dark, fear of strange noises, fear of being alone, fear of encountering dangers of any type, fear of encountering strangers, or the fear of being bullied by a mountain cyclist or a fit runner. *Fear is not knowing what something is and in what precise and mature way one can relate to this unknown.* Mature attitudes and stances are gained with experience and knowledge, everywhere. A close cousin of fear is discomfort. If not as unnerving as fear itself, the attempts to insure a 24/7 homeostasis of security and comfort are at least troublesome enough that, ensemble, they prevent us from walking in the rain or snow, or going camping more often because one misses one's Jacuzzi or warm shower, or because one cannot get to the preferred neighborhood's Starbucks coffee shop to drink one's habitual mega Moka-Macciato-topped-with-a-chocolate-covered-coffee-bean. Let's face it; it is usually easier to rest on a comfortable couch eating some pleasurable thing than to be out gardening, digging potatoes under a merciless sun. If some of these situations resonate with you or I, it is because the resonance indicates a symptom as well.

If LIFE can be said to be archetypically, ideally, naturally represented by wildness, why then do we reject it?

For all the reasons given earlier plus an additional reason, again, not new. The archetypes of LIFE have changed their masks and clothing and are no longer recognizable or useful as guides for healthy natural values and/or ideas. The ancient-wise supporting casts of archetypical characters we once depended on for meaningful development (the ancient water-earth-wind-fire heroes, our animal totem spirits, and the green men and fairies) do not necessarily fight for a return to ecopsychological balance, nor sacrifice their lives in the pursuit of ecological science. If our ancient archetypes of the hero/heroine, diverse totemic spirit psychologies, the mother goddess, the wise old man/woman, the feminine, the masculine, all desert their original and telluric semiotic mythical function, and we fail to recognize their timeless importance, then we don't understand or trust their lessons either. On the other hand, if the new archetype of the hero is someone who kills, maims, wears expensive jewelry, rapes, and burns forests to a crisp, why would any boy want to grow peas in a pot, or sing a song of respect after killing for food? If the new archetype of the feminine is an impossible body-frame of bones and skin, covered in exotic fur (grown in torturing cages far away from the stores that sell them) and on the lookout for the latest fashion, the Paris Hiltons of the world, why would girls want to get muddy by collecting frog eggs or berries in the rain? If the new archetype of an old wise man is himself driving a Ferrari in his late fifties and chasing after Paris

Hilton-type models, when will he teach orienting skills to both boys and girls? If the new mother archetype is a woman put in an impossible situation of having to excel by taking care of her family, being a corporate head, and looking like Paris Hilton 24/7, how will girls learn to run after butterflies or travel to Antarctica with boys as co-equal companions and friends?

If it can be said that there are archetypes representing the sanctity of LIFE, these might be blood, breath, or even green sprouting things. But when the blood of animals and human-animals is tainted or spilled indiscriminately, and breath willingly consumes smoke or breathes it, and finally, when there are less and less examples of greenness sprouting, or of diverse greenness sprouting unimpeded or unattended, when these things happen and more, everything seems to indicate that LIFE is DEATH. With that suicidal equation in place, teenagers kill or kill themselves and we live for the entertaining moment that will kill us, but it is nevertheless fun. The equation allows for maximum tolerance of atmospheric contamination as an urban norm (or we accept the fact that less affluent communities must pay the price for our relatively clean suburban air) or as a sign of "progress." Finally, LIFE is archetypically and concretely represented in our physical bodies. We can alchemically (Metzner, 1999) express LIFE through our bodies or choose to neglect this process.

What is wrong with a perfectly good and deserted island to escape to?

Fiction, reality and the expression of our own fantasies create interesting ambiguities on the road to cynegism. Pi, the character boy in the *Life of Pi* (Martel, 2003), was never neurotic in the sense that we have been using the word to describe our shared *Lebensneid* condition. Equally, Brian, the thirteen year-old character in *Hatchet*, another of Gary Paulsen's fine cynegetic stories, also achieves cynegetic transformation (see 4a). Both characters, inspirational examples of Fifth Order cynegism, are young and that gives them a leg up in ecopsychological BECOMING. Fictional also is Tarzan, a child rescued by apes, literally, from the dying text, achieving a complete cynegetic transformation, albeit without a human support base of other cynegetic individuals to create a lasting community. The real Robison Crusoe, Alexander Selkirk, an adult marooned on a perfectly good deserted island, on the other hand, curses his existence until he is able to escape it having only achieved a mediocre identification with his natural spaces. The character that American actor Tom Hanks portrayed in *Castaway* is also obsessed with leaving his small island paradise and equally ignores the developmental gains obtained during his stay. Like my earlier excerpt, he comes back with his own souvenir: a FedEx box in need of delivery. The difference between all these cases is age of course. *The earlier the transformation toward cynegetic mind begins the better chances that it will take root.*

I have personally, failed many times at overnight-types of cynegetic conversion. A recent failure occurred while considering a teaching position in the Bahamas and being told by my potential employer that I should not consider making this move if I was not prepared to bring a lot of cash with me. Affluent teachers were welcomed to apply. There went my opportunity, I thought, of reverting to cynegenic existence[95]. I fantasized too about moving to a deserted island, jobless and marooned, as the only situation in which I might be able to practice cynegetic existence. But then again, I had a family to consider and their idea of cynegenic progression did not involve such a radical approach. Neither was I sure that I would not end up talking to a ball rather than becoming part of a community of cygenetic buddies. But each failure was a learning experience and a new toughening of the spirit.

One of the opening quotes and excerpts of this paper is also Pi's recollection of sighting a deserted island after languishing on the sea for many weeks. In that book, the island does not turn out to be such an idyllic and permanent paradise. And such is the case with most of our romantic ideas of primeval existence: we believe them to be either personal or utopian versions of benign Edens or heavens-to-be and imagine ourselves walking naked on a bleached white beach or in a luxurious, tame green forest (of course, after having lost our excess weight or after having increased the size of our breasts considerably) browned by a tropical sun to the point that we resemble a local native wearing colorful yellow bandanas. All right, this is my personal cynegetic fantasy but I am sure you have one also. That is not an impossible dream, but that confident naked walk in a real paradise is first earned, perhaps in our backyards, today and tomorrow, by practicing and preparing to be the dark native in a real jungle some day. Apropos, a biography of the famous Artic and Antarctic explorer Roald Amundsen tells us of how, when very young and growing up in Norway, he would sleep with his window open in order to get accustomed to the intensity of inclement, cold weather. At fifteen he abandoned a career in medicine and embarked on his first great adventure.

As a more general description, the real native wisely stalks and kills, aesthetically and compassionately, lo live. LIFE and DEATH dovetail, creating an irrevocable dance, and our part in this existential and inescapable "deal" is to be fully prepared to understand and accept this responsibility. That is why he/she walks with confidence: she/he can procure food at will and will never have to wait for french fries and third rate meat to be delivered by servers who have forgotten all the power songs. *Soylent Green* burgers aside, his/her stride is definitely upright and confident.

Conclusion: The Medicine(s)

It is difficult to find a medicine that everyone can take. It is harder still to find a medicine that, once ingested, can cure us all. But, the instructions to most ecopsychological "pill boxes" I have read commence by describing what sort of individuals could benefit from the "pill." The unfolded bit of fragile paper and miniscule writing begins with the assumption that one lives in a city or the suburbs; that one spends far too much time sitting or driving; that most of one's entertainment or "sports" is watched passively and does not qualify as exercise; and that much of this entertainment is meaningless at best, and psychologically corrosive at worst. The instructions inside the pillbox assume that we are, like children, continually on the verge of being bored (mostly because our zoo cages were never constructed to feed cynegetic needs) and that we are almost totally dependent on others, often in a superficial manner, for satisfying basic survival, emotional, aesthetic, and mobility needs. The instructions say that the medicine they are offering us is for individuals who have forgotten how to prepare complex meals in the company of others and that the nutritional content of these meals should be varied.

The frail multifold parchment says that wandering, walking, or exploring in natural spaces alone, or with company, without the excuse of having to eat some barbecued thing, or competing in a race to see who gets to the top of the hill first, is medicine. The medicine also warns us to "Beware of the dumb-down world!" It clearly states that a golf park is a playpen and so are many parks that are not self-sustainable as genuine wilderness is. Sand traps may make a golfer very mad but they present no real danger or threat. Indoor gyms cannot replace the reality of frigid winter air while walking in the snow. Halfway through the instructions they assert with confidence that indoor plants are poor substitutes for virginal forests. They say that cats and dogs are not tigers and wolves, particularly if we treat our pets like children. They are confident in declaring that cars are not legs, that elevators are not legs, but that bicycles, on the other hand, are round legs. They repeat many times that micro-waved food is efficient but it does not allow for complex motoric routines that strengthen the hands and center the mind while preparing even a simple salad.

The medicine, they say, is always more exercise; more understanding of life-death circles that feed the bisophere; independence and freedom of personal movement; clean air; clean water; and no noise or noise types and levels that we can control.[96] One could perform a hundred shamanic passes until one passes out but they alone won't make you a warrior. A warrior hunts; a warrior kills for a living. The modern warrior-hunter is also schooled in the complex deconstruction of text. As his/her ancestors in the primaveral wild, he/she understands semiotic complexity and is not fooled by fake text. This also requires having mathematical statistical knowledge in order to make sense of certain types of complexity.

All of these examples, by themselves, are mere decontextualized actions and wishful thinking rituals. They have a better chance of taking hold and of igniting ecopsychological transformation when we surround ourselves, around the clock, with other individuals who are on the same path. Whether totally revisiting cynegetic ways, or by small degrees and steps, we can significantly modify our unnecessarily overculturized habits, or influence our communal leaders toward the deconstruction of a proliferating synthetically constructed city environment; it is the case that actively seeking and creating solutions rather than waiting for a change is in itself progress of some measurable type. Individually or collectively, at least, we might feel better and somewhat reassured that we are on the path toward wellness and ecopsychological recovery. The active engagement in all these facets of life are also models for our children, for their own ecopsychological RETURNING and/or BECOMING. Borrowing from Hermann Hesse again, we are unfinished and incomplete creatures:

> That man is not yet a finished creation but rather a challenge of the spirit; a distant possibility dreaded as much as it is desired; that the way towards it has only been covered for a very short distance and with terrible agonies and ecstasies even by those few for whom it is the scaffold today and the monument tomorrow-all this the Steppenwolf, too, suspected. What, however, he calls the "man" in himself, as opposed to the wolf, is to a great extent nothing else than this very same average man of the bourgeois convention

The deconstruction of this false tinsel self has been the guidance of many religious practices for as long as civilization has robbed us of our true nature and enlightened folks have noticed it. I also interpret Hesse's passage here to indicate that as civilization creates a fictional human being of *bourgeois convention*, it only compresses an ancient *Steppenwolf* mentality that sooner or later re-emerges in its pristine and innocent form, unrecognized and accused by modernity, or is distorted into the absurd or the very dangerous. Discovering and then channeling the *Steppenwolf* amongst the civilized is never easy. In some cases it may simply take the form of arriving at an acceptable truce where the *Steppenwolf* is fed a frequent and consistent diet of wildness. In other situations, dictated by individual temperaments and dispositions, it may mean an outright severance from bourgeois convention and accompanying absurdities altogether and relocation to wildness. Thus this becoming, if it is BECOMING, culminates in a complete reorganization of one's life, from the inside out.

". . . The Caribs are better off than we are."

J.J. Rousseau, Emile, Book One, No. 43

Appendix A

Five Cynegetic Trait-Clusters

Trait-Cluster I, or *first order* cynegism, is reserved for authentic hunter-forager-horticulturalist individuals, past and present, who must defend themselves, procure food, and pass on their culture with a minimum of technology. In Section Two I referred to an idealized ensemble of human values that might emerge from this kind of existence. I called it a *hunter-forager spirituality* based on specific activities and practices such as: stealth, frugality, gratitude, resourcefulness, strength, seasonally meaningful rituals, courage, patience, and perseverance. These, I ventured further, give rise to genuine pride, other values and virtues and then to the concept of morality. Thus morality must naturally emerge from these basic attitudes. Without reading my earlier caveat, this passage and description may sound as yet another romantization of the "primitive".

Trait-Cluster II: Are characters such as the Robinson-Crusoes wanting to return to civilization in a hurry, pseudo hunters like Theodore Roosevelt and the likes, and the occasional vacationers to tropical paradises may very well acquire new and useful perspectives and improve their neuroses by *killing,* somewhat, but they are not true cynegetic individuals if they turn back to civilization or if most of their existence is engulfed by it.

Trait-Cluster III: These are the individuals who might who dress in colorful attires, paint their faces blue or red during ball games, get drunk and scream "bloody hell" with the aid of alcoholic tonics, drive on autobahns at 120 miles an hour—all this in order to feel a bit of wildness inside them. These are understandable behaviors, regrettable circumstances, even the object of our compassion for it could be very difficult for them to recapture the authentic cynegetic, psychological core. These "lords of the flies" that pass me on the autobahn at 120 miles an hour remain the rulers of insects without having attempted psychological individuation.

Trait-Cluster IV: This group is represented by the chronic sickness of an ecologically stripped down and dehumanized ape whose longing does not go away even with affluence or moderate life styles, also deserve our compassion, as the persons who can never "let their hair down," who feel dirty in natural spaces, who must wash away the mud of an hour's hike (the most they will ever attempt), or otherwise society will reproach (a Superego reaching out from a "proper" past—*prop* as implying *clean* in French) their "wild ways."

Trait-Cluster V, or *improbable/rare cynegetic* caricatures, that is, the Tarzans, the wild-boys and girls of Avignon and other places, are either fictional characters and/or incomprehensible (and even reprehensible) real cynegetic models, but even they began their transformation early in development. They are equally important sources of inspiration or study.

Appendix B

Why is most of humanity accepting living with less, rather than much more, wildness?

Practical and existential necessity

Having forgotten how to live in harmony with wilderness and/or natural spaces, having lost a traditional and instructional line with these ways and past, most of us now depend, like infants, on an artificial world and are almost, existentially speaking, indentured slaves to sometimes meaningless jobs, health infrastructures, educational and civil bureaucratic services in order to survive, prosper and to define ourselves; to define BEING and being in the WORLD. *Many of the principal social/urban easy-to-access and convenient services and our interactions with more official social/urban infrastructures (e.g., mostly their human bureaucracies) are themselves the origins of our self-worth and self-esteem, and to the extent that their values are distorted and their services conditional on our servitude and automatic deference, so are the interpretations of our self-image.* These services, and proposed ways of living, are also constantly offered to us through the media and manipulated by institutions to insure comfortable corporate profit margins or promises of prosperity. In tandem, these two forces present (sell) these services and ideas as essential, or valid and "good." We have become akin to zoo animals grown accustomed to a prefab and artificially prescribed environment that even when benign and well intentioned, sacrifices a truer legacy, cognitive complexity, and the psychological fortitude that might emerge from that "wild" legacy. If we generally agree with Karl Marx and others that the quality of *being* depends on our existential doings and actual manipulations of reality, then the signing away of these responsibilities to others means that we have diminished personhood and *being* to a degree commensurable with our dependency on these services. It is ironic that the actual practice of capitalism and soviet style communism, that both ideologies, espousing liberation-paths of different sorts, fell down the same trap and hole making their citizens helpless automaton-manufacturers rather than free-roaming enlightened hunters.

Natural and cynegetic values resources are depleted, abused, or misunderstood The desire, hunger, and cost of maintaining a relative "high standard of living," civilization, "progress," and the affluence that allows increased comforts and temporary psychological patches, are fed by natural "things," systems, and systems and "things" in precarious biological balances. Either dominant cultures (capitalist or communist) have abused and ransacked other "lesser developed" societies and plundered their territories in pursuit of these natural resources with impunity, or many overpopulated territories and a bursting-with-people planet have used up their "free" natural-resources ride, never free to begin with. There aren't enough "things" and "goods," resources, for all people on Earth to maintain the above levels of gluttonous and capricious prosperity, and/or to survive. When the human population was low and small bands of cynegetic bands were living within diverse natural spaces and seemingly endless ecosystems, even careless humans did not impact dramatically—biospherically and globally. There are fewer and fewer lands to hide in as coyote did, in shame, after eating the forbidden red berries destined for the "children of the future." The psychological and physiological health impact of this senseless appetite has claimed uncountable lives and it produces death and neurosis in seemingly prosperous societies as well as those who disregard these concerns and avoid day-to-day ecological commonsense and scientific understanding; ecoethics. We are now beginning to feel and realize the ecological and ecopsychological impact of doing what the inhabitants of Easter Island did to their smaller territory, after upsetting their island's ecological stability during generations of egomaniacal religious and political competing propaganda. In short, the original matrix that allows for an embedded, 24/7 cynegetic enterprise is being corrupted.

Ideological propaganda that utilizes empty meanings or oversimplifies complex issues

Citizens of many nations accept, unquestioned, without proper educational training, intangible labels and poorly understood concepts sold by the dominant ideology, influential politicians, family members, and even misguided scientists. Bad text is accepted at face value. These intangible labels seem to acquire a certain meaning in the lips of and behind the charisma of leaders who are equally in the dark or simply nefarious and greedy. Labels and motivating rallying chants such as "growth," "prosperity," "the future," "nation," "patriotism," "the fatherland," "the motherland," "evil," "foreigners," "traitor," "inflation," "oil (we need more of it—you want more of it)," can move masses into antiecological, antiecopsychological, antiorganismic action. We are also at war with the planet every time we are at war with each other through ideological frenzy. In short, any specific agenda, and consequences thereof, for "prosperity" that pits a certain type of "good-for-you-development" against nature (e.g., hard technologies are better, versus, soft-green ones are expensive; or, uncontrolled growth is better than relying on sustainability that insures a good life for most) are sure signs of misguided and/or perverse leadership. If the formula for success always includes the propaganda "wilderness is bad and the civilized/progress is good," then this formula makes even the willing patient a bit cautious in finding a remedy for fear that he/she has turned "wild" in pursuit of a medicine. Not wanting to offend, and being a socially pragmatic and cautious individual—a member of a conforming herd—individual, he/she accepts the arbitrary and artificial moralized definition rather than the cure.[97] (Chomsky, 1968; and Mannheim, 1936)

Dysfunctional ontological bonding with all the wrong things

Rampant consumerism, superficial relations, wanton violence, or psychological depression are consequences, as Paul Shepard suspects, of ecopsychologically defunct development and a wounded psyche. Other than heeding Montessori's, Erikson's, Rousseau's, Freud's and other developmentalists' (and many sensible parents) advice of leaving the civilized behind (cities in particular), during early, middle, and later stages of childhood development for a total immersion with natural spaces, only a deep desire for the natural and to escape from city life, or accidental discovery of ecopsychological truths, or an ecopsychological diagnosis can help in the beginning of this transformation. *The transformation from juvenile patterns of consumption and materialistic and empty-hedonistic fixations can be long and arduous enough, even without a well-defined ecopsychological wellness goal in sight, judging by mainstream clinical standards. The transformation will have to include recognition of complex behavioral and cognitive patterns, a dysfunctional semiosis and biosemiosis, that will interfere with and impede a trajectory toward wellness.*

Individual and/or collective limitations

Considering that many flavors of nature-affiliation of my earlier simplistic characterizations of cynegism are possible, then the path toward complete cynegetic wellness will be impossible, very difficult, or a receding goal with obvious improvements along the way, without ever accomplishing a total revamping of the psyche. *In cases of extreme and incurable psychological dysfunction, the total depletion of ecosystems to unsustainable conditions, or even physiological and genetic impediments, it may be impossible for an individual to achieve prosperity of spirit of any kind, capitalistic or otherwise. For all the other reasons stated up to this point, individually or collectively, we may find more opposition than support, more discouragement than solutions, more ignorance than credible and practical information to begin the transformation.* Perhaps many of the variables that are now used to anticipate recovery and healthy adaptation in mainstream clinical practice, can be useful in predicting an ecological transformation. A caveat to this approach will be that most of the variables that might be useful in predicting a recovery originate within a psychological practice that aims at merely patching up individuals toward integration and "adjustment" back into collusive madness. It would be like using therapy only to send the patient back to the insane asylum. Moreover, there simply aren't enough individual teachers and guides working within the ancient legacies and who possess authentic traditional ecopsychological wisdom to go around to instruct us all. There are but a handful of practicing ecopsychologists. We are mostly viewed with suspicion, or as troublemakers, or as heretics, and/or upset the comfortable orthodoxy of mainstream psychology. But even we are at best, novo-shamans, and other than having rescued ourselves from a total immersion in insane societies, and having protected ourselves and families from most brainwashing, we lack an authentic cynegetic core: we don't kill for a living, we don't suffer very much in our academic posts, and it is always easier to preach to the converted from a computer screen and oracle than to stand in the cold rain naked, singing a prayer. More beneficial perhaps, but harder to accomplish in a single generation, would be that societies so structure themselves, via well-defined and implemented social support and educational programs, that have a more direct, ecologically beneficial, influence in all manners of wellness. This would include social policy conducive to maximizing the possibility that a bonding with natural spaces or wilderness will take place. That is, preferably, true, *first order* cynegetic adults, must inculcate these norms and ensure that normal development proceeds according to well-defined tracks. In my opinion, the American people missed a decisive historical opportunity (and privilege) by neglecting to elect Al Gore as a genuine representative of this progressive change, and instead made it possible to regress eight years[98] (a century or two in terms of ideology) into further madness and mayhem. But this election outcome can be now studied as the logical and expected collective will of a people who might be ecopsychologically ill.

The inability to relate to wildness (mistrusting or fearing "Mother Earth")

What guarantees are there that a child who is learning to walk will be caught in time by her mother before learning the hard way that walking, although exciting and liberating, involves a few bruises? No guarantees whatsoever. *This has always been the dilemma and the continuing challenge of the cynegetically immersed individual: how to interpret the role and function, real or projected-animistic, of the mother "out there" in the daily, yearly, and generational actions and functions of survival. The solution to this challenge is rather simple in my understanding. Life should be as challenging as learning how to walk; thus exciting, liberating, and fraught with the RIGHT type of danger toward a desired outcome: freedom on two feet or racing with the wind at full gallop. That is because only such a life provides our complex cognitive and physical systems with the necessary alimentation for normal development that can eventually be cashed-in as courage and wholeness. This self-initiated and courageous excitement and sense of liberation, with the additional and mature understanding that all natural things have their hallowed place and are indispensable to an ideal developmental process, is the only assurance that the child or we, on our way to transforming our sickly psyches into cynegetically nimble constitutions, can ever hope for.* With a small promise: even zoo tigers can go back to being feral or wild. This is the case because the genetics of our biological constitution ceased to evolve radically (into a new homo species) 150,000 thousand years ago. And even if our transformation is only partial, of the feral kind, *at what point, when is the feral thing wild?* Is there any need to use the word *feral* anymore if the consequences of running away from madness, from a pig stall, and returning to wildness propitiates a measurable increment of cynegetic wellness? Personally, I would rather be a feral pig than a penned pig even if I can never become a tusky *sanglier*.

Religious traditional stances about human nature being special and separate from telos

Religion has played and can play a valuable role in bonding the individual and societies to telluric origins. This is good religion[99]. Indeed, many first-nation peoples have/had such religions and their doctrines, mores and taboos act/acted as a self-correcting (Conesa-Sevilla, 2005b), thoroughly tested, and built-in ecopsychological set of principles that almost guarantees normal cynegetic development and thus an authentic affiliation with telos. A bad religion, on the other hand, is anti-nature; anti-wildness; propaganda and ideology supplanting respect for and worship of the organic origins of the human mind and spirit with illusions of grandeur and impossible transcendence. If the spirit emerges from a balanced communion with telos, if ecoethics emerge as a natural consequence of acting "justly," "mindfully" with regard to the entire complexity of life, then this spirit must be GOOD. If, on the other hand, we are promised a surrogate type of tame wilderness-in-the-sky, more of a country club or a harem than an original innocence and responsibility to THIS palpable Eden, then religion is bad and serves no ecopsychologically real purpose. The god that says to humanity, "You are more than the rest of creation," is a false god and eventually undermines our naturally good psychological balance. The interpretation of this line and bad text as originating in an ultimate supernatural power is a failure to use our reasoning capabilities to sense, perceive, and come to the conclusion that we are just one more species, no more and no less, that has not changed much in the last 150,000 thousand years and which requires the same intact environment in which it developed and needs the ways of interacting with this environment to be healthy, to feel whole, to understand the spiritual life. Coyote or Crow may be better gods because they teach a richer existential story about the folly AND about the stability of continued existence on ONE earth. Once, the myths were GOOD until bad text corrupted it as when old Inuit Oogruk replies to the cynegetic aspirant Russel, in Gary Paulsen's *Dogsong*:

> [Russel] What happened to the songs? Why don't we have them anymore? . . . [Oogruk] We had those songs until the first missionary came. He said they were wrong for some reason or another, like dancing was wrong. At first nobody believed him and we laughed at him . . . It

was not that we were stupid, just that we didn't know about hell. So he told us. About fire and pain and these demons—as he called them—who would tear the strip of meat off us. So, many of the people quit singing and dancing because they feared hell. And even when the missionary went crazy with the winter and we had to drive him out the damage was done. People were afraid to sing and dance and we lost our songs.

Appendix C

Sigurd Olson's "Flashes of Insight"

"Yesterday while on my skis, pausing on the high ridge north of Grassy Lake and overlooking twenty miles of wilderness valley to the great range to the southward, for a moment I had the sensation of harmony with the infinite. As Hudson expresses it when he had climbed a hill to look for the sunset, "I sat down and waited for it to take me." This being taken expresses it so perfectly that any further attempt would be superfluous. One is taken body and soul and while the illusion lasts one is filled with an elation, transported as it were into another world far from the strife of this. It does not last long, can be broken as mine was yesterday by the approach of a truck along the road a quarter mile away. For perhaps a full minute, I stood on my skis steeping myself in the glory of the scene before me. All thought of time had flown or of past and subsequent events, for a moment I was transported. Then like an unpleasant memory I was aware of a hostile influence approaching and I began to retrace the way to the matter of fact. It was nothing but the click, click of a chain striking a fender but it was enough to break the spell. It drew closer and closer until the air was filled with the unpleasant clangor of metal upon metal. I looked up in disgust but the truck was hidden by the trees. It grew fainter and fainter and at last was lost entirely. I stayed for a moment to try and recapture what I had lost but although I did for a brief moment, it was impossible to regain the complete beauty of the first. I pushed on my ski sticks and slid down the trail toward the lake. Once more I had had one of the moments for which I go out. Not always am I so successful. Some days I see nothing, hear nothing, on others every view gives me a glimmer of the goal . . .

. . . I remember a sunset on the top of Robinson Peak alone as I must always be if I am to receive the vision in its entirety. The sun a round red ball on the horizons separated from me by leagues and leagues of primitive wilderness. It hung suspended swelling glowing palpitating with energy. For a brief moment I experienced the sensation of feeling the earth move away from the sun. Nothing akin to it had I ever felt. Here was I an atom of life on the rim of the world watching it turn. Never before had I experienced anything which placed me so in harmony with the infinite. The play of gorgeous color on water sky and land no doubt helped to creat the setting but the main sensation the illusion governing the whole was a union of myself with the plan of creation. Then more than at any other time did I feel that I was a part of the beautiful life I loved. From that moment on I was a spiritualist. Nothing could ever take from me what I had found.

Years passed before I could analyze those moments and know in what their attraction for my lay. Now that I know I can see the explanation of many things I have done.

There is no doubt that others have the same feeling though I doubt that they have it to the same degree. Many have a certain appreciation of nature but fail to recognize or if they do recognize do not permit themselves to submit to it thereby losing its completeness. Those who do not see it scoff and call it sentimentalism. And how the sentimentalists are derided. It might hurt that criticism were it justified, but how can such criticism hurt when one's intellect can see so far beyond the pale of ordinary human perception. Could any criticism of jibe take from the me moment on Robinson Peak or a moment in a canoe in the path of moonlight. Nothing ever said or done can rob me of those moments. I am beyond criticism for I know.

The feeling of the supernatural comes not only on rare occasions but may come at any time lasting perhaps only a fraction of an instant. These fragmentary glimpses into the infinite are fully as inspirational as the longer ones but are not always recognized. The difference between living a drab and uninteresting life and one filled to the brim with thrilling adventures is just that, being able to see and know life's great moments when they come to you. Someone has said that to be happy one must know that one is happy and supremely happy. One cannot be happy wondering if one is lacking something. To get the full benefit out of anything one must abandon oneself entirely to it to the exclusion of everything else. Through long effort it is graduatlly becoming possible for me to get the maximum of pleasure and enjoyment out of my moments when they come. My greatest moments of happiness are then. I come from them with a new vision of the beauty of life. That is no doubt the secret of my devotion to the outdoors. It is not fishing and hunting or the physical enjoyment of being out but the knowledge that perhaps I will get another one of those glimpses into the unknown. Of late years it has become a mania with me and I will go to any lengths to satisfy it. A day that does not have at least one opportunity to satisfy it, seems to me a day wasted. Days when I have seen my vision are glorious beads on the chain of my life, the others are drab unbrightened stones.

There are few who see what I see, very few. Even the great writers of nature, many of them have failed. Occasionally there crops out an inkling of it but none of the clearness of perception and depth of feeling that I know. Why I should have it I cannot know, perhaps it is an inherited instinct from some far ancestral mystic. Surely none of my family have it, if they do it is hidden and unrecognizable. In me has been concentrated the natural mysticism of centuries of my race. I have been given the Seeing Eye. It is my mission to give my vision to the race in return for the beauty that has been shown me. I cannot go through life keeping it to myself. That would be rank ingratitude to the nature, I worship . . ."

—Sigurd Olson, *The Singing Wilderness* (*Silence*), 1956

Chapter Four References

Burroughs Rice, E. (1914). Tarzan of the apes. Chicago: W.F. Hall Printing Co.

Chomsky, N. (1968). *Language and mind*. New York, Harcourt Brace.

Conesa. J. (1999). Ecological Outcome Psychological Theory (EOPT): Application of Human Developmental Theories to Other Scientific Fields. NY: Forbes Publishing

Conesa, J. (1999). Matricial ontological universals allow for seamless "Is-Ought" logical transitions into ecocentrism. (http://www.geocities.com/jorgeconesa/Biosemiotics/MainOnto.html)

Conesa-Sevilla, J. (2005a). The realm of continued emergence: the semiotics of George Herbert Mead and its implications to biosemiotics, Semiotics Matrix Theory, and ecological ethics. *Sign System Studies*, Tartu University, Estonia.

Conesa-Sevilla, J. (2005b). The singularization of reality: Implications of a synnomic evolution of language to semiotics, biosemiotics, and ecopsychology. *GATHERINGS: Journal of the International Community for Ecopsychology*. (http://www.ecopsychology.org/journal/ezine/gatherings.html)

Defoe, D. (1995). Robinson Crusoe. (Adapted by Anthony Masters). Oxford, UK: Oxford University Press.

De Saint-Exupéry, A. (1995). The little prince. Translated by Irene Testot-Ferry. Great Britain, Chathan, Kent: Mackays of Chatham plc.

Devall, W. and Sessions, G. (1985). Deep ecology: living as if nature mattered. Layton: Peregrine Smith Book.

Dunn, M. (2001). Ella Minnow Pea. NY: Anchor Books.

Fromm, E. (1955). The sane society. New York: Holt, Rinehart, & Winston Printing.

Hesse, H. (1929/1969) Steppenwolf. Translated by Basil Creighton (Updated by Joseph Mileck). NY: Bantam Books.

Horney, K. (1942/1994) Self-analysis. NY: W. W. Norton & Co. Inc.

Jenson, J. (1992). *Fandom* as pathology: the consequences of characterization. In L. Lewis' (Ed.), *The Adoring Audience*. London, UK: Routledge.

Kaplan, R. (1983). The role of nature in the urban context. In I Altman and J.F. Wohlwill, (eds.), *Human Behaviour and the Environment: advances in theory and research*, Vol. 6 pp. 127-161. New York: Plenum Press.

Kaplan, S. (1987). Aesthetics, affect and cognition: Environmental preferences from an evolutionary perspective. *Environment and Behavior*, 19 (3-32).

Lopez, B. (1986). Artic dreams: imagination and desire in a northern landscape. NY: Charles Scribner's Sons.

Mannheim, K. (1936). Ideology and utopia: an introduction to the sociology of knowledge. NY: A Harvest Book.

Martel, Y. (2002). Life of Pi. NY: Harcourt.

Metzner, R. (1999). Green psychology: transforming our relationship to the earth. Rochester: Park Street Press.

Naess, A. (1973). The shallow and the deep, long-range ecology movements: A summary. *Inquiry* 16: 95-100.

Naess, A. (1979). Self-realization in mixed communities of humans, bears, sheeps, and wolves. *Inquiry* 22: 231-241.

Nash, R. (1982). Wilderness and the American mind, 3rd Ed. New Haven: Yale University Press.

O'Dell, S. (1960/1978). The Island of the blue dolphins. NY: Bantam Doubleday Dell Books.

Orians, G.H. (1980). Habitat selection: general theory and applications to human behaviour. In J.S. Lockard, (Ed.), *The evolution of human social behavior*. New York: Elsivier.

Orians, G.H. and Heerwagen, J.H. (1992). Evolved responses to landscape. In J. Barkow, L. Cosmides and J. Tooby, (eds.), *Evolutionary Psychology and the Generation of Culture*. Oxford: Oxford University Press.

Paulsen, G. (1987). Hatchet. NY: Viking Penguin.

Paulsen, G. (1995). Dogsong. NY: Aladdin.

Roszak, T. (1992 & 2001). The voice of the earth. New York, Simon & Schuster.

Shepard, P. (1973). The tender carnivore and the sacred game. New York, Scribners.

Shepard, P. (1982). Nature and madness. San Francisco, Sierra Club.

Steen, L. A. (2005). Data, shapes, symbols: Achieving balance in school mathematics. Unpublished. St. Olaf College, MN. "Penultimate draft of a paper that appears in *Quantitative Literacy: Why Numeracy Matters for Schools and Colleges*, Bernard Madison and Lynn Arthur Steen, editors. Princeton, NJ: National Council on Education and the Disciplines, 2003; Washington, DC: Mathematical Association of America, 2004; pp. 53-74."

Ulrich, R., (1981). Natural vs. urban scenes: some psychophysiological effects. *Environment and Behavior*, 13, 523-556.

Ulrich, R. S. (1983). Aesthetic and affective response to natural environments. In I Altman and J.F. Wohlwill, (eds.), *Behavior and the Natural Environment*, New York: Plenum Press

Ulrich, R.S. (1984). View through a window may influence recovery from surgery. *Science,* 224, 420-421

Ulrich, R.S. (1986). Human Responses to vegetation and landscape. *Landscape and Urban Planning,* 13, (1), 29-44

Wilson, E. O. (1984). Biophilia: the human bond with other species. Cambridge: Harvard University Press.

Chapter Five

Tracking as a biosemiotic exercise, ecopsychological practice,

and a transpersonal path

When the Nandi men are away on a foray, nobody at home may pronounce the names of the absent warriors; they must be referred to as birds.

—Sir James Frazer

While writing "Meet Heinz Droz" and *Biophilia Versus Lebensneid*, it occurred to me that I had not disclosed anything (expect for "wandering," and everybody "wanders") about my own ecopsychological practices, something more personal. A form of deliberate "wandering," tracking, has been my central ecopsychological and transpersonal practice since I was fortunate enough to work for the California Department of Fish and Game in the mid 1980's. Not that everything I have learned about tracking and its effects on ecopsychological unfolding were in my mind or developed at the time. But tracking seriously, with a purpose, began in those days.

While on an extended sabbatical leave, I have been able to track more animals and for longer durations in the last two years living in this isolated valley in Switzerland than in the last fifteen years in beautiful Bellingham, Washington, Alaska, or California. This prolonged practice, in combination with an interest in the local fauna, has made me rethink my skills as an extended, ancestral and more important ecopsychological *doing* that anybody can adopt as part of their own explorations of their woods, desert, or mountain.

By learning to track we answer some questions that unaccustomed urbanites may ask while initiating their own ecopsychological practice: *What am I doing here? What do I do now? How do I even begin to comprehend the complexity that I am now seeing?* Tracking combats this inertia and fear. Tracking may be the easiest way to deal with that complexity, to assimilate new biosemiotic text, and to feel at ease in the wilderness by studying and then comprehending some of its signs.

For accustomed trackers, it is an opportunity to rethink their tracking of *game* as something more. Without wanting to give away the contents of the next article, the opportunity is there to make tracking a *transpersonal task*. Namely, by de-emphasizing its more practical benefits and focusing on animal cognition as contributing to our own, we might enter, from time to time, an ancestral mind frame of totemic reverence. It is argued that when practiced from this orientation, this totemic frame of "reverence" is an important ingredient to ecopsychological unfolding.

Thinking in Animal Signs: tracking as a biosemiotic exercise, ecopsychological practice, and a transpersonal path[100]

Abstract

Tracking, or *signcutting*, of human and non-human animals is a skill that is still being taught and endures in our modern world. The argument is made for the obvious immediate cognitive and affective benefits inherent in the functions of tracking: a trans-species and biosemiotic communicative exchange. Moreover, *signcutting* is revisited as one of many valuable ecopsychological practices that allow the modern mind, assuming usually an urban mind, the opportunity to identify with wild animal intelligence in its own natural semiotic space and PLACE. Finally, it is argued that both the ecopsychological and the biosemiotic aspects of *signcutting* are intrinsic to its practice and, when approached deliberately, *signcutting* continues to be a powerful tool for transpersonal work. Anthrozoologically speaking, *signcutting* is one aspect of *totemic doing* and thus of identification with animal forms, habits, spirits, intelligences, and virtues. The tone of this presentation is impressionistic by choice.

> *"The human mind came into existence tracking, which for us creates a land of named places and fosters narration, the tale of adventure. Perhaps the quest began as food search. But in scrutinizing the details of the potential prey, competitors, and predators upon ourselves, and all the signs they leave, it seems more abstract, like scientific curiosity, communicated in art and narrated in myth . . . The whole sequence of brain and mind evolution by attention to animals constitutes a unique twist in the primate obsession with the self and society."*
> —Paul Shepard, The Others: How Animals Made Us Human. (1996)

Introduction

Yes, tracking is literally following some creature's footsteps, but the perspective-taking act, a theory of mind in action, also becomes, if artful and effective, following some mind's footsteps. In that ultimate predator-prey *venatic* game or dance, and as Paul

Shepard alluded to in the opening quote, the human mind *jumps tracks* [101] and the abstracted game is over-regularized toward, yes, a one-to-one totemic identification with the mind afoot, but also with an extended ground of natural history and myth. The *transpersonalization* sequence (alchemy, or association) moves Zen-like from the ABC's of toe sounding; from the practical and intellectual "bear is hungry" to the mythical; and then back to the commonality of the universal human mind. All archetypes can be chased after in this way and all dreams are vectorial movements toward something or some mind expressing truths. The multiplicity of signs associated with "minds thinking something," creates a *biosemiotic coda* where scat, tracks, hair, plumes, sounds, blood, wind direction, ground texture, and weather, communicate in gestalts to a person who, wittingly or not, will, at the end of the chase, think in ecological "wholes" and be forced out of its human shell, sooner or later, to become something better.

The "wholes," as Levi Strauss noted [102], in addition to assisting the individual tracking mind, become the seeds for totemic kinship relational systems, structuring societies the world over (1966). The seamless ecology of creatures afoot or on wings, mythical SELF, and a sustainable and meaningful society begin with the sensuous caressing of a concavity of soil and blood in snow or dust. Human language, and its cognitive envelope, reflects like a historical mirror, whether the mind is in synch or not (Conesa-Sevilla, 2005a).

As we humans became increasingly literate, we both lost and gained tracking skills, or traded quarry. From an ecopsychological perspective, it is no coincidence perhaps that as we began making and reading signs or marks on paper, we did less and less foot tracking.

It might have begun almost innocently with cuneiform writing: it seemed to be almost the same thing, imprinting little marks on soft clay as if playing at chasing big game. But then, the writing became very boring and monotonous—all that record keeping of how many cattle one had, and never seeing the variety of species and tracks. This is the *synnomic evolution* of language trading functions as it went to, finally, being impoverished to an act of singularized false propaganda (Conesa-Sevilla, 2005a). However, foot tracks never lied. What we lost with the de-evolution of language we gained when "new trackers" rediscovered and co-opted foot tracking, once again, in the service of life. While tracking the origins of life itself, Maurice Wilkins and Rosalind Franklin used the basic inferential skills of an able scout, and with X-ray crystallography as mud, allowed others to tell the story of the serpent of life: DNA. The same inference abilities (and using the same medium as the previous researchers, photographic plates) helped Edwin Hubble prove Einstein's insights. Stars left their own tracks, and a *red-shift* meant, like a fading print in the desert sand, that they were moving fast away from us. Moreover, an entire soup of exotic subatomic particles and their behaviors are also inferred, post hoc, as if they were strange animals themselves. Their beautiful and short-lived arcs and collisions may someday help tie the BIG cosmos to the micro-universe. Recently, a host of new exo-planets have been discovered, and while using similar tracking techniques as Hubble's, it may be possible to know if LIFE exists elsewhere. It is not a trivial point that the same basic set of perceptual-cognitive skills has allowed for so many other discoveries. But all this looking OUT THERE and DOWN HERE has also limited and distracted its original use from looking INWARD.

Sidetracking a bit, a little about the profane. When I worked for the California Department of Fish and Game in Humboldt County,[103] tracking was more or less a mundane job skill that was useful in explaining the behaviors of predators such as the otter. On the muddy riverbanks of the Klamath, we interpreted tails swashing, webbed weasel feet, and steelhead body parts as "one kill," wrote it down on a chart, and moved on to the next sign and checkmark. Before setting up salmon weirs, it was wise to check for signs of black bears and their cubs. The human-like tracks of bears gave me the same feeling as when I found human tracks in a lonely grove and I wanted to be alone: cautious annoyance. Encountering bears face to face never gave me the same feeling. Many times I tracked our exuberant Australian Shepard through the redwoods while she was giving chase to Roosevelt Elk. There, I saw bobcat and knew its mark. I saw skunks and knew their marks. I once saw, and then confirmed with her tracks, a deadly ghost: puma. Since then, infrequently, I have seen puma tracks and the same first animal comes to mind, every time, looming larger in my dreams (Conesa-Sevilla, 2005b).

That was many years ago and thousands of tracks before I started to understand their minds and mine. The "fish and gamer" was after all, only a worker who, yes, was having fun, but who was getting paid also. It was, however, the tracks of a chamois two years ago that consolidated all this perfunctory tracking into *totemic doing*. The tracks were of a large male chamois with an asymmetrical right front hoof. The longer right toe was similar to my longer middle finger. So I began *animalizing* his print and HIS human-like hoof marks began *humanizing* me. When I encounter his track still, his unique signature, I bring my own right longer middle and index fingers upon it, and "hoof" in the snow the movements of his legs. Sometimes, if I am really stealthy, hard to do at 50 with an arthritic left knee, I find him[104] resting under a Jurassic rock overhang. He looks down from his sunny perch and probably thinks, "So, you are the scent I smell touching my tracks, what do you want?" If I walk on a higher ridge, his fleeing distance is shortened and I only get to see the fat tail end of a mass of muscles tumbling down like a soft avalanche, but surer of itself.

It is true that I am anthropomorphizing but that is the point: This particular chamois is an ambassador of sorts to a mountain I hardly know at all and knowing HIM allows me, if not safe, at least a passage through it because I know where and how he walks that space. To the degree that I interpret his tracks and those of OTHERS, this landscape is revealed to me in a way that a compass and binoculars cannot. More importantly, I am no longer an unknown human crisscrossing a frigid landscape on his hurried way to beer or chocolate, but a slow and purposeful "knower" who has shed the human to become a chamois or a red fox. Their tracks, chamois' and red fox's, mean that and much more. The red fox in particular assists the chamois with his instruction and adds a mind much more feline-supple than goat-like: pouncing here, mating there, hiding around here somewhere.

Finally, the red fox (*Vulpes vulpes*) is the only canid, out of 35 known species, that leaves a unique sign: a paw pad print with a chevron pointing in the direction of its walk. The chevron is made by a callous formation, again, not found in any other *Canidae*.[105] For as long as the human mind has wanted to know the mind of the red fox, imprint with it, and recognized its 'arrow' paw prints, the human mind has interpreted and reinterpreted even more abstractly this chevron sign, one presumes, as the prototypical vector of direction. Even more, the fox being one of several animals, as Paul Shepard (1996) identifies, that are "at the edges" of human animal cognition, neither cat nor dog, neither friend nor foe, it also represents a cunning magical trickster. That the ambiguous trickster is also able to point to a precise destination for the human mind to follow is equally the subject of biosemiotics and of ecopsychological unfolding that eventually leads into a transpersonal quest. (Figure 1: Red fox tracks, Switzerland.)

Figure 1: Red fox tracks

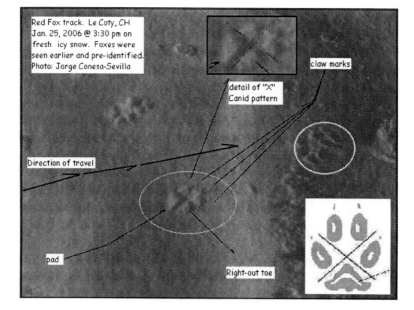

The Biosemiotics of Tracking

Tracking is a *biosemiotic* endeavor and skill to the extent that animal behavior leaves "signs" that can be later interpreted. Being primates, and obsessive about *seeing*, we see the 'signs' and read their syntax. In this sense, tracks are like words and sentences that inform, when correctly interpreted, a great deal about the authors of these prints. Tracks are TEXT in a truly semiotic sense, and more accurately, they are an example of biosemiosis, or *natural signing* (Conesa-Sevilla, 2001). It makes sense, at many levels, to begin an ecopsychological practice by learning how to track humans and non-human animals, by accepting this task as biosemiosis. There are at least three aspects of the interplay between the need to start and deepen an ecopsychological practice and its biosemiosis.

First, individuals committed and starting an authentic *ecopsychological unfolding* practice, especially if they do not have a lot of experiences in the wild, find that nature is mute or silent and does not transmit meaningful or comprehensible messages. In city life, humans are used to "reading," (bombarded really—Conesa-Sevilla, 2005a) interpreting, and acquiring meaning from the written word from multiple sources. Their transit through cities is full of information. In contrast, the apparent silence of nature, or the mysteriously sonorous, or the immensity of nature, can be, at times, foreboding because it does not seem, at first, to convey these meanings, or even any meaning at all. Nature looms silently and we escape to the comforts of our home. By learning how to track, an entire new universe of natural gossip, potentially useful information, and new meanings are clearly understood and can later become significant elements of a transpersonal journey.

Second, knowing what other animals "say" with their tracks, and how their behaviors engage the behaviors of other animals (*the venatic dance*), immerses human cognitive and affective processes in a kinship with their lives and life histories, allowing for the opportunity of rediscovering the totemic power of the animal spirit. From here on, identifying with an animal's choices, pursuits, and overall pattern of decision-making, not only informs our own intelligence and teaches us specific skills and useful bits of information, but in time, it becomes part of a genuine transpersonal exercise: I am no longer the human that follows signs but a red fox on its way to its den. Through their tracks non-human animals become the ambassadors of a world that may once have appeared forbidden and mute. They avoid unsafe trails and so must we, they find great places to stay dry and so we invade their homes, they find food and share it with us.

Third, animal tracks not only inform us about the meaning of the particular attitude or personality of an individual creature, or of its immediate pursuits, or of a group of animals, but ensemble, tracks crisscross into meaning-paths and thus generate a *semiotic coda*, a more complex and grander story that is dependent upon the ecological situation of a particular bioregion. Through tracking, we also learn about geology, topography, weather, hydrology, botany, predator-prey relationships, food items, and a host of other natural phenomena, interrelated into a GREATER KNOWING of a PLACE. Afterwards, we can never feel "out of place" in nature because we will be able to read Her signs.

Transpersonalization through tracking:
from concrete to abstract, from profane to spiritual

During some ecopsychological practices that I have participated in, individuals are exposed to a variety of exercises that are meant to sensitize a deeper self or make it leap, automatically, into the "spiritual". Most of us go through the motions, do these decontextualized shamanic passes, and some people do or do not experience the transpersonal moment promised in the brochure. Short of hallucinogenic induced states, how can the "average" individual learn readily available practices that they can then teach to others during eco-counseling or ecopsychological practice? Paul Shepard (1987), heeding the immense research and practice of human development, tracks ideal development toward a *cynegetic*[106] being. If all goes well, after the age of 18, and moving into his 20s, the *cynegetic* person has transcended his egotistical self and has acquired a mythical sense where his actions and experiences are echoed in totemic representation. This is both a rich and simple life. As Levi-Strauss (1966) indicated, this totemic identification is transpersonal, by definition, and existentially so. But before then, the *cynegetic* child was acquiring, day-to-day, a vocabulary, a lexicon of meanings that only later were integrated into a mythical gestalt that can be described as 'transpersonal'.

Realistically, except in very few and rare cases, the path toward individuation is paved with little stones and small steps. By that I mean that simple, mundane, prosaic, or even profane but precise and DELIBERATE ACTS eventually culminate in transpersonal experiences. Zen Buddhism emphasizes this path encountering that no duality exists between the humble act and the profound insight or the profane and the spiritual. Using tracker's terminology, we will call the easy, lazy, or shortcut type of approach "jumping track." But it matters greatly from phylogenic and ecopsychological perspectives WHERE this "profanity" takes place. To walk like a car is stupid and impossible. On the other hand, to walk like a fox, coyote, or wolf, is to breathe like any of them. The panting, the sniffing, the focusing on their nasal life, is a type of yogic practice, perhaps the most ancient of all. To do so deliberately, is to inhale the *prana*[107] of the wild and to cleanse a morbidly civilized and ailing persona.

Tracking is, literally, following LIFE, step by step. At the end of the trail, at the end of many trails, we might begin to understand the tracks we ourselves make. Tracking is an intense perceptual task that combines exercise with the deciphering of many *koans*. It can be akin to walking meditation while deciphering a *koan*: What is the sound of coyote walking backwards? If one is focused on the track and in trying to understand the animal brother/sister, then one is no longer focused on little self, on selfish self. If we forget about little self, everyday, then there is a chance that big SELF will come-a-visiting, wearing a coyote, fox or a wolf mask, dancing.

How tracking is really "signing," how signing is really BECOMING

In the context and intent of the arguments made thus far, an animal does not leave tracks so we can find them—we follow tracks so that we can find ourselves. Equally, the tracks are normally the means to a kill or for setting a clever trap; but the killing that counts is putting out of its misery the distorted ego, and the trap is for capturing defunct personas acquired during an over civilized and pampered life.

According to California's Humboldt County tracker Kim Cabrera[108] (1999), tracking is, "Following the very subtle signs of tracks and staying on the trail of your quarry . . . If you find every step and learn as much as you can from each track you will be a better tracker . . . Skipping the difficult tracks teaches you nothing about how to see them." Given her definition then, learning how to track is very similar to learning a vocabulary where no particular appearance or form of a word should be ignored. "Jumping track" is the easy and lazy way of tracking where, having secured *prime sign* or after being *on good sign*, an imaginary and distant path is assumed and followed. Thus the actual set of tracks is pre-empted, circumvented, in an attempt to kill quickly. Only experienced trackers can jump track, the rest of us have to study each individual print on the way to redemption.

Tracking is, like other complex human and enriching endeavors, both art and science. The front paw prints of the beaver, raccoon, muskrat, and opossum are so human like: gnomes playing in the mud. Their miniature "us" are industrious, adroit, fussy, and manipulative, but we know, empirically, that these are not busy gnomes but creatures with their own natural histories. And yet, during their tracking and recognition, the human mind fantasizes and imagines fairy tales, forgets about the furry creatures and imbues their prints with the magico-realism of Irish and Finnish tales.

The ease with which animal tracks, the written word, and human imagination easily trade cognitive spaces with each other is Paul Shepard's (1996; 1998) strong argument for the necessary co-evolution of the human mind in tandem with the minds of all the other animals. To him, this was an indispensable argument for the development of human cognition above and beyond what any other cognitive-linguistic theory might have said about the origins of our intelligence. It is hard to find counterarguments to many of his theses. But while tracking, the realization that human and non-human animals have pushed their original reptilian and shrew-like cognitive spheres to their present limits is plain to see. Biosemiotically speaking, NATURE is inter-semiotic and thus inter-interpretative from the molecular to the air/water-broadcasted communicative levels (Hoffmeyer, 1996). But hearing, smelling, tasting, and feeling (a combination of *autocentric* and *allocentric* sensorial skills) did not signify enough for the primate who abandoned the forest or was forced to forage out yonder in plain sight.

This ancestor began life in the plains working from the capital accrued in arboreal, three-dimensional, and color-vision life, and he/she "saw for a living". The ancestor stood up and was able to see a texture gradient of art prints disappearing into the open horizon. Who could resist such an invitation? It also *saw* for a heart and for his/her spirit. And *saw* in the savannas they did, the hooves of so many hoofed animals: curving inward, dancing outward, digging deeper, sprawling, pointing, or forever resting dead in the air, which signified the gold of nutrition: bone marrow. These primates also *saw* each other in malcontent, in sex, in nurturing, and in war. And they always *saw* other non-primates doing the same while leaving their tracks. And it must have been very easy, not only to *see* the visual cacophony of multiple beasts cavorting on the African soil, but to *see* his/her own prints doing the same dances. And it must have been very easy to continue to dance and to continue making marks on the sand, all sorts of marks, and to replicate these for other primates. Who among them could resist the tracing and re-drawing with nimble fingers around the edges and inside the profundity of wildebeest tracks, so geometric, so safe to touch? As if saying, "Here I am, touching your soul and there is nothing you can do about it." Of course, he/she must have also touched his/her own tracks and felt, by comparison, the same intuitive depth. If I can touch your soul, couldn't I touch mine as well?

And during those dances, who remembers under what song, a primate learned about a spirit that was grander than all the soil marks put together. It did not have to be a complicated thought, just the intuition that my footprint is one among so many others, no more, no less. *And that is the beginning of transpersonal psychology: first I acquire a self or a center, then I crowd it or delude it, and finally, I transcend it.* The hydrology of redemption and forgiveness helped too: the rains always came and washed the sin prints, all the errors of visual cacophony away. The earth as soil was renewed. There was clarity once again and new prints to step into and to follow. Physical anthropologists make us share their sense of awe when discovering humanoid prints fossilized on ancient "fresh" volcanic ash. A line of dainty feminine steps is boldly walking into a vast psychological vault. With the clarity of hindsight we gasp at her courage and almost warn: stay!

It is almost an obligation to be impressionistic when describing a primal, and very distant past. But what yokes their *seeing* to ours is a common primate visual predisposition to read signs on surfaces. To spot fleas doing their own jumping dances on skin-soil and to remove them is to be like them. To read these very words on paper is, as the American aboriginal peoples described, reading *tracks* on paper. Their primate ancestral ecopsychological wellness was almost guaranteed by their perilous sustenance and total reliance on perceptual gifts. Our ecopsychological wellness seems, more and more, to be a re-inventing and co-opting of their ways. *Thus tracking is all things true: historical glue, enduring dirt art, perceptual and cognitive challenge, physical exercise, encyclopedic and ecological knowledge, dirt cheap, a source of self-esteem, a diet for an obese self, and a vanishing act of man/woman turned into a fox-like creature: neither cat nor dog, neither friend nor foe, slit-eyed and slicing through forests. All ambiguity is embraced, all contrasts erased, all pointing toward individuation.*

Tracking can be, once again, the semiotic act that binds the eye to the heart, to the self, to the mind, and to the OTHER. It is so easy! Look for a track and follow it. If you lose the tracks, ask why. Then learn how to do it better. Keep going, following and learning until you forget yourself and you miss dinner. Do bring plenty of water and matches, though, Nature is no 'mommy'.

"In the book of the earth it is written:
nothing can die.

In the book of the Sioux it is written:
they have gone away into the earth to hide.
Nothing will coax them out again
but the people dancing."

—Mary Oliver, "Ghosts," from New and selected Poems

"Let cavillers deny that brutes have reason;
Sure 'tis something more, 'tis heaven directs, and stratagems inspires
Beyond the short extent of human thought.

—Somerville

Chapter Five References

Conesa-Sevilla, J. (2001). Topo-existential equilibrium: Constraints of Energy, Safety, and Possibility on 2-D and 3-D terrestrial foraging, predation and defense of city and fossorial systems (Application of Semiotic Matrix Theory to the Biosemiotics of Territorial Dialectics). *Paper, Gatherings in Biosemiotics 1,* May 24-27, 2001, Copenhagen, Denmark.

Conesa-Sevilla, J. (2005a). The singularization of reality: Implications of a synnomic evolution of language to semiotics, biosemiotics, and ecopsychology. *GATHERINGS: Journal of the International Community for Ecopsychology.* (http://www.ecopsychology.org/journal/ezine/gatherings.html)

Conesa-Sevilla, J. (2005b). Lucid dreaming, aesthetic expression, and ecopsychological unfolding. *The Lucid Dreamer Exchange, December 2005, #37, 8-10*

Hemming, B. (1999). Buckshot's Modern Trapper's Guide for Xtreme Safety, Survival, Profit, Pleasure. Quiet Wheel Books.

Hoffmeyer, J. (1996). Signs of meaning in the universe. Bloomington, Indiana University Press.

Levi-Strauss, C. (1966). The savage mind. Chicago: University of Chicago Press.

Oliver, M. (1992). New and selected poems. Boston: Beacon Press.

Shepard, P. (1978/1998). Thinking animals: animals and the development of human intelligence. Athens and London: The University of Georgia Press.

Shepard, P. (1982). Nature and madness. San Francisco, Sierra Club.

Shepard, P. (1996). The others: how animals made us human. Covelo, California: Island Press/Shearwater Books.

Additional Commentary on Tracking by Sigurd Olson:

"I hadn't gone far before I found a deep, well-beaten trail coming from beneath a pile of old logs, laying where the grass had been deep and still covered with a good drift of snow. The trail led from a sort of burrow going under one end toward a swamp nearby where I knew there were plenty of meadow mice and other things that might be of interest to an animal that hadn't eaten a good meal for months.

I could see by the trail that the skunk had made the trip from its hideout to the swamp many times, for the runway was well trampled. No doubt the warm nights and the warmer days had had their effect and that hibernation was probably over. On one of his first trips out, when still on edge and nervous, something had frightened him, perhaps the hooting of a horned owl, or a branch creaking back in the woods, just enough for the warning protective odor to be released."

—Sigurd F. Olson, *Skunk Tracks,*
America Out of Doors (circa 1940-1943)

Chapter Six

Ecopsychological Education: Is That Possible?

An educational practice in which there is no coherent relationship between what educators say and what they do is a disaster.
— Paolo Freire, Teachers as Cultural Workers

I think J. J. Rousseau, M. Montessori, H. Hesse, P. Shepard, E. Erikson, or S. Freud might have all been in agreement that it is in the formation of the young mind, pliable as it is and eager to internalize a natural lexicon, that societies are transformed and/or our planet can be saved. Most clinical psychologists and school counselors would agree with the idea that mental ilness prevention, growing up loved, happy and grounded, surrounded by sea, wood, or prairie, beats last-ditch therapy. In their combined insights their answer to the opening title would be "Yes!"

We might be in unanimous agreement that education does not have to be loaded toward an MBA or economics[109] degree and in that, definitely, children should not be formed toward this narrow teleological end in mind. Let's face it, too many individuals with technical or engineering degrees, and almost as an afterthought, decide to tack an MBA degree (online or otherwise) to their names almost as if saying, "I suck at being an electronics engineer so I might as well manage and make money." Now that they are "marketable" some of these folks go from a life of selling switches to fancy valves to wide girth retirement in Florida while the world collapses.[110] Both switches and valves may be appropriate metaphors describing their psychological lives, but synthetic controlling devices are abhorred by Nature: ultimately she does all the controlling.

Ecopsychology then must work at both ontological ends: in early ecopsychological education up to 12th grade, and when "best plans" fail, or when adults were not so lucky to partake of ideal development; with therapy or counseling. But it is far easier (and more natural and authentic) to do exercise and have fun with kids while chasing and identifying butterflies, than to treat a reluctant obese adult on the verge of suicide. It is more economical and less dangerous too. Therefore, *we may conclude that the lion share of ecopsychological work to be done is educational more so than therapeutic.* Since our first meeting of the European Ecopsychology Society, we identified education as a central focus of the society's labors. Five of seven founding members are or had been educators. In this we wanted to heed Freire's admonition (opening quote) that we walk our talk.

In *Biophilia Versus Lebensneid* I made a special case for the fact that, novelistically at least, the cynegetic child and youth are central figures and characters. Rousseau's *Emile*, also novelistic, has been a template for ideal education for some of these authors and subsequent generations of educators. Rousseau and these authors understood how the pliable minds and hearts of their characters could develop in more profound ways toward a total comprehension of a natural lexicon and how their characters could be permanently affected by this formation.[111] The repercussions of these fictional ontological experiments lead to unexpected and novelistically exciting ends to the extent that corrupted, civilized society waits around every corner, to undo and to challenge *telluric wisdom*. But what about real life development or education? What about the practical matters of implementing such a vision? Fortunately, many educators have tried and succeeded in implementing *ecoeducation*. (I have provided the reader with a short list of these schools in the United States, at the end of this book.)

I have been fortunate enough to participate in and to observe schools that closely adhere to *a flexible ecopsychological educational program*. More often they are not so bold as to advertise themselves by that description and prefer safer and more marketable subtitles such as "environment," "ecological," "farm," "nature's laboratory," or "wilderness,"—"school." Usually, but not always, they have been farm settings and Montessori schools. Even if my perceptions are correct, then I still have some questions: *What philosophical, developmental, or pedagogical core elements were in place to make Montessori, or any other schools, credible, valid, and competitive? What sort of blueprint if any did they follow? Are their founders happy that they tried, or offered their school? Are their students any different by these experiences? Do they fair equally, better, or worse in post K-12 education? Would these children, as adults, choose the same type of formation? Are they happy, loving, grounded, and environmentally conscientious individuals?*

Perhaps there is no better way to answer at least some of these questions except by embarking, with soul and blood (some cold cash helps too), on the enterprise of opening, running, and dealing, day-to-day, with the realities of a top-to-bottom ecopsychological program. The rest of the chapter is a narrative about some of those experiences.

An Erdkinder (Earth Children)/Cynegetic Model for Education

My wife and I recently attempted to open an "environmental farm school" (code phrase for a *"flexible ecopsychological educational program" after cynegetic principles*) mixing the Erdkinder vision of Maria Montessori while tempered and sensitized by the important work of American Ecophilosopher, Paul Shepard. We attempted to do this near the city of Neuchâtel, the birthplace of developmentalist Jean Piaget. We thought to ourselves, "If there was a place on earth that may be open to these progressive ideas would be the city of Neuchâtel." We thought, "If anybody will appreciate the need and the idea for a "farm school" would be Switzerland, the land of tingling "happy cows" and goats and Heidis running around milking them." Well, that was our market analysis anyway.

To bring back an earlier point, we were clear on the vision and notion that too many schools already pre-prepare (badly) students for MBA or economics school and that the world is not better for having too many MBA majors running around making money. That would be the first sentence of our mission statement, or something to that effect. Most students lack, it seems, the breadth of a liberal arts education with an emphasis on real world problems and with students at the center of these solutions. To illustrate this deficit, in a recent Christian Science Monitor article by Mark Rice-Oxley, Dr. Geoff Hayward, lecturer at Oxford University's educational studies department was quoted as saying:

> [there are] genuine concerns about young people and their capacity to benefit from higher education . . . Part of the problem lies in the way teenagers are taught in school, prepped assiduously for exams at the expense of broader understanding. [112]

To continue our personal story, at first, there seemed to be some indication of parental support, a must in educational ventures. At first, there seemed (still is) to be a great need to have a secondary English school in this area. At first, a foundation representing major foreign companies and investors were warm to the idea (still are). At first, there seemed to be political support for the idea as well and the possibility of the City of Neuchâtel contributing to our project. Certainly, two experienced educators well steeped in environmental and ecological science with extensive certifications to boot would had made the whole deal a very sound social investment on an entire generation of ecopsychologically evolved individuals. Or so we thought.

To make a long story short, mostly to avoid embarrassing decent folks or revisit bad and incomprehensible moments, the economist who decided to support a preparatory, curriculum driven IB[113] school was forced to quit amidst the veil of an undisclosed "scandal"—Apparently, they failed to bring more MBA's and company money into the village. The local companies, the parents, and the canton still need and want a secondary English school, and by the time these lines reach the public eye they probably would get one. It just won't be a Montessori-Shepard farm-cynegetic curriculum or school.

To be fair, many other factors contributed to our decision not to pursue this idea in Neuchâtel, including the fact that we decided to invest in the birth, promotion, and maintenance of the now operational European Ecopsychology Society. But during this process of about nine months of pregnant possibility it became apparent that other fundamental reasons were driving this process to its failure. As my more philosophical wife is fond of saying, "The train came and the train left."

In retrospect, perhaps it was foolish to think that two American educators, even with demonstrable credentials, could be so bold and presumptions as to try to teach the Swiss to be ecopsychologically attuned, well, their children. Perhaps it was another case of selling ice in Antarctica (but with fast melting ice sheets it may be a nobler venture). There was also a strong cultural aspect of Swiss French or of cantonal insular politics that prevent foreigners to step on cherished and guarded territory. And there was also the famous Swiss procrastination slowing every little thing down to a miserable snail pace. If you think I am kidding, go and live there for two or more years. Clocks in Switzerland, I found out, are made to be exact for slowing time, for procrastination. Einstein lived here too and fled after having a slow clock relativity insight.

Ultimately it was both our inability to "sell" this vision as the best education a child will ever have or, and at the receiving end, a glittery fascination with programmatic or curriculum-driven education such as the IB preparatory model that may have dissuaded folks from our vision. To be honest, I don't think the parents got to choose anyway. According to the economist who was nudged to give up his job, his decision (I am reading the minutes I took from two meetings) to take the IB bid hinged on the fact that he much liked the IB suited man who spoke in a pseudo-British accent and two, apparently it was a sign of high metropolitan status to market IB curricula and education to the many foreign families who seem to country hop for jobs and happen to speak English.

I am no cynic. But I understand that the implementation of great education is often trampled by or impeded by political or personal ambition, or even pedigree reasons given by non-educators, and that these reasons have nothing to do the value of a good education.

So this chapter is about second chances. Namely "selling" this idea to you the reader. If we fail to "sell you our school" then the public has finally spoken.

Montessori's Erdkinder "Earth Children" and The Cynegetic Child/Youth

According to Maria Montessori, the three goals of an Erdkinder "Earth Children" Curriculum are:

1. To open the way to the possibilities of the adolescent for personal expression, that is, to facilitate, by exercises and exterior needs, the development of the interior personality.
2. To supply that which we consider to be the creative elements necessary for the physical being of man [woman] in general.
3. To put the adolescent into relation with present civilizations by bringing him [her] general culture and by experience.

These general goals, as stated by Maria Montessori near the end of her professional career, never fully developed by Montessori herself, have been the subject of debate even among Montessorians. That is, the under development of these ideas, in contrast to her other more defined pedagogy, has left much room for subjective interpretation and idiosyncratic creation of schools. Even when committees of Montessorians write a contemporary curriculum, it may not reflect what a living Maria Montessori might have meant by this new approach. The imperfect idea as originally presented in her book, *From Childhood To Adolescence*, could have progressed to include modern day ecological science, and Ecocentric ideas as well. Although her emphasis on the socialization of the adolescent into a responsible, loving and compassionate member of his/her society are aspects of her earlier education program, these qualities or virtues take a special meaning and priority in the final development of the adolescent into a mature adult.

Her emphasis of the almost teleological development of human culture and technology without an ongoing criticism of its accompanying anthropocentrism, leaves her idea of Erdkinder an unfinished product, even in present-day interpretations. To name a few, human-centeredness, an uncritical view of the agrarian legacy, obsession with human civilization and culture, and the failed notion that Earth was "made for" humanity, are some of the anachronistic and environmentally antagonistic notions that still persist in Montesori education and in Erdkinder models today.

To reiterate, absent from her approach, and the approaches of her successors, is the fact that a humanistic emphasis, without an ecological grounding, may slip very easily into anthropocentrism, and a blind eye and heart is created to the full complexity of a biosphere and community that shares (should) equally in our development and ethics. This is the same blind spot associated with other scientific attempts to understand ethics itself. Lawrence Kohlberg, interested in Piaget's ideas of the development of ethical reasoning, discovers moral reasoning and development that amazingly excludes relationship and ethical obligations to non-humans or to the natural world. With this example as illustration, lays most of the limitations of a human-centered cultural education. If altruism is not for the non-human or the natural world, not present in a discussion of ethics or in a psychology of ethical reasoning and moral development, then the education of the child must go outside this human-made world for more encompassing and real answers.

Paul Shepard's[114] cynegetic approach reflects contemporary views of human development that have made a far reaching and stronger case (e.g., Erik Erikson, Theodore Roszak, and Erich Fromm) for the fact that mental health, normal development, caring politics, sound economics, and meaningful science are all connected to the successful bonding of the child and the adolescent to, and the integration of his/her identity (cultural and personal) with a living world that exists intrinsically, that is, a world that has existed without being manufactured, coerced into being, or selfishly exploited by this one, now predominant species: Homo sapiens *sapiens*.

The educational philosophy and pedagogical practice of the cynegetic child assumes that the ecological challenges that the new Montessori child faces were not even formulated at the time when Maria Montessori wrote about education. By logical implication, the cynegetic child and vision does not appear in her under formulation of Erdkinder, nor does it appear in full rendition in present-day Erdkinder models. Montessori herself offered a general plan for an Erdkinder education, contending that a more specific plan would establish itself naturally based on the experiences of the community. If by the "experiences of the community" we mean the entire biospheric community of human and non-human inhabitants, then Erdkinder practice must include an encompassing Ecocentric approach and method.

Being that the education of the child/youth demands all the help it can get, our hypothetical school, let's call it Elsbeth's Farm, has synthesized all approaches and sources of education, psychology and science into a more encompassing and realistic educational model that aims to prepare the child/youth, not only for the world of human culture and its challenges, but also for the real and more ancient world of an entire biosphere which includes geophysical, biological, and chemical processes. For us the "cosmic" in Montessori means real and complex interconnections of a larger community of species, including Homo sapiens. So a "cosmic purpose" must be reinterpreted as the questions: What is the role and function of the human species on this planet given our cultural activities? Which of these activities do not seem "cosmic" in the sense that they are anti-nature? and How does one form and educate a new community of humans who understand, with an understanding that is not simply academic but that is internalized as personal ethos, that this planet has a "history" that precedes our short one, and that this history gave rise to our very consciousness? In the answers to these questions lies the beginning of maturity, healing, and finding our more pressing and real "cosmic purpose." With Montessori we agree that:

> The stars, Earth, stones, life of all kinds form a whole in relation with each other, and so close is this relation that we cannot understand a stone without some understanding of the great sun! No matter what we touch, an atom, or a cell, we cannot explain it without knowledge of the wide universe.

Mission

Given the above observations, then the mission statement of such a school may be something along the lines of:

> Either the learner is at the center of learning or the curriculum is, but neither can occupy the limelight meaningfully without a harmonious integration that interlaces environmental science and ecopsychological unfolding as The Education for the 21st Century. In the real contexts of environmental collapse, mindless consumerism, selfish or petty nationalistic politics, and global corporate rape of Nature, guiding and preparing the youth 'for the future' demands a total rethinking and overhaul of the 'average' curriculum. If revamping the public educational system is not possible, environmentalist and Nature bonded families must devise a new pedagogical plan that prepares their (our) children for the chaotic realities that these ills will surely unleash.

The above mission statement can be used to draw up a set of learning or formation outcomes that would, at a minimum, address the following:

1. To assist and train youth learners in acquiring specialized scientific methodology without which students cannot evaluate personal, socially complex, and natural information accurately.
2. To involve learners in epistemological criticism (a critical dialogue about ways of knowing) in all skill areas and fields of inquiry (*metacognitive reasoning).*
3. To inspire learners to contribute their personal commitment and reasoned judgment so they can solve, or inspire others to solve, real problems in the real world: economical, humanistic, artistic, environmental, social, or political.
4. To be planet citizens with an existential awareness that includes, without second thoughts, the welfare of non-human animals, the plant world, and their physical environmental requirements predating human life.

5.   To rejoice in frugality, to curve consumer appetites, to make do with what you have and value it, to be sustainable and self-sufficient, to think twice about joining passing trends and fashions that do little to invigorate the human spirit.

These and additional outcomes, although written in general terms, underscore a creative and adaptive curriculum that keeps a straight keel against fad educational winds by adhering to a robust ecological and credible developmental agenda. Important aspect of this developmental progression were outlined and then described by Paul Shepard in two of his greatest works: *The Tender Carnivore*, (1973) and in *Nature and Madness* (1982). The following section outlines these ideas.

The Cynegetic Child/Youth

American philosopher and ecopsychologist Paul Shepard (*The Tender Carnivore*, 1973 & *Nature and Madness*, 1982), while using Erik Erikson's and Erich Fromm's models of human development and psychology, traced an historical path of mental and physical health deterioration from an original Paleo-hunter past to present-day industrialized societies. His writings were the first voice, echoed since in medical and psychological-environmental science, about the impact of rapid and drastic environmental and societal changes to our evolutionary past and genome.

In essence, he argued, the physiology and psychology of modern humans, for the most part, has not changed from those of Paleo-humans. We are still they, therefore, physical and mental health needs have to be understood in this context. While using ecological science, developmental psychology, archeological evidence, and historical data Shepard argued, similarly with Rousseau and Maria Montessori, that educating children, youth and adolescents toward a healthy and grounded end, necessitated an immersion in a real and original natural world of rich and complex geography and natural history where human intelligence can maximally hone in its perceptual and intellectual capacities, achieving, after this training, the peak of its natural species-specific talents. Thus nature, they argued, and its predictable cycles and processes, offers more enduring, more in-depth, more authentic, more real, and ultimately more satisfying lessons than the fickle and transient, disposable, material-bound and capriciously fabricated man-made synthetic environments.

Paul Shepard and others argue that it is the natural world (as well as the intense interpersonal dynamics with a small band—20 to 25—of humans) that gave rise to and perfected human intelligence to begin with and so it is the natural world (and a small and intense social group) that best serves as the classroom for the authentic, original mind. This is a mind that is perceptually and cognitively quick, compassionate, and that understands the ecological interplay of non-human and human companions alike. At the end of this ideal development and training, the cynegetic individual, have argued J.Rousseau, Paul Shepard, Maria Montessori, Erik Erikson, Sigmund Freud, will achieve a level of maturity, self-control, love of the complexity of the natural world, independence of thought, and compassion for others, unparalleled by present-day mental health and personality standards. Thus if achieved, the cynegetic progression leads to the opposite end of arrogance, narcissism, or self-centeredness. The cynegetic individual is at the same time an educated and practical individual who can solve real problems in a real world using whatever special talents he/she is able to offer.

Although this developmental path is hard to achieve in present-day urbanized settings or industrialized nations, given the appropriate environment of relative freedom of choice, independence of action, and a high expectation of abiding to ethical guidelines, all in the backdrop of a natural school environment, this developmental feat can still be achieved. Thus a special environmental setting that exemplifies these natural qualities and allows for such a developmental opportunity AND the unique and loving support of a group of adults who manage this high quality development ARE the alchemy that transforms the child into the integrated adolescent, an adolescent who understands himself/herself as part of a complex web of social and natural interactions where he/she will be called to participation as a mature partner.

"Distant" Learning: Where have all the good teachers gone? The implications of Paulo Freire's "Teachers as Cultural Workers," to Montessori Education

Addressing the selfish needs of businesses, corporations, and local politicians to educate what amounts to "drones" seems to be the idea behind many preparatory curricula. Instead of using the words, *drones* or *docile automatons*, parents and politicians switch to euphemisms such as a *good education*, *the best education money can buy*, or *I am investing in his/her job early*, etc. There is nothing wrong with considering the practical aspects of any education, but in making them the horse rather than the cart, a lot of opportunities for *teaching with development* are missed. Worst of all, environmental and ecological preparation appear later or are diluted as footnotes to a much premature and generally useless MBA career.

But simply teaching to utilitarian or political objectives, using environmentally sterile outcome based educational approaches (also lacking a heart and a clear ecophilosophical direction) tends to increase the incidence of teacher burnout. Children and youth notice little things like a teacher who, in the vernacular and vulgar, 'does not give a damn'. Teaching, being an intensely and overly prescribed social transaction (as Vygotsky and Paulo Freire described our profession), is more sensitive to the quality of people than to stand-alone ideas or a straight jacketed curriculum. Case in point, both Christian and Islamic fundamentalist outrageous and irrational views are taught by passionate and 'caring' teachers who obviously succeed in creating new generations of haters. Devils and gods can teach any curricula with equal persuasive impact.

Instead, a liberal arts education, on the other hand, with a curriculum that correctly identifies the formative elements that give rise to healthy normative psychology, one that transcends the local cultural selfish needs in the greater service of the harmonious integration of human activity in synch with natural processes, should be the pedagogical target.

Prescribed curricula, curricula that are not flexible or open to the reflection and criticisms of teachers and learners are bad curricula. The imposition of a pre-packaged, static, dumb down or restrictive curricula that did (does) not receive the creative input of the teacher-implementer, creates a learning situation where both the teacher and the learner are neither, and both are equally passive dialectical agents. *That is, as passive and uncreative teachers and learners, they share only partial consciousness. If so, how can partial consciousness remedy the foes of this world or challenge the status quo when this status quo demands automatic compliance to social conventions that are themselves rooted in partial consciousness?*

"The child comes first": Child Centered Pedagogy

If an educator cannot put himself/herself in the child's developmental, cultural, emotional and intellectual situation, and teach and love from that space, then they have no business in education. Surely, and by definition, they are neither modern educators nor Montessorians. Ecopsychologically speaking, this means that any educational format that decontextualizes learning from time-tested ancient, natural, easy, and efficient human relational models where children are provided with plenty of physical activity and are allowed to experiment with natural objects, may very well serve the techno-autocracies' labor needs but it may impede the development, as Rousseau correctly pointed out, of a self-sufficient morality.

It is a form of false advertisement "to sell" a school as such if these principles are not believed in and practiced wholeheartedly. ("Child centered education".) Lacking the professional training (modern pedagogy and child development), the personal commitment, or the patience to exercise this maxim, day-to-day, any other institutional changes will only be "surface" deep or merely cosmetic, "Team Building" included."

The developmentally modern emphasis on child-centered pedagogy also alters the traditional hierarchy found in most schools. We are all valuable and equal contributors of an agreed upon pedagogical program that we adhere to child centered principles. A school's hierarchy begins and ends with the student and her needs. The mantra to be repeated, over and over, is the following:

IT IS NOT MY SCHOOL, 'TIS THE CHILDREN'S
IT IS NOT THE DIRECTOR'S SCHOOL, 'TIS THE CHILDREN'S
IT IS NOT THE VICE PRINCIPAL'S SCHOOL, 'TIS THE CHILDREN'S
IT IS NOT OUR SCHOOL, 'TIS THE CHILDREN'S
IT IS NOT THE COUNTY'S SCHOOL, 'TIS THE CHILDREN'S
IT IS NOT THE STATE'S SCHOOL, 'TIS THE CHILDREN'S
IT IS NOT THE COUNTRY'S SCHOOL, 'TIS THE CHILDREN'S
IT IS NOT THE PARENTS' SCHOOL, 'TIS THE CHILDREN'S
IT IS NOT PHILIP MORRIS' OR AUTODESK'S SCHOOL, 'TIS THE CHILDREN'S
IT IS NOT . . . , THEY ARE AT THE CENTER, ALWAYS!

The New Ecopsychology School Hierarchy

In this new ecopsychological hierarchy, teachers who consider themselves "cultural workers"[115] do not belong to facile "teams". Rather, they choose to work in schools that, like themselves, work for children, the betterment of societies, and for the future of our planet. If they are on that team, they don't have to play bridge or drink Margaritas in order to be effective and excited about what they do each day. The latter are examples of bonding with all the wrong things.

More strongly said, and to paraphrase Paulo Freire, *teachers as cultural workers do not submit to ineffectual authority nor teach children to be submissive of inadequate psychologies or bad social policies.* Equally important, *teachers as cultural workers first protect children/youth from dysfunctional forces and then empower them to challenge and heal these tendencies.*

Along the same lines, education should not follow corporate/political-ideological organizational models or aims because their aims and procedures are seldom the same. Corporations sell products, whereas schools are entrusted with helping to shape nobility and increase knowledge, understanding in individuals so they can challenge, for example, the very idea of 'corporations'. Corporations often adhere to an economical "bottom line" that is detrimental to humanistic, spiritual, or environmentalist ideals. Schools and learning are not products. *A human being is not a product.* Education, by definition, has been a vehicle for social dissent and critique when societies have failed to live up to the highest human ideals. Teachers do not belong to corporate "teams".

What follows are examples of discourse used when administrators, un-willing teachers, or politicians dictate policies or make self-serving decisions. That is, lacking rational and child-centered arguments they choose rhetoric rather than dialectics, and intrigue rather than genuine collaboration. So in addition to not addressing serious questions and problems (and remaining silent for long periods of time) they present themselves as "above the fray" in order to imbue a false sense of dignity to their office, self, or post, or focus on banal things. Be alert to the use of and be wise to deconstruct administrative or supervisory language that resemble the following constructions:

". . . I refuse to get into *polemics* with you about this"

". . . I think you are being too *emotional, too serious* about this issue, Ms. Malcontent-visonary"

". . . we all have to give and take (but usually it is they or their favorite teacher who do all the 'taking')

". . . you are not being a *team player*"

". . . sometimes the needs of children have to be sacrificed in order to insure institutional well-being" (A similar argument: ". . . sometimes little things like 'Freedom,' 'The Right to Privacy,' or 'Civil Liberties' have to be sacrificed in order to insure national stability and security")

". . . the curriculum is the curriculum and that is that! Little Julia has to conform to all this testing"

". . . let's meet in my office, alone, and have a heart-to-heart conversation"

". . . creativity has nothing to do with real life, Math scores do!"

". . . creativity has nothing to do with real life, S-p-e-lli-gng good does!"

". . . there is only enough money for boy's football, the girls will have to play with balloons and fake, paper tennis rackets"

". . . we have to consider the needs of our community (code phrase for pleasing 'X' or 'Y' politician or corporate donor), that is why I am installing a soda-pop machine for our children"

". . . let's all go to the bar and have a few Margaritas and everything will be better"

". . . Mrs. secretary, scratch Teacher 'Malcontent-visonary's' comments off the minutes"

". . . influence is mightier than the truth"

". . . I think you need to wear a little more make-up and dress better ;)"

". . . Do you know how much bicycle racks cost!?"

". . . install a shower for teachers and students who want to run during their lunch, outrageous!"

". . . no child in this school will grow potatoes in a school/community garden for as long as I am the . . ."

". . . pass the punch . . . let's dance!"

". . . what global climate warming issue?"

If these or similar commentaries are used frequently around your school, to address you or others, it is perhaps time to leave and insufferable situation and start your own Erdkinder. The "good old boy network" will prevent you from disarming their "wit."

Recommendations For Establishing an Environmental/Liberal Arts, Normative Psychological Educational Setting that is respectful and Pro Human Growth

COMMUNICATE FACTUALLY
(rumors kill . . . the spirit)
Discourage/penalize ineffective, defensive, defective, deficient, not factual, and unproductive modes of discourse

BE CIVIL AND PROFESSIONAL
(be yourself, be assertive, but in a civil way)
Discourage/penalize unprofessional and/or not civil interpersonal communication and exchanges

KNOW WHAT YOU BELIEVE IN
(train and re-train—lifelong learning)
Agree on clear, contemporary, scientific-based, Child Centered pedagogical and psychological guidelines. Stick to them!

APPLY WHAT YOU BELIEVE IN
(despite all obstacles)
Consistently implement (enforce/reinforce) Child Centered pedagogical and psychological guidelines

TEACH IN THE 21ST CENTURY
(against antiquated and obsolete/absolutist "preformationism")
It is not usually clear or obvious that Child Centered pedagogy is practiced by all educators, administrators, or staff consistently

TEACH IN THE 21ST CENTURY
(against antiquated and obsolete/absolutist "preformationism")
It is not usually clear that all educators, administrators, staff, or parents share a commitment to Child Centered pedagogy

GOOD FENCES MAKE FOR GOOD NEIGHBORS
(ALL adhere to the same rules, ALL rules can be revised according to credible data)
Meeting minutes should be taken. Meeting minutes should be given back to all participants with the opportunity to modify statements. This practice reduces

hearsay, gossip, and characterizations that attempt, unduly, to put a person in an undesirable light. Robert's Rules of Order or similar meeting protocols should be studied and used.

ACT/WORK FROM JOY AND FAIRNESS, NOT FROM GUILT OR FROM INTRIGUE

(Nothing equals the empowering effects of education)

Administration should be proactive with a clear and humane developmental vision that is Child Centered

BE FACTUAL, BE FAIR, CONSIDER THE CHILDREN

(If you don't belong in credible, modern education, get out!)

Administration should aim to examine real, root causes for challenges and problems and determine credible courses of action and correction based on developmentally sound and empirically confirmable facts, not personal reasons. (For example, to the extent that alcoholism is suspected and then confirmed, the teacher/staff/administrator should be removed from supervisory duties regardless of their present or past contributions . . .)

EXPORTING PHILOSOPHY AND PEDAGOGY

(be an evangelist of your heart and ideas . . . be contagious!)

All school personnel are equally responsible for the welfare of children and for adhering by (extending/exporting) Child Centered pedagogy and psychology outside the confines of the physical school. Adjunct, docent, and volunteered help must adhere by these principles.

In Case You Missed It!

In case you missed it, the preceding section was supposed to address these questions:

What philosophical, developmental, or pedagogical core elements were in place to make Montessori, or any other schools, credible, valid, and competitive? What sort of blueprint if any did they follow? Are their founders happy that they tried, or offered their school? Are their students any different by these experiences? Do they fair equally, better, or worse in post K-12 education? Would these children, as adults, choose the same type of formation? Are they happy, loving, grounded, and environmentally conscientious individuals?

In case you missed it, here were the answers, plus additional commentary:

1. *What philosophical, developmental, or pedagogical core elements were in place to make Montessori, or any other schools, credible, valid, and competitive?*
   18th, 19th, 20th, and 21th centuries education that was Child Centered. A balanced pedagogical approach where neither the teacher/guide not the

modern curricula are central to leaning but that *in their synergy*, and while being attentive to the developmental needs of each child, the child is able to discover and test relevant ideas. If the teacher/guide is central to learning he/she is so because they are funny, patient, caring, self-effacing, devoted, extremely intelligent, *did not choose teacher as a second or third rate profession*, and are at the top of their professional training and "game". The curricula must reflect real human, ecological, and environmental problems and the means (sciences, humanities, arts) for solving them. Empowerment and action, rather than decontextualized intellectual curiosity should be motivating factor for learning[116].

2. *What sort of blueprint if any did they follow?*

    A child-centered flexible one: *a flexible ecopsychological educational program*. From administrative practice to teaching, from curricula to field trips the questions should always be: What does this child, youth, or young person require of me? Am I optimally guiding their development, satisfying their intellectual curiosity, or sharing the most up-to-date and relevant information that I am able to obtain with them?

3. *Are their founders happy that they tried, or offered their school?*

    I think they will always be happy and tired. Teaching is a 24/7, energy demanding profession best left for very bright and caring persons. Impostors need not apply. Only the best of the best should attempt something so profound and exquisite as teaching. The satisfaction and your only "cash value" in teaching is always knowing that your labor is the most sacred, important, and nobler of all the professions. You will always be poor unless you have a rich wife or husband. In our family we are both teachers that means that we have to grow our own food! I have included the presentation dossier at the end of this section to get an idea of how poor, tired, and happy we would have been.

4. *Are their students any different by these experiences?*

    Most are. At their end of their school experiences children cry, parents cry, teachers cry, even the ducks cry. That is how you know, scientifically, that the students, the parents, and the teachers are different. Human growth is dialectics. If I am deeply and keenly interested, no, invested, in your growth and development, then I also grow and develop. In true dialectics, the roles "guide" and "student" are constantly morphing allowing each participant the opportunity to reflect, amend, and continue to grow. No curricula can ever teach that.

5. *Do they fair equally, better, or worse in post K-12 education (academically, socially, implied)?*

    All data and studies I have seen report good and bad stories. Stand-alone, internal data suggest that these kids are usually at a higher academic level across all disciplines. The caveat is that there are very few and comprehensive and longitudinal studies done on these schools. Many schools track their students and at least one school in Switzerland, La Grande Ourse, actually welcomes back their students for tutoring even when they have left their school at no cost to the parent. If the schools were outstandingly good and kids/youth move to schools where the standards are lower, then the student may get bored. The translocation to another school must be monitored by parents, students, and teachers alike so that early measures can be put in place to continue advancing at a developmentally preferred pace. In some cases, the expanded social life of the student may compete with past educational efforts and impede progress. Once again, parents, students, and teachers alike have to determine whether this is something developmentally normal for the age group and attempt to balance these new social awakenings with the expectations of academic progress. Kids that move from these schools directly to college are generally good students or excel.

6. *Would these children, as adults, choose the same type of formation?*

I have not seen any data that answers this question. But to the extent that the school is central to the life of a community and that the same leadership continues with renewed vigor and enthusiasm, there is no reason to believe that parents would not choose the same for their children.

7. *Are they happy, loving, grounded, and environmentally conscientious individuals?*

The ones that I have met are most of those things. I would qualify "happy" with general contentment. I have not met many HAPPY individuals in my entire life—life is tough. And the ones one seem to be HAPPY were faking it or are extreme extroverts on rum. As far as being *loving* and *grounded*, and since schooling is less a determinant of personality than family environment or peers are, some were more loving than others, at least they expressed *loving* more outwardly. They seemed more *grounded* than the average child/youth only insofar the curricula allowed for physical work, community learning, and a cooperative life. As far as being *environmentally conscientious*, they were all planet citizens who continued on and projected their activism into the professions they chose to pursue.

Relevant Educational Commentary and References Related to Questions 1-7

Barron, M. (1992). Montessori in the twenty-first century. In Margaret Howard Loeffler's (Ed.), *Montessori in Contemporary American Culture*. Portsmouth, NH: Heinemann, pp. 267-279.

Chattin-Mcnichols, J. (1992). *The Montessori controversy*. Seattle, WA: Delmar Publishers, Inc.

Chattin-Mcnichols, J. (1992). What does research say about Montessori. In Margaret Howard Loeffler's (Ed.), *Montessori in Contemporary American Culture.* Portsmouth, NH: Heinemann, pp. 69-100.

Johnston-Coe, E. (1992). Montessori and the middle school years. In Margaret Howard Loeffler's (Ed.), *Montessori in Contemporary American Culture.* Portsmouth, NH: Heinemann, pp. 239-261.

Louv, R. (2005). *Last child in the woods: saving our children for nature-deficit disorder.* Chapel Hill, North Carolina: Algonquin Books of Chapel Hill.

Chapter Seven

Deep Ecology and its Influence on Ecopsychology

The term deep ecology was coined by Arne Naess in his 1973 article, "The Shallow and the Deep, Long-range Ecology Movements." Naess was attempting to describe the deeper, more spiritual approach to Nature exemplified in the writings of Aldo Leopold and Rachel Carson. He thought that this deeper approach resulted from a more sensitive openness to ourselves and nonhuman life around us.

—William Devall & George Sessions, *Deep Ecology*

The above general description of Deep Ecology by two of its influential co-founders, William Devall and George Sessions (1985), identifies two key elements of its philosophy that lead directly to an ecopsychological practice or therapy: spirituality and a certain *practice* that opens the human psyche to itself and to all of the natural world. For most co-founders of the movement (including Gary Snyder and Robert Aiken) this meant extending and bringing Buddhist principles and zazen practice to bear on ecological issues. That they did this in a coherent and lasting way says more about the inherent teachings found in Buddhism than about anything new or revolutionary in deep ecology. Thus Deep Ecology, at its core, is an actualized ecopsychology and ecology based on an Eastern spirituality that readily accepts and easily partakes of nature as an intrinsic element for becoming, not only in an aesthetic sense but in a spiritually grounded sense of living *purposely* "as if Nature mattered."

The deep ecological phrase, "as if Nature mattered"[117] is an odd one. From the advantageous perspective of our own presumed ecological ethos, the phrase almost minimizes the total influence of Nature upon us, as a force that leads the way for the rejuvenation, rebirth, and transformation of our psyche. From the disadvantageous (ignorant or combative) perspective of the proverbial "man on the street" the phrase is equal parts radical propaganda, utopia, and hopeful mantra.

Ecopsychology could have been birthed by other fields and was to some extent (transpersonal psychology). But when filtered through the deep ecological movement, ecopsychology as theory, science, therapy, and personal practice became much more and simpler. Ecopsychology, by not being filtered through the worst of (or the perturbing average of) psychology in the 20th century, bypassed anthropocentrism, *computercentrism*, monotheism, monarchism, and a lot of machismo. Its stronger and wiser feminine voice was saved as a pure and open-ended thought: "Live purposely, as if nature matters."

Grounded on the empirical empowerment of zazen practice (Zen Buddhism), aided by a rich and long religious history, transformed in Norway and in California by disciplined free spirits, feminism, and the 1960s-1970s, and developed by eager psychologists into actual therapies, deep ecology gained in all their strengths and simplified their collective message to "Live purposely, as if nature matters." This is not an esoteric sentence or a mystifying koan. It says "Do It," first of all, better than a Nike commercial. It is a prescription for action and not an idle philosophical argument to be ingested with cigars and brandy. It also explained what the *doing* was about while allowing the possibility for multiple interpretations of *doing*.

It is also reminiscent of William James' discovery of the *Will*, the practical philosophy that might have saved his life. But again, William James took nature for granted as did many other 19th and 20th centuries thinkers who had plenty of it. In *psychologizing* Deep Ecology as Ecopsychology we meet the Buddha or Saint Francis of Assisi on the road pointing the way back to mental health. All these roads lead to one place: NATURE.

However, there are both differences and similarities between Deep Ecology and Ecopsychology, and the differences are growing to the extent that more and more psychologists reinvent ecopsychology, as it should be. A big tent now, it accommodates many personalities, styles, and local necessities. Some of these differences and similarities will be drawn out in the next two sections.

Finally, and as I disclosed earlier, I had been practicing zazen meditation when I took courses from William Devall, shortly after the release of the co-authored and aforementioned title in 1985. My ecopsychology is therefore still very much grounded on Deep Ecological values and principles. It is fair that you, as the reader, know this. But this disclosure matters more in the context of writing this book for students and colleagues. It sets up expectations about the things that *I will be doing* and about the fact that you can call me on *behavior* and *language* that do not adhere to these professed values and principles. That is, by this disclosure I can always count on the fact that if I were to deviate from this course, you are not only entitled to alert me to this fact, but perhaps also obligated to do so. I call this *self-correcting therapy*.

Deep Ecology's Basic Tenets

As narrated in the book *Deep Ecology*, the basic tenets of the movement were born in a desert, Death Valley, California, while Arne Naess and George Sessions were on a hiking/camping trip. It is both odd and fitting that in such a desolate wilderness so much was accomplished by two minds. It rings as prophetic that a simple and clear-toned message was hollered (or written down) in the austerity of one of the most inhospitable places on Earth. That two Buddhists (or Buddhist-friendly) could see natural diversity in a few shrubs, rocks, and lizards and see a paradise, is remarkable enough. Perhaps only Buddhist compassion could have seen, embraced, loved, and been determined to save a few shrubs, rocks, and lizards while thinking about the planet Eden. Perhaps this is what all prophets do, Buddhist, Christian, Hindu, or Muslim. But perhaps this was god's way to undo other desertic and failed prophetic events that led to the uncaring belief that shrubs, rocks, and lizards should have no place in our spiritual lives. Perhaps this was god's way of rectifying many wrongs that have resulted in many more wrongs. And god said, "I will take this Norwegian visionary and this California poet and re-write history." (I do not know how to do "god." This is as close as I can get without risking upsetting some folks.)

From these two compassionate hard heated heads and softer hearts came the following principles:[118]

- ☼ Non-human life has *intrinsic value*
- ☼ Species *diversity* contributes to this value
- ☼ Humans have no "right" to diminish this richness except to satisfy *vital* needs
- ☼ The richness and depth of human cultures is not limited by smaller populations
- ☼ Present human *interference* with the nonhuman world is *excessive* and worsening
- ☼ Policies must be changed resulting in societies that would be very different from present ones
- ☼ New societies and their success are measured in "quality of life" rather than a "higher standard of living"
- ☼ Those who agree with the above points have *an obligation* directly or indirectly to try to implement the necessary changes

Again, to those of us who are already invested in saving planetary LIFE across the board, for its intrinsic value, the above set of values and principles are not too far apart from other ecological manifestos. I take this to be a sign that some progress has been made. If the above are a higher multiple of Buddhism's Four Noble truths, then their Eight Wheels of action, their ecopsychological *doing,* are the following:[119]

☼ Humans have a *vital need* to cultivate *Ecological Consciousness.* Humans *need* direct contact with wilderness and undomesticated places.

☼ Working on ourselves is the most basic and "real work" (Gary Snyder)

☼ AWARENESS: Of big and "little" things in nature that comes from learning during appreciation in SILENCE and SOLITUDE.

☼ The habitual practice of attentive contemplation in silence and in solitude leads to the basic ecological INSIGHT of *interconnectedness* or *interrelatedness.*

☼ The *insight* of *interrelatedness* leads to multiple and sustainable intuitions such as visions of non-exploitative science and technology and, in general, to ACTING from other clear principles.

☼ We cannot change our consciousness by only listening to others, we must involve ourselves and take "direct action."

☼ We take "direct action" after questioning ourselves and the dominant culture.

☼ We face the facts as they are and determine to "Live our lives DELIBERATELY."

The combined ecopsychological import, then, emanates from *inward contemplation in nature* and from our ability to *act from these clear principles and insights.* "Ecological insight" and "right action" become a looped feedback *noesis* where "faith and trust in our most basic intuitions" gives us in turn the "courage to take action." Again, we can see the Eastern religion influence in their trusting *insight* as an equal *noesis* on par with scientific ecological understanding. Ecological Consciousness then is (should be): a "joyous confidence that we can re-establish a basic harmony between individuals, communities, and NATURE."

In their active practice, deep ecologists vary from advocacy to activism, and from activism to militancy. All *active practice* is genuine and some of it provides for good memories and interesting discussions in ethics. My own fond memories are of seeing Dr. Devall picking a shovel from the trunk of his car, climbing the side of a hill by a roadside in beautiful Humboldt County in California, and commencing to uproot several purple *lupus* plants, foreign invaders and competitors of the local flora. I lost several arguments to deep ecologists. I keep losing them because their actions are stronger than my words are convincing. If we take to heart evolutionary theory, I would ask, then isn't the fact that *lupus* does so well and out competes the local flora part of a pattern of invasion and extinction that has been going on since time immemorial? Shouldn't we also "uproot" Anglo-Saxon or Spanish human influence from California, order them to leave under the threat of a shovel or pick? After all, it was these human intruders who introduced the "malignant weeds" to begin with.

I guess we all pick the fights, ahem, activism, we are likely to win. For Dr. Devall, eradicating *lupus* is probably as close as he would ever get to uprooting Anglo-Saxon or Spanish human influence from California. Being of Catalan origin, I can tell you that a lot of California looks like a lot of Catalonia and Spain, therefore I have never felt like a weed there—I always felt that I was born in its magical landscape and deserved a little niche. I am very fond of *lupus*, *Scotch Broom*, and all the *genistas* that flower in such a blinding profusion of yellows, whites, and purples.

But this boldness to *act*, besides being endearing in its impossibility at times, deserves healthy respect. It is, once again, a model for *action*, not theories. And when this model for action becomes ecopsychology, watch out—now we are talking Ultimate Force Psychology!

This last *Being* outcome, a "joyous confidence that we can re-establish a basic harmony between individuals, communities, and NATURE," is so powerfully psychological that it could only have led, as it did, to practical ecopsychology. This outcome has the potential, in the right hands, to undo years of wasted anthropocentric psychology, quaint-tea-with-biscuits psychology that barely patches up the soldier and pushes him back into battle saying, "Adapt to the boiling water and to the insanity of our malcontent and creation." "Pass the biscuits!"

Ecopsychological Interpretations of Deep Ecology

If you were to conduct a survey of the many ecopsychological services or schools that are now part of an international sisterhood for Ecopsychological wellness, I imagine that you would be impressed by both the idiosyncratic styles and how much they have in common with each other or with a deep ecological base. From Rumania to Australia, from Canada to Brazil, it is as if many mental health practitioners, who have never heard of ecopsychology before, are almost simultaneously, joyously, and sincerely embracing it as the new authentic "thing."

In this embracing there is also reinterpretation along a predicted continuum. In previous chapters, I have spoken directly or indirectly about an *ecopsychological unfolding* that runs the gamut from simply adding more plants to your alienated apartment and life style in the middle of New York City, to the final frontier of going "back to the land," or "back to the woods." So, the spreading of ecopsychology clinical practice or methodology can be described in terms of or from the perspective and the needs of the client. Each mushrooming ecopsychological service may be the idea or special project of an individual psychologist, but not always.

Thus ecopsychology is also outdoor or wilderness education, birth-trauma therapy, shamanism, plain old fashioned counseling, gardening with a stick, tracking and wandering, social or political activism, swimming with crystals, druid trance, Christian mysticism, Dervish dancing, moon worshiping, dowsing for spirits, petting snakes, liberating abused animals, and always shaking your right index finger at politicians who have failed us. And while reading about all these activities, you might have smiled a couple of times. I did not.

On the one hand, as much as I would like all these interpreters of "ecopsychology" to become trained psychologists or counselors first, or that they become intellectually grounded in disciplines such as philosophy, a big part of me says "no" to this desire (or elitism). All these activities (some are referred to as "New Age") suggest or are indicative of failed quaint-tea-with-biscuits psychology. As if saying, "Moses did not deliver the so-called Ten Commandments, therefore we are entitled to worship the golden calf," these spirited and serious renegades are inventing their own way back to nature via their own ecopsychologies.

I am ambivalent because I would like anyone to be able to choose the "back-to-nature" path they feel most comfortable with and be more successful at it. On the other hand, I am not an anarchist, and although rebellious by nature and birth order effects, I do believe that some order will add credibility to Ecopsychology, so that others take it seriously. I take it very seriously and high caliber minds take it seriously so that is all that matters to me for now. But about all these activities, this ecopsychologist asks: Are they conducive to a deeper ecological understanding and insight that really puts natural processes first and human wants second—or to a sustainable balance? Or, Are these activities mere distractions from a much harder and important task toward individuation? Or even, Are these pastimes or The Passion of Individuation? If an "ecopsychologist" is leading some urbanite into the wilderness, he or she is totally responsible for that person. If a bear mauls the urbanite to shreds, then the "ecopsychologist" is responsible. If the poor swimmer is asked to swim in a pool with crystals and dolphins, and he or she drowns (or is mauled by the frisky male dolphin), then the "ecopsychologist" is to blame. If a client suffers a psychotic episode while undergoing birth-trauma therapy, then the untrained "ecopsychologist" is to blame. If a snake strangles the urbanite during a de-*evilization* apple tree ceremony, then the "ecopsychologist" better have a snake-strangles-my-client-the-urbanite insurance clause. As of now, there are few or no restrictions for using the phrase "ecopsychological counselor/therapist" in order to designate what a "practitioner" chooses to do. Shop around and be wise about distinguishing "quackery" from a genuine practice that aims to be responsible for your soul and thinks less of your dollars. And then again, quackery might just do the trick if you don't know that it is quackery and it does not cost so much. Swimming with dolphins among crystals IS costly!

Finally, there is no doubt that ecopsychology can and will benefit from empirical research. No doubt issues of how transference occurs, for example, to name just one area of inquiry, in different ecopsychological therapy situations, is useful information even for traditional therapists. I have raised this issue[120] in the past and it continues to be a concern for me:

> . . . Specifically, there is little empirical information about the differences, if any, in ecopsychological practice, regarding legal issues and psychological processes such as *Fiduciary Relationship*, *Transference*, structuring counseling time, *Power Differential*, and *Safety*, to name a few but important core points. Given that ecopsychological counseling and therapy are extremely varied, for example, issues of client or practitioner *safety*, need to be re-examined. For example, riskier procedures need to be identified and professionally *protocolized*. The issue of *transference* is ubiquitous to all psychological and body manipulative wellness enterprises. The diverse settings of ecopsychological practice (indoor-outdoor, psychodynamic-psychedelic) could either foment or diminish its portent. These ideas are in need of examination for curiosity's sake and for responsible ecopsychological practice.

Considering Big Questions

No mainstream psychologist can read the above statements casually or dismissively without having to answer the harder questions: If I consider myself a standard, eclectic clinician, shouldn't I consider ecopsychological practice, its aims, as part of my general palette of services or "tricks"? Am I considering the totality of BEING in my practice—Raw Nature included? If not, why? Am I up to speed with radical ecology, radical only because it has to shout louder to be heard above the cacophony of easy-busy psychological noise? Am I doing any *Good*? Am I any *Good*? Am I dead?

As I am writing these lines there is furor and rage in the Muslim world, perhaps justified, over cartoons that are described as blasphemy. As I write these words there is furor in the world over something and everything. As I write these lines there is less fury about saving our planet. This furor about something and everything but not about the ONE THING reminds me of a silent movie I once watched (or was it a black and white dream?) where two lumberjacks are slugging each other hard on a tipsy and rickety boat that is about to go over an immense waterfall. In the last shot before the boat is disinclined to fall but falls over the falls anyway, there is a close up shot of the two overly dramatic and overly made up men holding still in a pugilist position, looking into the camera but in the opposite direction of the falling boat. These pugilists and that boat represent the misplaced interests of much of psychology and humanity. But then again, psychology is at least supposed to be responsible for humanity, or isn't it? The day that psychology takes Nature as seriously as it does the little, decontextualized simian black box, on that day humanity and the planet will have a fighting chance.

I know what the word BLASPHEMY means to this ecopsychologist. I will always use it in the context of *some selfish or thoughtless word or action that diminishes the historicity of the natural world for the lazy convenience of a moribund maniacal ape.*

Deep Ecology Implies Philosophical Arguments

Many ecopsychology counselors or therapists who I know are less interested in making "philosophical waves" over a movement that they see as a necessary and last-ditch practical task for making folks feel well and the harder task of facilitating *transpersonalization.* That is why they are extremely good at what they do. I accept their impatience, disinterest, or disdain with understanding, knowing that they are very busy saving the planet and us. Nevertheless, as a philosopher-scientist-ecopsychologist, I meet dozens of individuals from all these areas who seek, ask for, and need philosophical arguments from our bunch. As if a dying planet and rampant ecopsychological alienation were not arguments enough in and of themselves, philosophers, for example, are sometimes more sensitive to well-put arguments than the reality of a car careening their way. Thus, we must "play their game" as best we can, if for nothing else, to say with a clear conscience that we tried.[121]

In environmental ethics, a course typically taken from a philosophy department, the jury seems to be still out regarding the Deep Ecology tenets, values, and arguments presented earlier. One of the accusations, if we can call it that, hinges on the central deep ecological idea that natural things, beings, etc. have "intrinsic value,"—a Buddhist fantasy to some philosophers. Philosophers argue, astutely and with face value sagacity, that as far as anybody knows (we can't ask a wolf these questions), only human beings can *evaluate* their reality, thus all natural objects *have a value relative to a human need, from aesthetic to profit-based.* This is a good argument to the extent that only humans can use language to describe the value of things to each other and make comparisons about the relative worth, significance, and reality of any values at all. This is a good argument to the extent that philosophers assume that wolves have no value systems of their own, have no aesthetic sense, or are incapable of hierarchical or classificatory cognition. But because wolves live in highly regulated and hierarchical packs, even the dullest philosopher must admit that wolves have *social evaluative cognition,* otherwise there would be no need to describe readily observable behavior in terms of an alpha or omega "something." *Social evaluative cognition* has been studied and reported in many animals. But even at a more basic evaluative level, animals such as the South American macaw, have even been observed making *utilitarian evaluative choices*. (Wolves and many other animals as well: the choice of a place to sleep in the cold at night for example.)

If empirical research is of any use to philosophers, the questions get more complicated for them: Does a wolf that has a readily observable sense of social hierarchy, have intrinsic rights to have, to express, this social sense of hierarchy? If a wolf decides to fight for an Alpha role, how does he do that? Is this some kind of lowly instinctual behavior that has nothing to do with having evaluated first his social status and the entire panorama of his social pack structure?

If we twist their arms and they admit that intelligent and social animals have more intrinsic rights than, say, a rock, then they have lost their sagacious argument already. Because the rock and its minerals feed the deer that the wolf hunts in an interrelated ecological pattern. Remove the rock, the water, the lowly plants, the forest, and what do we end up with? Nothing to evaluate or to philosophize about! Now here comes our important counterargument: *The value has never been on any single thing, but in the ensemble, on the ecological pattern.* That is the wisdom of ecology that was the wisdom of the humans who bothered to understand it.

It is a petty and decontextualized question, from thinking in ecological totalities, to ask whether wolves, plants or rocks have intrinsic value in and of themselves. I think they do, in and of themselves. Deep Ecologists, arguing as they are from Buddhist insight, are not really saying that a single rock has an absolute, unrelated intrinsic value, but rather that everything has value because everything has Buddha nature. If you don't like the *Buddha nature clause*, then rephrase this claim in ecological whole terms as saying that everything contributes to a majestic pattern of life, TOGETHER.

The other important element of this discussion hinges on *the relative evaluative role that each evaluative being has in the WHOLE*. Should we give more weight to humans evaluating their *umwelten* than to wolves and foxes? If so, why? By what fair rule do we make the human a hierarchical superior evaluative being? If nothing else, greater consciousness and self-awareness pins that mind to a tighter commitment to the rule: "I, out of all evaluative beings, shall not, cannot evaluate above them, for my own selfish wants." And the reason for this is rather simple and the subject of the full-fledged argument presented below: A being with greater consciousness and self-awareness is in a position to understand ecological interrelatedness as a pervasive existential principle. That understanding should continue into an extended morality of natural inclusiveness, that clearly grasps and acts for the principle stated above: everything contributes to a majestic pattern of life, TOGETHER.

Thus the following argument is another application and defense of SMT but equally, it brings back SMT to bear on deep ecological and ecopsychological issues and arguments.

I end the chapter with this argument still hoping to find, after seven years of its publication, a counterargument to its positions from the philosophically inclined.

Ironically, the above paragraphs and arguments, if true, bring both Paul Shepard's cynegetic life and "hunter" morality and Buddhist practice to an equal Kholbegrian moral reasoning level: Postconventional Morality. That is, both argue from a recognition that LIFE is sacred, that ecological WHOLES are more important than the singular gluttonous creature, and that MINDFULNESS of both the sacredness of LIFE and of the WHOLE that it inhabits preserves the intuition and the awareness of a higher order and hierarchy of which humans are only one aspect, one component. From this Postconventional moral level the hunter can kill as a sacred act and be holy, and the Buddhist can choose not to kill; either way their actions follow from an intrinsic RIGHT: to preserve the WHOLE.

To continue this argument and anticipate the ones that follow arguments, I will try to show that ecocentric ethics and the morals prescribed by them can be derived from ontological constraints that are ubiquitous and lawful in Nature-at-large (therefore empirically corroborable). I shall do this by borrowing an approach by Alan Gewirth[122] called an *internal model*. The *internal model* for evaluating is-ought arguments depends on the assumption that "Ought" is not external to "Is," and therefore that moral action logically follows from a lawful and empirically derived set of premises. The full argument and its checklist against Gewirth's *internal model* will be presented later in this monograph. But first, I would like to spend a few moments on my definition of matricial *ontological universals* [123] as the "Is" factual premise that would give rise, naturally so, to what I call *ecocentric* moral reasoning and subsequent action, our "Ought." Secondly, I will try to show, that "oughts" necessarily follow from these constraints on being. I will end this monograph arguing that ecocentric "oughts", even when violated by necessity, self-interest, or ignorance nevertheless remain internally ecological, universal and unchanging.

Matricial Ontological Universals Allow for Seamless "Is-Ought" Logical Transitions into Ecocentrism

Matricial Ontological Constraints: "Is"

The cart, the "Is", is the *beta* ontological constraints of *Energy*, *Safety* and *Possibility* and their interactive potential that give rise to the myriad of behaviors or to the manner of cognitions in basic, sentient and noetic organisms alike. That is, organisms are in the constant pursuit of energy, protect themselves and their kin, and fulfill their genetic and cultural potential while procuring and securing the earlier two. In our planet at least, this matricial ontological strata provides the common ground for interconnection, affiliation, and communal exchanges. These three *beta* elements are present in organisms and define these as living matrices (the *alpha* category). The outer existential dynamism of *beta* synergy is thus expressed and reflected—no, embodied—as developmental needs recognized by psychologists such as Abraham Maslow.[124] No metaphysical "sky hooks"[125] are needed to instigate proper ecocentric moral action.

An individual is thus itself an evolving matrix interacting with other matrices, from wombs, to mother to nations, existing within the confines of these interactions. The affinity between matrices is such that health and well being are dependent upon the contribution of each matrix or organism to the larger patter of interactions, to matrices-at-large. Furthermore, and important to the formal argument presented later, physically, developmentally and psychologically speaking, most (nearly all) of the matrices explored by humans (and other organisms) tend to be closed systems that can be impacted detrimentally by excessive demands.

The phenomenological and/or empirical evidence to the absoluteness of the matricial existential space can be obtained by observing how the *beta* elements, *energy, safety* and *possibility*, shape the organismic behavior from which all other patterns of existence are manifested. In this sense, my present claim is a Naturalistic one since it agrees with Naturalism that human existence is embedded in an "alma Matter", or nature matrix, its strict adherence to empiricism, and the view of natural matricial constraints as amoral. In short, creatures with a mental life are matrices; think about matrices; feel within matrices; know something about matrices and want to achieve maximum efficiency as matrices and within other matrices. The ontological *beta* constraints define the organizational patterns which imaginative creatures construct, from corporation to church hierarchies, from movies and story-telling to family dynamics, and to morals.

Ecocentric Morality: "Ought"

The matricial imperatives briefly sketched above are, as Santayana would say, my "brute facts." If we can accept this sketch, at least momentarily, we now can move to an evaluation of a set of conclusions that follow logically from these matricial imperatives.

If organisms are yoked to an existential wheel of *beta* dynamics and are themselves expressing these principles in thought or action then it follows that an understanding of these dynamics and their prescription for life could provide insight into the ground of morality. To be able to move seamlessly from universal natural law to a justification of the singular organismic act, it may necessary to first show how life-generating universes such as ours must have a common engine that transcends the indigenous planetary life of superficial diversity of moral form and act.

I have argued before [126] that such common prescription would be highly efficient for the preservation of information and learning from simple reflexes and tropisms to noetic enterprises. That is, the *beta* constraints and their dynamics provide, cognitively speaking, a transferring vehicle that facilitates the teachings of survival to nascent, inexperienced, or advanced organisms. To live in adherence to *beta* dynamics is to prosper; to violate its principles is to perish. This simple lesson is effectively acquired, irrevocably so, to the extent that we are born and develop in an existential matrix. The moment we define something as being alive, define it as an organism, it is so because it must operate within, it is trapped within, an existential matricial wheel of cause and effect. Any organism, conscious or unconscious of its 'aliveness' must do the work of life: it exists within a predetermined ecological and environmental context; it must, feed itself, protect itself, reproduce, discard catabolic waste and continue seeking existential avenues of sustenance and protection either by retaining adaptational gains that worked in its evolutionary past, or by changing survival strategies. These changing survival strategies may be serendipitous events such as novel and adaptive mutations, or self-motivated and intelligent goal-oriented behavior. Being both defines and is defines by the *beta* interactions.

To reiterate, the relative ease to acquire important universal laws for survival is an efficient way to transfer this learning and wisdom to generations of developing creatures. The ecological efficiency of the *beta* constraints imbues natural processes and its products with a built-in self-regulating momentum, making the universe, as far as we can think and see an interdependently efficient process. Here comes the seamless part: although organisms can bonk sometimes at ecological self-regulation, instinctively or in a premeditated way, they cannot help or pretend that they not obligated to this interconnection without, in the long run, affecting others and eventually themselves detrimentally. The *beta* ontological universals, by definition, are not idiosyncratic even though the myriad of adaptations that emanate from their interactions might be. Organisms as matrices are forced to seek support, balances, alliances, compromises, and adventure in nature-as-a-matrix and in other matrices. The very act of existence forces, teaches, cajoles, and even deceives us into moral compliance.

And all the bets are off when self-aware, complex organisms such as humans, partake of creation. The obligation to matricial dynamics is our existential *angst*. Such creatures as us have *dasein*: we are in the world, we are of the world and we have the knowledge that we are defined by it—by its TOTALITY and by its interrelatedness, not by any one isolated thing or property, including human language. This self-aware animal entity is egocentric by nature, for sure, by virtue of being engendered in limited social matrices. These initial womb and mother matrices are physically limiting, and/or fail, in the end, to provide every need. This situation leaves the human spirit in wanting or at least in a perennial state of reminiscence. The existential wanting or reminiscence can be dealt with, mitigated even, either by accepting the incertitude and incomplete satisfaction of accommodating to others, or by stealing from life. But stealing from life leads nowhere in the long run. All other social matrices that follow human development can be physically or cognitively limiting.

This predicament, a moral one, forces the subordination of self-interest while accommodating to other matrices. This accommodation assembles a field of psychic and biological tension, what Kurt Lewin [127] referred to as *life space*. Therefore, any human struggle in relationships, for identity, or with itself is essentially an ecological battle. It is out of this *life space*, in which self-aware creatures are the protagonists, that the movement from "Is" to "Ought" takes place. Wellness of being, survival, and prosperity are played out according the book of matrices. To act against it is to act against nature. To deny it in us is to deny nature in us, human nature.

Moral acts are efficient and necessary because the universe is efficient and it is necessary to have them in order to maximize organismic potential.

From "Is" to "Ought" in Six Easy Steps

First, I will present my ecologically driven "Is-Ought" argument and then proceed to use Alan Gewirth's test for establishing whether in fact a given moral argument can logically jump from statements of 'fact' to a prescription for moral behavior. The preceding sections can be summarized by the following ontological argument:

First Premise.—A brute fact: The matricial dynamics of the *beta* elements constrain organismic behaviors and mental life to a finite set of behaviors and thought and forms of interactions.

Second Premise.—These *beta* constraints are: securing *safety* (self-and kin protection), maintaining *energy* levels to optimally functional standards, and the exploration and monitoring of the environment for opportunities that maximize existential *possibility.*

Third Premise.—The interaction of *beta* elements, their function, in matrices and as matrices interact with other matrices, seeks ideal ontological states, a homeostasis that defines well-being.

Conclusion One.—All types of human moral engagement, from self-interested to altruistic, help humans in achieving a homeostatic state of well being. That is, humans cannot escape their moral singularity because it is a flight from being itself.

Conclusion Two.—Ecocentrism, as a reflection of affiliation with nature and as an expression of *beta* dynamics, brings the most good, the most well-being to the greatest number of organisms in creation-at-large.

Conclusion Three.—A self-aware moral agent *ought* to behave biocentrically to derive and procure the most good and well being for itself and others.

Conclusion Four.—To behave biocentrically is to extend intrinsic value to the whole of creation and to consider the impact of our actions on all matrices we encounter.

For the remainder of this section I will show how these premises and conclusions meet Gewirth's criteria that avoid the *naturalistic fallacy*, or moving from statements of fact [128] to statements of value. According to Gewirth there are six "interrelated conditions or tests that must be satisfied by any solution of the real "Is-Ought" Problem." The argument that 'solves' the "Is-Ought" Problem must have *oughts* that meet the following criteria: they are *moral, prescriptive, egalitarian, determinate, categorical* and *non-circular*. First, by virtue of being *moral, oughts* must be outer oriented and serve the needs, interests, and the well being of others. Second, the *oughts* must be *prescriptive* in that moral action follows logically from premises and makes moral action mandatory. Third, *oughts* are *egalitarian* because they aim to distribute well being equally between the benefactor and the recipient. Fourth, value statements are *determinate*, that is, they obligate a particular action while negating another (e.g., if we are dependent on matrices, we can not kill them. We are interdependent with all matrices therefore killing is immoral). Fifth, ought statements are *categorical* as opposed to being hypothetical. By being categorical Gewirth means that we are locked in reciprocity with others and that this state is irrevocable. To these five conditions he adds a sixth one, *non-circularity*. By this he means that the "Is" premises must not be moral or prescriptive themselves, must remain statements of fact.

I think that my earlier argument, an ecological ontology based on the *beta* matricial constraints, meets all these criteria. Conclusions one through four are obviously moral, egalitarian (and utilitarian), categorical, and prescriptive because they inspire a commitment to interrelatedness and clearly define the benefits for benefactor and recipient. Furthermore, the argument meets the criterion of non-circularity insofar the premises are not value statements but naturalistic brute facts descriptive of an existential process I called matricial dynamics. Energy, safety and possibility declare no value. They simply stand for events that are phenomenologically observable in nature.

What remains is to decide if these ontological *oughts* are also determinate. I think that this test is the hardest to pass because it is at the crux of all moral dilemmas—which action must I take and be called a moral choice? Even when the dictum of a moral argument is obvious (God all-mighty exists, therefore one must do X, W or Z), there might be numerous circumstances when the choice to be made does not clearly negate a path in favor of another, thus the *ought* is indeterminate (e.g., the tribulation of Abraham in whether or not to sacrifice Isaac). Conclusions one through four also meet the criterion of determinacy insofar matrices are obligated to associate. Such an obligatory affiliation, regardless of the ultimate outcome of such affiliation, forces an irrevocable existential engagement. There is no alternative to affiliation, and non-participation is negated by the very command to interact at all costs. It is not surprising that this obligation is existentialist in nature, that *being-in-the-world* forces us into action. Yes, neglect of other matrices happens routinely. But neglect is itself a disclosure of affiliation. "I shall not engage them" decides simply between me-as-a-matrix, what is best for me-as-as-matrix, and they. I say simply because the moral agent has not really escaped the ecological *life space.* Hermits, more radically, try to dissociate from society and end up choosing instead a micromatrix called self from which they cannot escape. They forgo affiliation-at-large and confront instead the matricial dynamics within. Whether the affiliation is intrapsychic or external, the moral agent must always choose to affiliate and pay notice to the demands of matricial dynamics. It would first appear that only in cases of suicide or homicide does the moral individual terminate affiliation. Qualitatively speaking, it is certain that both suicide and homicide erode the ground of potential affiliation for the murderer and the rest of us. But even in death, even through death, a matrix intensely focuses onto itself and just like the antisocial and the hermit, it is obligated to 'preserve' safety, energy and possibility, however misperceived, in an act of annihilation.

To conclude, the ground of well being can either be spread through continued commitment and connection to nature-at-large, in order to maximize potential being, or it can be withheld. The former describes a moral act the latter an immoral one. Because matricial dynamics extend, as far as we can infer, into the universe, a moral continuum is established which declares that *more affiliation is better than less and that caution in affiliation is better than rushed unreasoned contact.* Courtesy to all beings is courtesy to self because we all employ the *beta* ontological template in repeated actions and through their infinite variation.

Additional Commentary by Aldo Leopold:

"We can be ethical only in relation to something we can see, feel, understand, love, or otherwise have faith in."

"There is no ethic dealing with man's relation to land and to the animals and plants which grow upon it . . . The land relation is still strictly economic, entailing privileges but no obligations . . . Obligations have no meaning without conscience, and the problem we face is the extension of social conscience from people to land. No important change in ethics was ever accomplished without an internal change in our intellectual emphasis, loyalties, affections, and convictions. The proof that conservation has not yet touched these foundations of conduct lies in the fact that philosophy and religion have not heard of it. In our attempt to make conservation easy, we have made it trivial."

"That land is a community is the basic concept of ecology, but that land is to be loved and respected is an extension of ethics."

Chapter Eight

What Does Shamanic Lucid Dreaming

Have Anything to Do with Ecopsychology?

"Grandfather," I asked, "does it bother you that the younger Indians do not learn the old ways? That you have no student to learn your plants? That your medicine is not given the respect is due?"... "It is true the youngsters do not want to learn. That is not my problem, but it will be theirs. One day the medicines that the missionaries send from the city will no longer arrive. The people here will come to me to relieve their pains, to protect their crops, to conquer evil spirits that kill their children. But I will be gone and I will have taken my plants with me."

—Mark J. Plotkin, *Tales of a Shaman's Apprentice*

Of Freud's psychoanalysis it is said that it was a modern copy of counseling techniques widely used by Hassidic Rabbis long before Freud put them into practice—and he knew it but never told! His co-opting included a rich Jewish religious culture of dream interpretation. C. G. Jung could not keep his hands off archetypes—archetypes in dreams, aboriginal statues, western paganism, and eastern religions. To say that they were fascinated by the primitive is an understatement. As we will see later, we could not say the same for the average modern psychologist and clinician. Being interested in shamanism, as it pertains to the WHOLE of human psychology, ecopsycholoy, requires courage.

Real shamans may have been the scariest humans any person ever encountered other than rabid killers—sometimes they were both (and later, enchanted Rabbis.) If they did not scare you into living they scared you into dying with dignity. (By some accounts, they also visited (visit) the patient inside his/her dreams.) It might have been akin to walking into a psychologist's office and finding him/her hanging upside down from a roof beam wearing furs and feathers and smoking a cigar asking, "How's your Id these days, child?" The more things change the less things change. Short of modern fur-and-feather shamans many of the healing roles or practices associated with aboriginal mental or physical health medicines have been taken over by modern-day shamans, who somehow have misplaced their original plants[129]. I think they have misplaced more than their botanical burlap sack. But to the extent that this shaky historical bridge exists, and more importantly that the niche for a "mental health practitioner" exists, it suggests that fragile simian psychology will always be in need of some sort of shaman—or a new DVD player.

There is also fierce competition between aboriginal shamans, modern-day shamans, and between university-trained shamans and their jungle counterparts. In the Amazonian jungle, competition between two powerful shamans is easily resolved: I put a curse on you, you put a curse on me, and the stronger curse wins. Sometimes both shamans are equally powerful and both die. Competition between modern-day shamans is resolved by dropping a few mean-spirited hints here and there—that the other fellow does not have a Ph.D. or that the competitor used to hang around with Timothy Leary in the 1970's. Gossip is as lethal as the evil eye or a curse. Now, competition between modern-day shamans and aboriginal ones is downright nasty. Until recently, with serious studies in cross-cultural psychiatry or psychology, the jungle shamans were seen and depicted as the incarnation of the boogeyman. Now, quaint-tea-and-biscuits psychologists who drive Volvos and wear a tie[130] to work that matches their Ids can be merciless against the soil-and-mushroom forest shaman. If not directly merciless, they can vent or re-direct their suspicion or fear onto a straw-man version of the forest shaman: the ecopsychologist.

We must understand their fear and need of reprisal. By all accounts, Freud and Jung would have been happy to be confused with forest shamans, after all, they read extensively and their encyclopedic minds were walking Encartas seldom produced in clinical training anymore. And so are forest shamans: walking encyclopedias of botanical lore, spirits, gossip, and forest lore unequalled by their peers. Mark Plotkin (1993), and other ethnobotanists have corroborated this fact in other parts of the world, estimates that an "average shaman" (even an "average aborigine" without shamanic training) can identify hundreds of botanical specimens and know two or more curative or utilitarian functions for each. They can estimate proper dosages of curative plants and administer them without killing the patient, more often than not, and be very effective in mitigating or curing tropical diseases still unknown to modern medicine. They can do this from memory without having to consult a pharmaceutical manual or the DSMV-IV bible of mental anguish and disgust. That they can do this without scales, beakers, couches, background elevator music, fake fountains hidden behind fake bamboo curtains, or needing to go through a middleman of an insurance company, is remarkable and reassuring.

Then, there must be a real and profound intellectual and knowledge divide between the cookie-cutter clinical psychologist and the Freud's, Jung's, and forest shamans of the world. And they know it! Hence the explanation for their envy, fear, arrogance, and patronizing of anything *overwhelmingly wild or natural*. I think that both Freud and Jung looked forward each day to uncovering something overwhelmingly wild or natural. In this sense, they were fearless shamans.

The point of this *intervention* is to anticipate the next sections and suggest that when it comes to mental health and therapy, when it comes to *getting dirty*, to doing the work of the seemingly unfathomable human mind, it is best to understand EVERYTHING related to its natural habitat and origins. To the extent that quaint-tea-and-biscuits psychology has become an insular vocation of some grander enterprise and life-and-death career that required more than a few years in college and a short and obligatory internship in a mental institution or similar facility, then not only are our points defensible and fair, but they indicate that a radical transformation of our field is required toward the ecopsychological end of the spectrum.

The most observable casualty of the "old burlap bag of authentic tricks" is the reluctance, by the quaint-tea-and-biscuits psychologists who drive Volvos and wear a tie to work to match their Ids, to say the word "dreams." While eager to deal in all morbid aspects of sexuality, the fantastic dream world of the patient (pardon me, "client") seems to many of them as the most obscene ambit of human consciousness-unconsciousness. Even when personally attracted to dream work and therapy they may lack the confidence and training to do anything useful or therapeutic with this interest. Maybe it is that dream work and therapy takes time and interdisciplinary training, none of which is rewarded by insurance companies. If your voice is sweet-enough, you smell nice, and you can quickly wrap up the counseling session within fifty minutes, then you can have a "successful practice."

What follows is a plug for and the ecopsychological interpretation of why understanding dreams, if not dream therapy, is so essential. But more specifically, I will address the need for paying attention to what traditional shamans have considered the *visionary* or have learned to manipulate in order to move into the animal mind: the *lucid dream*. With significant revisions, most of the text that follows was originally copyrighted under another book title.[131] The fact that it reappears in this book, albeit with necessary contextual revisions, suggests that I find it very relevant to the ecopsychology of dreaming, especially "Big" dreaming.

The Scientist Shaman

> "Dreams, from a shamanic point of view, are of two types: ordinary dreams; and nonordinary, or "big" dreams. Shamans are normally only concerned with big dreams. A big dream is a dream that is repeated several times in the

same basic way on different nights, or it is a one-time dream that is so vivid
that it is like being awake, an unusually powerful dream."
—Michael Harner, *The Way of The Shaman.*

When it comes to the "Big" dreams, and specifically, the lucid dream, we are all forced into a sort of personal sorcery. It is 'sorcery' from the point of view of the dream content itself to the extent that new frameworks of knowledge exchange are possible beyond the non-dreaming reality. This is simply a fact that must be accepted, and it occurs for millions of individuals on a nightly basis. It is a fact whether my spouse believes it or not; it is fact whether my neighbor believes it or not; it is a fact whether psychological or dream research and science address these experiences adequately or not. Our "Big" dreams go on manifesting themselves in our psychological reality despite the limitations of dreaming "Big" Dreams elsewhere.

Because these dreams are a unique psychological reality, as well as a significant element of the whole of consciousness and even perhaps the very seeds of what is called the mythical[132], and because the new frameworks I have suggested employ mythical symbols or occur around ancient themes under the highly impressionable state of the lucid dream experiencer, they gain a certain irrevocability and validity beyond objective science. One can dismiss these knowledge frameworks, if one chooses, as nothing more than bizarre states of consciousness. However, their *noesis* remains. Diminishing their import flies in the face of contemporary research on dreaming and REM states that specifically argues for the role of these processes in memory consolidation, maintaining a modicum of higher order reasoning states—a pilot light for consciousness if you will—and for problem solving. So at least some of the research shows that cognition is doing something constructive when the lights seem to be out. Generally speaking though, *it seems that a profound experiential and experimental chasm exists to the extent that the "shaman" specializes in the "Big" dream and most dream research has been devoted instead to the "little dream."* This chasm has been almost convenient for both parties, but it does little to bring the entire study of dreams under a singular and ecopsychological satisfying umbrella. Another falsity, originating in western scientific paradigms of sleep research, is that of dichotomizing consciousness into ordinary versus non-ordinary, or consciousness and altered states of consciousness. I will address the latter limitation at the end of this section.

Even when this unfortunate classification, little dreams-big dreams, is addressed in the scientific literature and dream research community, there seems to be little interest, and/or limited personal experience of "Big" dreams. They are just another category of interesting dreams, no more no less. But even when investigated, "Big" dreams are only inadequately explained, or not at all, by dream theories such as Hobson and McCarley's Activation Synthesis Theory which views dream events as the result of random activation of medullar and pontine cells. Even when these authors make allowances for the creative abilities of cortical systems to organize this random activation according to some personal agenda and interest, their explanation remains a description of actual dream physiology and only that, since it does not attempt, ecologically speaking, to explain the psychological and cultural regularities of "Big" dreams (recurring lucid dreams for example).

In other words, what others and I call a "mythical" or an "ecopsychological" dream language that makes sense to the dreamer, or to a collective of avid vivid dreamers, may be gibberish or the product of random activation to others who, interestingly enough, might not experience these dream states and might not understand these experiences no matter how many neuron clusters they investigate. I grudgingly accept and understand their limited position for the reason that an experiential chasm exists between the journeyer and the outside, passive, and so-called "objective" observer.

We can put this argument a bit more strongly. In fact, contrary to the orthodoxy of "squeaky clean" dream research, and as an argument against present hyper-technology driven empirical trends in sleep research, I claim that there can be no "objective" or "outside" observer in, particularly, lucid dreaming research who does not have an intimate and credible hold on these phenomena. So-called "objective research" can at best be an outside and clouded window into a real and extended phenomenon that can only be understood inclusively from an existential and ecologically grander point of view. This is in fact no different than attempting to understand the psychology of "Big" love by studying neuronal activity, hormonal changes, or moist secretions. One has not "captured human love" in an experientially valid sense.

Additionally, to be sure, there is non-randomness in being routinely frozen (as in sleep paralysis), or in learning specific rituals/behaviors to induce lucid dreams, or even in participating in the exact dream as many times as one wishes. A three-part lucid dream is anything but random. At the very least, *what these experiences suggest is that, with practice, some less interesting neuronal random activation can be yielded and controlled, once in a state of self-awareness, to enlist the activation of specific brain systems needed to elaborate upon a "Big" dream experience.* If some individuals are capable of doing this, then some of the dream research has to explain how this is accomplished.

To be sure, achieving conscious lucidity or self-awareness sometime during sleep is no small task or common. But when it occurs, one should assume that lucid dreaming is another state of consciousness along a continuum begun in no-dreams, passivity, and true randomness dream states. Now, when the SP experiencer is able to produce or manage the circumstances required in achieving a singular event, then he/she controls, even owns, the non-random story. Also, REM dreaming itself does not "spontaneously" appear "sometime" during the night. Most mammals dream roughly within a 90-minute non-REM—REM cycle; so in this sense, there is nothing random about the "spontaneous" excitement of pontine, and later, sub cortical and cortical areas. What I mean is that this adaptation has a mammalian *purpose* that culminates by a force of *will*, in humans at least, in a singular and repeatable experience: the uncanny dream.

To reiterate, even if we can call these neuronal events "physiologically random" *the subsequent cascading effects of this spontaneous cause are further restricted by mental habits and impressions peculiar to the individual and the species. This experiential funnel reduces the scope of randomness even more.* Finally, probability is obligated one step beyond when the dreamer dreams "Big" dreams as a matter of course. *This probability enters into the realm of repeatable conjuring when the lucid dreamer is involved in genuine ecopsychological practice* (or zazen meditation).

I concede that several acts of "neuronal randomness" end up being a purposeful and singularized non-random event. But the volitional and self-aware quality of lucid dreaming experiences amplifies an initial and less consequential sort of randomness and makes this psychobiological explanation recede as not very useful for the "shaman" dreamer. LaBerge's (1985) well-known criticisms of Activation Synthesis are reflected in statements like this:

> As for meaning and nonsense, the Activation Synthesis model of dreaming seems to completely disregard the possibility . . . that dreams could have any intrinsic or even interesting meaning whatsoever.

We must agree with his criticism here as well, as being major obstacles to any bottom-up theory of dreams which disregards the complexity of a self-aware and fully embedded ecopsychological mind to get to work, for a reason, on any stimulation that goes on during its watch, day or night, or more importantly, a mind that seems to carry intentionality, *purpose*, and goals into the mythic realm of dreaming.

The Dreaming Skills of a "Sorcerer/Shaman"

In an effort to continue to close a western rationalization and arbitrary gap between the aesthetic, the mythical, the scientific, or the shamanic I will be using the words "sorcery" and "shamanism," broadly speaking, to mean ancient hunter-forager and shamanic practices and disciplines that scientific methodology only co-opted or thinks it has perfected.

Historically, dreaming "the shamanic way" has important and useful antecedents that form an important archival and experiential background for the exploration of hypnotic or meditative techniques that have an origin in these ancient practices. As we suggested at the beginning of this chapter, both Freud and Jung saw this connection when they set out to organize and invent a science of dream interpretation and exploration. I must admit that I will fail to keep up with these two formidable minds and their scholarly syntheses in this book; but we nevertheless owe them a great deal and must strive to borrow the best that they can offer us.

In the context of this grander literary and scholarly field of wisdom, sometimes using the word "shaman" is more appropriate if we have reports that lucid dreamers utilize these skills in the context of dealing with or being "assisted" by other animal forms and entities, for example, to heal. Sometimes the word "sorcerer" would be more appropriate. Officially sanctioned or not, moreover, these practices we refer to as "sorcerous" or "shamanic" are also part of elaborate mystical traditions across all the major religions. However, we shall see that there might also be *sound empirical (ecopsychological) reasons to focus on shamanic practices.* The often-found shamanic link in the literature of lucid dreaming attests to this appropriate and obvious inclusion. Regardless of the cultural, historical, or religious context in which these terms are found, I specifically mean all the ancient and pre-scientific empirical methods that included, and include to this day, the following principles:

1. The disciplined or routine *observation and study* of a particular phenomenon, *internal or external* to the shaman.
2. The delving into the particular "mystery" *wholeheartedly, with the totality of one's psyche and body*, as an authentic process, and sometimes despite terrifying obstacles: the risk of social or family ridicule, punishment, injury, banishment, or worse, death.
3. The hindsight design, pre-determined devising, or accidental bumping into a particular set of acts, actions, rituals; *any conjuring* that attempts to direct, control and obtain some "grace" or favor from the phenomenon observed and its continued exploration and testing.
4. *Transcending* the initial facts and details of—as well as internalizing and automatizing the acts and rituals; any conjuring—the phenomenon in order to reach a higher humanity or understanding of self and universal motifs. *Transcendence* includes the understanding of general principles and lawful processes which most organisms know only as particulars.

In these enterprises, and when abiding by these four principles, a devoted scientist and the proficient shaman see eye to eye. Thus, this ecopsychologist and scientist feels quite comfortable borrowing, if effective, any results and practices that derive from these sound and holistic principles.

Assuming that the lucid dreaming experiences are taken to be indicators of shamanic potential in cultures worldwide, and because these "Big" dreams can occur spontaneously without the use of hallucinogenic agents, or trance-inducing exercises, they may also share elements of *transcendence* common to both. In the words of Michael Harner again:

> His experiences (the shaman's) are like dreams, but waking ones that feel real and in which he can control his actions and direct his adventures. While in the SSC (Shamanic State of Consciousness), he is often amazed by the reality of what is presented. He gains access to a whole new, and yet familiarly ancient universe that provides him with profound information about the meaning of his own life and death and his place within the totality of all existence. During his great adventures in the SSC, he maintains conscious control over the direction of his travels, but does not know what he will discover. He is a self-reliant explorer of the endless mansions of a magnificent hidden universe.

The Unity of Consciousness and the Extension of Consciousness

The premise inherent in the last quote is that consciousness incorporates a larger continuum of experiences even though it appears, phenomenologically speaking, that there is discontinuity of mental states. One apparent discontinuity in the west is that between normal and altered states of consciousness. But on the other hand, we all accept that when we are tired and fatigued, or when we are engaged in daydreaming, all these states, although different from being perky-awake and alert, are part of a GRANDER consciousness we deem unitary. If so, then a psychological proposal that presents consciousness vaguely, or incomplete proposals of what consciousness is or is not, originating mainly within a modern western culture, are limiting *noetic* exercises because, in reality, *consciousness exists as a vast continuum of human experiences for many cultures and times.* The cherishing of nature as the source of the "spiritual" and the continuity of nature into an ecological conscious and unconscious that we demote to an inferior cognitive status, that of *animism*, is nevertheless evidence that consciousness was perceived by ancients to be, if not seamless, at least continuous and interacting with its many layers.

So the complexity and continuity of consciousness, even when refused and ignored by dogma or law, even when we have forgotten what to do during the transitions between these states, is nevertheless safely and securely represented in the experiences of other cultures or individuals who wish to expand their *noetic* horizons. The simplistic and debatable classification of these experiences into a consciousness-side and altered-states-of-consciousness side sets limits to what "normal" consciousness could be about, and at the same time reduces the other side of this dubious dichotomy to something less than an ideal sort of mental state.

To borrow and then re-apply a wonderful sentence I quoted earlier from Harner, if the purpose of consciousness is to serve "a self-reliant explorer of the endless mansions of a magnificent hidden universe," then the scope of consciousness itself needs to be rediscovered and expanded *to include all of the mansions within and their interactions with the natural world—the ultimate source of who we are.* Specific to the shamanic experience Dr. Benny Shanon (2003) writes:

> The dynamic nature of consciousness should be borne in mind. Consciousness is a system that spans an entire range of possibilities along which, at different times, different profiles emerge. Throughout our lives, the values associated with the parameters of the system consciousness are constantly changing. The values in dreaming differ from those in normal wakefulness, those encountered when we are fresh and alert differ from those encountered in fatigue, and all these differ from those exhibited in the extreme states usually referred to as 'altered (or alternate) states of consciousness.' Since consciousness is always changing, always alternating, the term 'altered/alternate states of consciousness' is, I find, deceptive.

Shanon proposes a theoretic reformulation of consciousness where it can be "defined by a set of parameters that can take different values." He writes that his statement is in opposition to William James' presentation of consciousness as consisting of a more exclusive or restrictive "set of features." To the extent that these *features* are defined and prescribed by a western mind that can be seen as MIND-bankrupt or that fears the open-ended consciousness of dream lucidity, it is understandable that it belittles, demotes, and under-represents its aesthetic possibilities, for example. To paraphrase Shannon, the parameter "self-awareness," takes on different *values* between awake and sleep states in a cyclical fashion with respect to those individuals who dream lucidly. If consciousness is defined by yet another parameter, "bounded-by-the-idea-of-a-body," then consciousness so defined is equally cyclical between awake and sleep states in the lucid dreamer. For example, the lucid dreamer can project a *dreaming body*, or not, but this freedom is not even an option for the physical body during awake consciousness. But even when we adhere to a more orthodox account of consciousness, the lucid dreamer is more awake than asleep; therefore his/her explorations need to be investigated more seriously because now they have entered the realm of waking phenomenology.

If a complete understanding of consciousness still depends on an explanation of dream lucidity, then philosophers or psychologists who demote and oversimplify dreaming to a footnote about "the dream experience" as an exception to a certain rational-when-awake rule (in order to be dismissed from a grandiose consciousness-explained scheme of their own invention) are surely on shaky ground simply because their theory is non-inclusive.

If *aesthetics*, for example, endures beyond the awake state into dreaming-with-volition, and aesthetics is a purposeful human enterprise that maintains ecopsychological balance, then the aesthetic products that result from lucid dreaming are as important as the ones obtained and explored during the awake states, or any other state for that matter. Once again, Shanon arguments seem to support these ideas when he refers to the shamanic journey resulting from taking the hallucinogen ayahuasca when he says:

> The phenomenology of the ayahuasca experience suggests that within the definition of human consciousness exist some parameters that are not part of regular contemporary discourse. I refer to the parameters of aesthetics and sanctity. I propose that these are basic determinants of human cognition; correspondingly, they might be grounded in the very structure of the brain.

Shanon's claim is all the more reassuring not only because it echoes the case I have already made for revisiting *aesthetics* as an undercurrent for the mythical, the shamanic or lucid dream, but because he finds it so fundamental to a definition of consciousness. The aesthetic component of consciousness is part of his "semantic parameters" or what I have been referring to as the *semiosis of dreaming*. Because this aesthetic element can be that much richer and informative during psychedelic or lucid dreaming experiences, then it is attended to with fuller and greater *attention-consciousness*, and thus new meaning is not only derived, but also expanded and created. The aesthetic experience itself can move seamlessly into the mystical experience. I ask once again: *If mainstream aesthetics is valued and written about, and mystically produced aesthetics is valued and written about, and even if the hallucinogenic-shamanic experience is valued and written about, then why should a potent and naturally induced state of conscious lucidity and derived aesthetics be any less valuable than any of the other states and products?*

Equally, Shanon makes a distinction between an actual meaningful and purposeful experience and disorganized, psychotic, mental products. To him the experiences of the shaman are well-structured and laden with meaning whereas those of the psychotic are often fragmentary and chaotic. If this distinction works for Shanon, then by logical extension, IT MUST BE APPLIED to the lucid dream experience as well.

If purposeful, non-chaotic mental operations are one of the measures by which we could assign a higher "production" quality or value to consciousness, *then the non-ordinary and willed lucid dream experience of a sober lucid dreamer is at least on equal footing as the willed journey of the shaman who ingests ayahuaska.* More strongly, I will argue with the religious traditions that employ meditation as a vehicle into the uncanny that in fact the lucid dream experience is that much more pure or honest because *it requires no pharmaceutical props and because it has a longer and more pervasive influence on the day to day life of the "shaman."*

Of course, to be naturally endowed to the shamanic is not the same as force-feeding the mythical with botanicals, but since they both share important visual and experiential elements, shouldn't we study in-depth the naturally occurring phenomenon with the same interest and scientific curiosity? It may not be the case as some authors have suggested that ingestion of mind-enhancing botanicals gave rise to the mythical and/or the mystical, but rather that a handful of individuals have always existed who tapped into these states regardless of whether or not they could find that "god herb" of magic mushroom.

To close this section, even Shanon, willing as he is to expand the construct of consciousness so the ayahuaska induced shamanic experience has a credible place in the firmament of what is accepted in western psychology and philosophy, oversimplifies dreaming. For example, when talking about the ability of the hallucinogen ayahuaska to enhance reality he says, "Dreams and imagination usually decrease the value assigned to this parameter [The conferral of reality]; the ayahuaska experience may increase it." Not so in the lucid dream!

Finally, only lucid dreamers know for sure and are qualified to talk about their "Big" dreams, and only lucid dreamers are in a position to evaluate the affinity that their experience has with other reported phenomena. All together, whether we know it or not, the inebriated shamans, sober shamans, artists who pretend to be shamans, philosophers of consciousness who wish to be shamans, are converging on a similar *noesis*: the mythical. One can only ignore mythos at one's own ecopsychological peril.

The Semiotics of Ecopsychological Dreaming

> *"The earlier culture will become a heap of rubble and finally a heap of ashes,*
> *but spirits will hover over the ashes."*
> —Wittgenstein, *Culture and Value*

The revolving door of everyday experience while awake, thinking that one is awake, dreaming that one is awake, and of recalling mundane dream material, with respect to the meaning transported between all four levels and their significance for person and culture, becomes a matter of *semiotic* interest. If *semiotics* is interested in deciphering the way in which these dream signs are generated, broadcast, and finally interpreted by individuals and culture, then dream phenomena becomes a special case for this field of inquiry with the added bonus that semiotics may be the only field umbrella and serious enterprise that is capable of encompassing the biology, psychology, geophysics, poetics, mythology, and cultural implications of the phenomena.

The complexity of the interaction between these levels of meaning and signification is what anthropologist and semiotician Lévi-Strauss means by *bricolage*. Lévi-Strauss co-opts the word *bricolage* from a more mundane meaning that suggests an incongruous mix that seems to hold together. By using this word Lévi-Strauss wants to convey how it is that myths might be constructed. For him (Joseph Campbell speaks to this as well) myths are essentially maps that assist a believer or user to use their symbols and metaphors in order to resolve or to address an experiential contradiction or conflict (always developed in the tale-myth itself). But these symbols and metaphors must come from somewhere. Lévi-Strauss thinks of the obvious—that myths are built from the kaleidoscopic multiplicity of social and environmental facts or activities. The difference between the mythic and dream compositions of reality is that the myth is more static than the *bricolage* of the dream. The bricolage of the dream, especially when it is aided by the dreamer's willful control of the dreamscape, ceases to be simply another social item, becoming a transcendental tool, often times risking facile social interpretations. In traditional cultures where taboos are respected and the norms are tight and inflexible, the bricolage of the controlled, self-aware dream may be one of the few methods of challenging myths that cease to guide with wisdom precisely because dreaming is itself, if not a shamanic journey, an ancestral form of communication.

Both myths and dreams contain creatively and synthetically formulated "truths" that have the potential of guiding the development of self. Joseph Campbell said, "The myth is the public dream and the dream is the private myth." In that sense both myth and dreaming need and feed off each other. *So there are enduring and universal existential realities apprehended by a personal and basic human psychobiology that can become heuristics or archetypal truths. It is certain that the personal and private dream machine reflects (acknowledges) these archetypal truths. But it is also the case that it has the capacity to invent new ones or provide new images for old ones. In this sense "Big" dreaming is an awesome undertaking and responsibility, on equal footing with any creative human enterprise because it uses the individual-as-a-dreamer as a new and contemporary interpretant of old mythology to infuse into old social patterns new rituals, signs, symbols and behavioral repertoires.* Logically, this process of mythical renewal also means that sometimes the private dream world is in conflict with the public myth, a situation that mythologist Joseph Campbell thinks can lead to trouble: *neurosis*. Campbell writes that individuals confronting this neurosis have been visionaries, leaders and heroes. Campbell further describes the resolution of this neurosis as follows:

> They've [visionaries, leaders and heroes] moved out of the society that
> would have protected them, and into the dark forest, into the world of
> fire, of original experience. Original experience has not been interpreted
> for you, and so you've got to work out your life yourself. Either you can
> take it or you can't. You don't have to go far off the interpreted path to

find yourself in very difficult situations. The courage to face the trials and to bring a whole new body of possibilities into the field of interpreted experience for other people to experience—that is the hero's deed.

At yet another level, the biological, humans are animals, designated by species, genus and family. We are primates, and our *uncanny dreaming* and dreaming states served in the adaptations of many species before us. If lucid dreaming, or a rich dreaming life in general, are phenomena still manifesting themselves in our experiential makeup then it is because they were useful ecopsychological adaptations. Particularly in the midst of our synthetic world, dreams may be the only authentic experience left of a once ecopsychologically deep grounding and biosemiosis with nature. Then understanding their genesis and potential for problem solving and personal unfolding becomes a practical and even necessary enterprise. But always, it seems to me, dream experiences are the precursors of what Lévi-Strauss calls the *mythical*. In this primal and important sense, people who are lucky enough to experience unusual dreams as everyday or continuing realities are privy to truly archaic knowledge modes that deserve to be understood even more so because of their primacy and their enduring status in addition to any tools they provide for problem solving and personal growth.

As the opening quote by Wittgenstein suggests, the semiosis of dreaming as a study includes the exploration of its permanent quality and intensity as a continuing experience, a common psychobiological cause, and its enduring manifestation: lifetime and historical psychological effects. That is, *even after the material elements of cultures cease, there remains a psychobiology of "Big" dreaming as hovering spirits that make their reappearance in another culture, in another time, described using vernacular terminology. The new and vernacular terminology and experiences can be adopted into new myths or can modify the old ones. Thus, the bricolade of myth is reconstituted anew.* Ecopsychological recovery includes understanding dreams for re-establishing old telluric connections.

Moreover, when aspects of dreaming become hyperconscious through lucid dreaming, then, semiotically speaking, convoluted, grasping-at-straws psychoanalysis has less to contribute to our study. Now I must interpret for myself or with the help of poetry, myth and culture what dreaming means *for me*. Furthermore, it helps the dreamer if others have made a similar journey and have practical advice to dispense. This is a semiotic process that owes some debt to psychoanalysis, as long as psychoanalysis or other clinical attempts are not second-guessing dreaming, always, as a sign of dysfunction.

We must then accept the likelihood that Freud is basically correct when he repeatedly makes the argument that dreams have an *energy charge that belongs more to the infantile* than to the rational or adult basically because the infantile registered its first universe, for months and years at a time, enveloped in purely perceptual and sensorial truths. Ecopsychologist Roszak may readily agree with the notion that dreams are the voice of "his" ecopsychological unconscious. By this *we should not infer that this infantile mode is less precise at conveying truths*, or remembering trauma, or that it has no role to play in adult life and in the development of self.

To conveniently deny this early and rich existence and assume that it plays no part in dreaming life—an experience inundated with pure sensation, perceptions, and undifferentiated scenes that are hard to discern and control—is at least bad science. Thus, leaving this developmental aspect out of the dream *bricolage* makes it more difficult to explain the phenomenology of the dream content as being expressed in strong emotions, in visual or sensorial tones, and always stuck in the present. More importantly for ecopsychology, as the biographies of many naturalists and philosophers and seem to indicate, *something about their early infantile exploration of nature endured strongly into their adult lives contributing not only to their choice of careers in the biological and ecological sciences but to insights that later where crucial in understanding more of Nature.*

The special shamanic dreamers are once again in a unique position of experiential advantage and potential psychological growth because they can continue to develop in dream states. *Using Freud's model again, these dream shamans can bring to submission the fuzzy and busy infantile aspect of the average dream, forge it at will, or by technique and daily practice, into another consciousness state where self-awareness has an extended opportunity to evolve with new experiences.* If one is troubled by the simplistic, imperfect, and unfortunate man-in-the-street rendition of Freud's idea of the infantile in the dream I urge you to consider an alternative interpretation. My interpretation, a thought experiment, asks that you pretend to be a big cat, monkey, or whatever animal you identify with (it has to be a mammal), and imagine what its dreams would be like. I imagine that its dreams would be about its strong *limbic system reactions* to its existence for sure, joys and fears, all these played out in an eternal tense: the present. Its ideas would also be rooted in the perceptual or the sensorial rather than in higher order, rational thought processes. Its motoric agility, real, remembered or desired, may take the form of a sort of flying, in flight or fight or chase. I am not saying that human dreaming, shamanic or not, cannot be more than these experiences, but I am saying that Freud, by looking at the "infantile" as a significant source of dreaming, *has connected all animal minds to our animal mind and made it possible to think about the origins of our human totemic experiences.* By sharing these evolutionary dreaming predispositions the shamanic is simply a natural and logical expression of that ecological collective. I will develop this point further in the next section.

Freudian and Jungian Bricolage

Freud, like a wise and savvy old shaman, ends *The Interpretation of Dreams* with what is, in my opinion, the best chapter in that immense book. He saves his best trick for the end. The long and complex chapter "The Psychology of the Dream Process" contains a revolutionary section (B) simply entitled "Regression." But his meaning of the word *regression* in this section is not what is usually and first thought of, as in a regression to infantile or juvenile behavioral or cognitive states. He means by this term a hypothetical neuronal mechanism of regressing to perceptual-sensorial states from conscious states involving motor volition and control during dreaming. The reverse order of this neuronal process is engaged while we are awake. At the risk of oversimplifying a 'must read' for anyone who thinks Freud is outdated and has little to contribute to psychobiology and cognition, he proposes, ahead of his time, a neurocognitive model that attempts to sketch a series of perceptual, memory and motoric systems arranged in a precise and logical sequence. These arrangements of systems representing the psyche are introduced as a theory of dreams that Freud thinks may account for empirically observable facts. For example, the flow of information to and from the ends of this processing of information (one end being the capturing of physical stimuli by sensorial mechanisms, the other being consciousness itself) determines whether we are dreaming, hallucinating or engaged in ordinary reality. In the same model, he not only provides reasons why this cognitive regression flow terminates during dreaming, in the exploration of images and old memories or the visual images of older memories, but argues convincingly why this is an "infantile" mode.

Simply put, Freud reaches the conclusion that *thoughts[133] are transformed into visual images when we dream*. Furthermore, in an important declaration he says, ". . . we may describe the dream as the substitute for the infantile scene modified by *transference* to recent material. The infantile scene cannot enforce its own revival, and must therefore be satisfied to return as a dream." The process of *transference* is important here for Freud as well because it is the bridge that will connect and recombine into a new bricolage two seemingly unrelated events that share common elements. *Transference is a semiotic process of association of meaning.*

Freud may have overreached with other psychological ideas, but he seems to identify important universals in dreaming that, if not related to a uniquely human ancestral ecopsychological source, point to primitive and animal-like cerebral processes we may share at least with all mammals. If so, then *it makes sense that dreams are more akin to traditional shamanic experiences and lore because they demand from the dreamer a different psychological attitude that includes and results in totemism, in the expression of universals in totemic form.* This pre-historical and historical process, in twists and turns that may not be recognizable to the modern or untrained eye, is the *archetypal psychohistory* discovered by Jung's insight into psychology and mythology, or as Edward F. Edinger puts it, "the self-manifestation of the archetypes of the collective unconscious as they emerge and develop in time and space through the actions and fantasies of humanity."

If totemic, the symbols and language signs endure, clamoring, as a connection to the animal within by representing its aspects through mythological pantheons that span human experience. If true, ignoring the rich ecopsychological vault of the dream world is akin to severing our soul in half and claiming that one side does not exist or should be ignored. Ultimately, dreaming, and particularly lucid dreaming, in tandem with artistic expression and ecopsychological unfolding can boost each other as transpersonal functions to reiterate and recapitulate one truth: ecopsychological balance and harmony—as a reinforced dialectics.

In the last section of this chapter, it pays to inquire further how this reiterative or recapitulative process (a positive feedback loop) has anything to do with maintaining ecopsychological balance. It may not be an exaggeration to say that knowing this process is taking place (or actively seeking ways to exercise its three components: aesthetics, lucid dreaming, and purposeful immersion in the wild—*itself a complete ecopsychological practice without any ecopsychologist telling you what to do*) and being affected by it may be the most widespread, authentic, and ancient ecopsychological practice humans have ever known.

Lucid Dreaming and Aesthetics[134]

In the previous section I claimed that the interlacing between lucid dreaming material, its artistic reinterpretation in diverse media, and these having a direct impact on *ecopsychological unfolding*, "may be the most widespread, authentic, and ancient ecopsychological practice humans have ever known." This is true insofar as many people experience lucid dreams on a regular basis and provided that they are interested in using this aspect of their mental lives for ecopsychological unfolding and then balance.

If so, what comes next may be something they are very familiar with. Also, many practitioners of Transpersonal Psychology are keen on the study and understanding of Psyche processes that I will attempt to describe in the context of lucid dreaming and its artistic representation. The interested reader can go to writers in this field for further information if you have not already.

I will continue to interpret *ecopsychological unfolding* as a more inclusive process of *personality individuation* (non anthropocentric and embracing of all nature and its processes) or being actively involved in the discovery and integration of as many personality aspects as possible that are said to be the inclusive of a real "me:" dark and light, somber and gay, or evil-tending and good-generating. Thus the full integration of SELF, even if it is an impossible task, requires that these dualities be stitched together into a larger and seamless SELF-quilt. Because this task is extremely demanding and difficult, due in part to the extreme dichotomizing tendencies of individual limited awareness, nationalism, and ideology, a lucid dreamer is on the other hand in a position of advantage over the regular dreamer. This is the case since dream content and the manipulation of a dreamscape by lucid dreamers allows for a *volitional returning to* and *controllable dialogue* with the depth of the psyche. Dreaming itself embraces ambiguity.

The simpler story is, to relate and reiterate in a few lines, that lucid dreaming can be for many a reliable source of perceptual and cognitive data, a source of novel interpersonal exchanges with imaginary or known dream characters, and a controlled exercise of social and personal "deviance." By *deviance* it is meant that lucid dreaming allows for cognitive and emotional free-play that could challenge comfortable and even orthodox relational cultural patterns. This inner dreamscape "deviance" can be and is expressed via another "deviant" enterprise, artistic expression, creating a powerful hermeneutic circle and maximizing the potential for SELF-growth.

The Surreal

It is more common to hear about lucid dreaming and its potential aesthetic products being defined in terms of "surrealism" than in any other way. In fact many of the personal accounts that describe lucid dreaming begin, elaborate upon, or end by paying notice to its surreal quality. I would argue that although this description aptly surveys the surface presentation, the fragmented nature, and even the overall quality of lucid dreaming experiences, nevertheless, this predominant surreal classification is less important or useful *in my art or in my ecopsychological unfolding.*

Surrealism is, as philosopher Paul Shepard aptly described (1996), the antithesis of the fully integrated-natural world and of its ecopsychological ideal: a fully embedded humanity, inescapably, in Nature. That is, surrealism is the reification and the ratification of components "in and of themselves" extracted from a larger original and organic context and elevated to a polished and exclusive category (a form of fetish). The rapidly shifting dreamscape itself makes this reification and ratification possible because oftentimes, even when we are proficient lucid dreamers, the fascination with a particular and singular element of a dream detracts attention from a larger and more dynamic scenery and meaning-content that the proficient dreamer does not pay attention to or cannot keep up with. When lucid dreamers recollect the vividness of a dream, it is often these surreal highlights that are mentioned.

Film has been the artistic medium par excellence that depicts dream life as surreal precisely because of its potential for control of temporal sequencing and image unfolding. Directors can artistically manipulate both temporal sequencing and image unfolding in order to create a close approximation of an original dream experience. I will only cite the work of the famous Czech filmmaker, Jan Svankmajer, who transferred the surreal work of his equally creative wife and artist, Eva Svankmajerová, to film, here, as principal exponents of the surreal artistic approach. (Eva Svankmajerová is well-known for her writing and plastic arts.) But hundreds of other film sequences emphasize the surreal quality of dreams. Even when the focus is not a single object, an entire dream sequence can unfold in exceptionally alluring and brilliant vignettes without an apparent connection between these frames. Surrealism is thus also *deviant*, intensely so, in my earlier use of that word, since it forces a new interpretation of time and space that can lead to unique and creative insights. Salvador Dalí made an easy juxtaposition of mathematics, time, and his visual rendition of these advances, as he understood them. Dream surrealism has been re-created or re-interpreted in dance, music, poetry, and architecture.

I will not argue here that a focus on the surreal quality of dreams is not important for other forms of artistic expression or even that it cannot contribute to *ecopsychological unfolding* in its own right. But I am saying that, at least in my case, the more humble aspects of lucid dreaming end up being the more important and pertinent messages that invite further discovery.

More Humble Aspects of Lucid Dreaming

The more "humble" aspects of a lucid dream that I am referring to are *content* as opposed to *surface* driven. Their lackluster "humility" lies in their often hidden and harder-to-arrive-at semiotic aspects, as Freud and Jung discovered. Instead of the surreally enhanced sensorial qualities that are often present in lucid dreaming, these more fundamental elements are of great significance to me. It is their potential *semiosis* that makes them more important. One word (its meaning), a face (as a mask suggesting my behavior or an ideal), the angle of an object (indicating direction), a text read (in a larger context), music heard (not only notes but what the song means to me or how it makes me feel), and a complete dream story that holds together logically and provides discernable meaning to the individual dreamer—this is the stuff of which *my dreams are made*. Particularly since 1994, my lucid dreaming has had a dominant *shamanic* import, to use that term both generally and technically. Of course this import has coincided with an equal interest during waking reality in attempting to understand global patterns of the human condition in mythical terms. For a given question in waking reality, for example, a dream being was encountered who wore a particular mask. This mask was later carved to achieve maximum approximation to the dreamt object. The dream being was also pantomiming or acting out various dances and manners of walking or flying or swimming. These dream manifestations and their messages were the answers I sought. By carving them afterwards I had the extended opportunity not only to reminisce about the dream and its message, but also to refine and elaborate further this message for maximum clarity and understanding.

Often, the depth of meaning inherent in these more lackluster aspects of a lucid dream echo a genuine interest in and detailed inspection of my natural surroundings. In fact the more slowly and deliberately I walk in my woods, the more detail I see in natural objects that catch my eye-spirit, the more vivid and the greater detail the dream object provides. This is walking meditation at its best with the expected and often reported effect of enhanced lucid dreaming. Thus, control of dream lucidity means more than a technical procedure that can quickly be learned from a CD. It is instead a prescribed and intense attentional state or movement, even a way of life, and perfecting it is the aesthetics of which I am most desirous.

Lucid Dreaming, Artistic Expression and Ecopsychological Unfolding

The complete dynamics that I have been trying to describe makes for a circular, self-feeding and grander aesthetics where no longer is there a distinction between the lucid dream, the dreamer, natural embeddedness, or the artistic product. All are complementary manifestations of a grander semiosis represented simply in Figure 2:

Figure 2

Lucid dreaming as personal and shared mythology

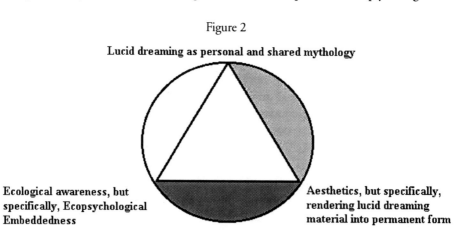

Ecological awareness, but specifically, Ecopsychological Embeddedness

Aesthetics, but specifically, rendering lucid dreaming material into permanent form

The concept of art as being separate and thus decontextualized from this circular relationship, itself a form of surrealism, or even as a necessary but incomplete inspection of nature when an original code is lost, is a western invention. This is aesthetics interpreted from a "deficit" model. Interestingly, many so-called primitive languages do not have a concept for art for they experience and express their existential and natural relationship as a grand process or even a cosmology, a process rather than an object.

Perhaps an imminent discovery, my view of the interplay between lucid dreaming and its artistic representation is, to my surprise and delight, more "primitive" than western. In this sense, I no longer follow or am interested in a western production vector that places an interesting lucid dream on a position "a" followed by production of art piece "b," however hypnotic, well crafted, and commercially viable this art piece may turn out to be.

Instead, the artist, the process of making art, and the art product itself are all fully integrated components of lucid dreamscapes and of the original life-nature-matrix that generates all dreaming. Paul Shepard (1967/1991) describes this existential and ideal cohesion: "The inner world is coextensive with the outer, the natural habitat a middle ground, lacing into each other like fingers of clasped hands."

Further Commentary: The Objiwe Dreamcatcher, Tibetan Dreams, Dream-Inspired Artwork by Odilon Redon

"The Ojibwe people tell of how, many moons ago, Spider Woman brought the sun back to the sky each day. But when the Ojibwe nation spread to the ends of the world, she began to find it difficult to make the journey for all of her people. Instead, she directed the mothers, sisters and grandmothers to weave a magical web for new babies using willow hoops. These dreamcatchers would allow only good dreams to enter the babies' minds when they were asleep. The circle of the hoop was a symbol of the sun. The web was to connect to the hoop in eight places to represent Spider Woman's eight legs or in seven places to represent *The Seven Prophecies*. A feather in the center of a baby's dreamcatcher represented breath and life. Adults did not have a feather in the center of their dreamcatchers but instead kept a feather in their possession."

—D. Blake, *Legends of the Native American Dreamcatcher*

"The Mother Tantra says that if one is not aware in vision, it is unlikely that one will be aware in behavior. If one is not aware in behavior, one is unlikely to be aware in dream. And if one is not aware in dream, then one is unlikely to be aware in the bardo after death."

—Tenzin Wangyal Rinpoche, *The Tibetan Yogas of Dream and Sleep*
(Mother Tantra of the Bön tradition.)

—Odilon Redon, *The Crying Spider*, photograph of original, 1881

—Odilon Redon, *Spirit of the Forest*, photograph of original, 1880

Chapter Eight References and Bibliography

Austin, J.H. (1999) Zen and the brain: toward an understanding of meditation and consciousness. Cambridge, MA: MIT Press.

Baars, B.J. (1988) A cognitive theory of consciousness. NY: Cambridge University Press.

Baars, B., Newman, J., & Taylor, J. (1998) Neuronal mechanisms of consciousness: A Relational Global Workspace framework. In S. Hameroff, A. Kaszniak, and J. Laukes, (Eds.), Toward a Science of Consciousness II: The second Tucson discussions and debates. Cambridge, MA: MIT Press.

Campbell, J. (1988) The Power of myth. In Betty Sue Flowers (ed.) *John Campbell The Power of Myth with Bill Moyers*. New York: Doubleday.

Conesa, J. (2002) Isolated sleep paralysis and lucid dreaming: ten-year longitudinal case study and related dream frequencies, types, and categories. *Sleep and Hypnosis*, 4 (4), 132-142.

Conesa, J. (2003) Sleep Paralysis Signaling (*SPS*) As A Natural Cueing Method for the Generation and Maintenance of Lucid Dreaming. Presented at The 83rd Annual Convention of the Western Psychological Association, May 1-4, 2003 in Vancouver, BC, Canada.

Conesa-Sevilla, J. (2004). *Wrestling with ghosts: a personal and scientific account of sleep paralysis*. Pensylvannia: Xlibris/Randomhouse.

Conesa-Sevilla, J. (2005). Lucid dreaming, aesthetic expression, and ecopsychological unfolding. *The Lucid Dreamer Exchange, December 2005, #37, 8-10*

Edinger, E.F. (1973) Ego and archetype: individuation and the religious function of the psyche. Baltimore, Maryland: Penguin Books Inc.

Freud, S. (1949-1989) An outline of psychoanalysis. (Translated by James Strachey). New York: Norton & Company.

Freud, S. (1900-1996) The interpretation of dreams. (Translated by A. A. Brill). New York: Random House Value Publishing Inc. (Gracemercy Books).

Harner, M.J. (1981) Hallucinogens and Shamanism. New York: Oxford University Press.(pp.134.)

Harner, M.J. (1982) The way of the shaman: A guide to power and healing. New York: Bantam Books.

Hobson, J.A. and McCarley, R. (1977) The brain as a dream-stage generator: activation synthesis hypothesis of the dream process. *American Journal of Psychology*, 134, 1335-1346.

Hobson, J.A. and Stickgold, R. (1994) A neurocognitive approach to dreaming. *Consciousness and Cognition*, 3, 16-29.

Hobson, J.A. and Leonard, J. (2001) Out of its mind: Psychiatry in crisis, a call for reform. New York: Perseus Publishing.

Jung, C.G. (1956-1976) Symbols of transformation: An analysis of the prelude to a case of schizophrenia. (Tranlated by R.F.C. Hull) Princeton, N.J.: Princeton University press

Jung, C.G. (Ed.) (1964) Man and his symbols. New York: Dell Publishing Co. Inc.

LaBerge S., & Levita L. (1986) Lucid Dreaming: The power of being awake and aware in your dreams. New York: Ballantine Books.

LaBerge S., & Levita L. (1995) Validity established of DreamLight cues for eliciting lucid dreaming. *Dreaming*, 5, 198-206.

LaBerge, S. (2000) Lucid dreaming: Evidence that REM sleep can support unimpaired cognitive function and a methodology for studying the psychophysiology of dreaming. HTML version of LaBerge's (2000) Lucid Dreaming: Evidence and methodology. behavioral and Brain Sciences, (23 (6), 962-963.

LaBerge, S. & DeGracia, D.J. (2000). Varieties of lucid dreaming experience. In R.G. Kunzendorf & B. Wallace (Eds.), Individual Differences in Conscious Experience. Amsterdam: John Benjamins.

Lévi-Strauss, C. (1962-1966) The savage mind—La Pensee Sauvage. Chicago: The University of Chicago Press.

Lévi-Strauss, C. (1977) Tristes tropiques. (Unabridged translation be John and Doreen Weightman.) New York: Pocket Books.

Metzner, R. (1999) Green Psychology: Transforming our relationship to the earth. Rochester, Vermont: Park Street Press.

Naranjo, C. (1967) Psychotropic properties of the harmala alkaloids. In Daniel H. Efron (Ed.) Ethnopharmacologic Search for Psychoactive Drugs. *Public Health Service Publication 1645*. Washington, D.C.: U.S. department of Health, Education and Welfare.

Nardi, T.J. (1981) Treating sleep paralysis with hypnosis. *The International J. Clincl. and Expimntl. Hypno.*, XXV, 4, 358-365.

Ness, R.C. (1978) "The Old Hag" phenomenon as sleep paralysis: a bicultural interpretation. *Culture, Medicine and Psychiatry,* 2,15-39.

Newman, J. and Baars, B.J. (1993) A neural attentional model for access to consciousness: a global workspace perspective. *Concepts in Neuroscience*, 4, 2, 255-290.

Payn, S.B. (1965) A psychoanalytic approach to sleep paralysis: review and report of a case. *J. Nerv. Ment. Dis.*, 140, 427-433.

Plotkin, M. (1994) Tales of a shaman's apprentice: an ethnobotanist searches for new medicines in the Amazon rain forest. USA: Penguin Group.

Roszak, Theodore 1979. *Person-Planet*. New York: Anchor Press.

—1992-2001. *The Voice of the Earth*. New York: Simon & Schuster.

Shanon, B. (2003) Altered states and the study of consciousness: The case of ayahuaska. The Journal of Mind and Behavior, 24, 2, 125-154.

Stewart, K. (1969) Dream theory in Malaya. In Charles T. Tart (Ed.) Altered States of Consciousness. New York: Doubleday Anchor Book. 161-170.

Van Eeden, F. (1913) A study of dreams. *Pro. Soc. Psych. Res.*, 26, 431-461.

Van Eeden, F. (1918) The bridge of dreams. New York: Mitchell Kennerly.

Van de Castle, R.L. (1994) Our dreaming mind. New York: Ballantine Books.

Wasson, R.G. (1983) Soma divine mushroom of immortality. New York: A Harvest/ Harcout brace Jovanovich, Inc.

Zinberg, N.E. (Ed.) (1977) Alternate state of consciousness: Multiple perspectives on the study of consciousness. New York: The Free Press/Macmillan Publishing Co., Inc.

Chapter Nine

A Student's Experience as a *WWOOFer*

(WWOOF: Willing Workers on Organic Farms)

"I only appreciated the dysfunctionality of my situation when I was removed from it. I went to spend a couple of weeks with my family in rural Switzerland, and the transformation being in the country was dramatic and elucidating. I didn't want to go back, but when I did, it was with a new sensitivity to the impact the city was having on me . . ."

Since the conception of this book I wanted to include a voice and an experience that was not mine, and that would speak to young readers in their own voice. At the time, our daughter, Kaliana Conesa,[135] was volunteering on a green technology farm in Ireland after having spent her first winter in Berlin, Germany. Her descriptions of the contrast between both experiences are a recapitulation of ecopsychological recovery and becoming. I have asked her to write a full account of those experiences for this book not only because I think many more students should know about the *WWOOFing* (WWOOF: Willing Workers on Organic Farms) program as an economical way of traveling and learning independence, but also because it offers a concrete example of the possibility of ecopsychological becoming or unfolding that is honest and immediately graspable.

Kaliana's Story

Berlin

Living in Berlin for six months is one of the most draining things I have ever done. These months were dominated by winter, which seemed to begin mid-fall and only mellowed out halfway through what is customarily spring. It is a miserable time not so much for the marrow-freezing cold, though I didn't enjoy that. What makes it really bleak is the particular way the concrete, an elementary constituent of the place to an extent I'd not noted before or since, shakes challenging hands with the sky and simply won't let go. If I'd had gray receptors in my eyes, they would have gone into an epileptic fit and perished a week into the season.

Winter can be gloomy anywhere, but a northern European winter, compounded with living in a metropolis for the first time in my life, finally did me in. Going out to do even basic errands got to feel like a battle with the entire city. The glowering people, treacherous "fast German cars," and the omnipresent, almost tactile roar of noise were all obstacles that weren't to be overcome, but resigned to. That noise in particular I almost came to fear—untraceable, *sourceless*, I only ever identified it as "the sound of the city." It was just there, seeping into everything, interfering with and altering the tempo of my whole self, sometimes to *unrecognizability*.

I eventually avoided leaving my flat unless I had to. I could only negotiate my way through the city given total resignation to its onslaught, an exhausting feat I avoided at all, and considerable, costs. My mental and physical resources were nearly always so thoroughly tapped I rarely had enough left over to pursue the things I loved doing. The real problem was that I got used to all of this. Immersed as you are in your own life, awareness that something isn't right can be elusive, especially when the effects of what is wrong have permeated all throughout your self.

So, I only appreciated the dysfunctionality of my situation when I was removed from it. I went to spend a couple of weeks with my family in rural Switzerland, and the transformation being in the country was dramatic and elucidating. I didn't want to go back, but when I did, it was with a new sensitivity to the impact the city was having on me, and a resolution to get out of there.[136]

Although I didn't yet know just what I was going to do, the general direction was clear. I knew that my greatest moments of lucidity whilst in Berlin came when insulated deep in a park or watching the resident pair of magpies from the flat balcony. I admired them and everything else that seemed to exist in spite of the place—trees engaging in *treeness* just as they would in a forest, blithely pushing their roots up through cement paving. Of course trees and birds could only be found because the city was in fact a suitable habitat for them. But I rooted for anything cyclical—the weather, animals, plants—that existed as they always have. They seemed to mock the static unresponsiveness of buildings and concrete, which, let alone, would crumble in a few decades. Honing my awareness to these little islands of vibrancy kept my sanity, and I knew intuitively that I needed to be in a place where "I would be surrounded by this" to repair the damage wrought by the city.

WWOOFing It

I think I was probably investigating farm work online when I happened upon information about the *WWOOF* program. As I read about it, I became increasingly excited. The premise behind the scheme is simple: you volunteer on an organic "farm" in exchange for food and accommodation. I say "farm" because the entities included range from backyard gardens to communities striving towards self-sufficiency. But they are unified, at the least, in their eagerness to utilize organic growing methods, even where their implementation is a work in progress. It is common for participants to go far beyond this, revitalizing and maintaining the land they inhabit to integrate it with, and contribute to the resiliency and health of, surrounding ecosystems. Many are also focused on preserving the traditional lifestyles, craftsmanship, and horticultural techniques of their area, sometimes in direct struggle against the industrial-scale, homogenizing farms encroaching on their (and every other) region. With *wwoofing*, one is directly contributing, albeit modestly, to the autonomy and resiliency of the local economy, via practices and crops that make sense at a local level. Even in relatively economically stable countries, the universal plague of atrophied localized sufficiency, beginning with the de-emphasizing of small scale farming and production, will take its customary heavy toll on community bonds, the land, and those who make their living directly from it.

So when people invite *wwoofers*, as the volunteers are known, onto their land, food and lodging are only the most tangible aspects of their offer. Volunteers will of course be exposed to a range of work that will almost certainly involve acquiring new skills and knowledge. Besides all that's necessary to learn simply to do the work, hosts usually have other facets of knowledge that they are happy to communicate. They may practice craftwork, alternative therapies or holistic medicine, or yoga. Many are artists, musicians, or excellent cooks. Some of the places *wwoofers* have the opportunity to volunteer are retreats and educational centers, in which case they may be able to participate in the activities and classes offered. But at the heart of all of this, *wwoofing* involves active engagement in natural and social communities. You experience a new place as a contributing participant in it, which makes it infinitely more demanding, intimate, and therefore rewarding than, say, increasingly popular eco-tourism, which, like plain old tourism, places the individual in essentially a spectator role, skimming off the top of what a community is made of, and sometimes even detracting from its complexity and vitality. Active participation is harder, but your experience is proportionate to your effort, and you can only get a true measure of the soul of a place when you've become a drop of the blood with which it pulses.

Wwoof hosts are found on six continents and span the range of climates, ecosystems, and geology; whatever considerations and interests you may have, there will be a place to suit. I didn't have a large travel budget, and, in all honesty, was nostalgic for an English-speaking country. I'd long had an interest in Ireland, which fit both bills, and so began my search there. Each host provides a brief description of their place and what kind of work volunteers can expect; some have websites you can refer to. They also include a handy key which provides such information as how many people, adults or children, are on the property, what kind of accommodations and equipment they can supply, special diets they can cater to, average hours of work per day and number of working days per week, and languages spoken. You get a feel for how remote the place is and what local transport is available. But for all the information, finally choosing a host is essentially an act of trust—that the situation will be as it's portrayed, that the hosts will provide the amenities they've promised, and, basically, that the people on the other end are going to act in a respectful and decent fashion. But then they put the same trust in you, and you have the benefit of knowing that if the hosts had acted questionably in the past, other *wwoofers* would have made complaints to those running the program. Basically, the contract between volunteers and hosts is of the oldest and most fundamental human sort—based on the knowledge that symbiotic arrangements generate the most beneficence for all concerned, and sealed with goodwill.

There was a superabundance of compelling choices, even being restricted by a *vegan* diet. In the end, I chose a host based on their location (near the dramatic southwest coast), and the fact that they generated all their own energy through an entirely homespun combination of wind, solar, and water power. Everything was arranged via e-mail (though I encourage everyone to talk to potential hosts over the phone if possible, to get a better feel of who you'll be living with), and I left with the somewhat discomforting assurance that once I got a bus to a nearby village, hitching would be easy and safe. But so it was, and after a moderately wearing journey throughout which I was buoyed by anticipation and awe of the land around me, I was picked up by someone who knew the very place I was after and delivered me all but to the doorstep.

Sneem, Ireland

I resist trying to articulate my confusion of impressions and emotions as I walked through the land that first time. But a big part of what I was feeling was simply relief. All the tension I'd accumulated from effectively being on the alert every time I stepped outside had no place here, and obligingly, almost instantly, drained away. It was like being in a cramped place for a long time and suddenly being transported to an open field, which was more than figuratively the case. And I'd never experienced a landscape like this before. It was defined by fierily indecisive topography that tried to go in all directions at once and somehow succeeded. The soil was dusty and knobby with stones, but abundantly fertile underneath, as evinced by explosions and expanses of green that very nearly glowed. A sea breeze was moving inland fast, scattering clouds and their shadows in slightly surreal patterns.

The inception of all the labor that'd gone into the land was the host's desire to live as self-sustainably as possible, while recognizing that complete, self-contained sufficiency isn't a practical aspiration. Perhaps in the context of a significant and very dedicated community with a sprawling collective body of knowledge and skills it can be realized, but beginning as he did with just his own family, he was primarily interested in doing what he could, and educating others based on his trials and experiences. In addition to the original family in the main house, two friends of the host now had their own places elsewhere on the land. All the structures were built by people living on the property, their friends, and *wwoofers*. One man lived in vaguely yurt-shaped structure that he'd built using nothing but local fallen timber, a hammer and nails, a level, and a little plastic for the base of the turf roof, pitched at a jaunty angle. The interior was all curving, raw beams, good for hanging and climbing, and the ceiling was woven just like a nest. I would end up spending a lot of time there, and have rarely felt so situated and cozy inside any structure, like a nest indeed.

The *wwoofers*, of which there were three others when I arrived, lived in "the pallet house," named for its construction of, primarily, shipping pallets. It's small, with two stories and very basic cooking and bathroom facilities. It would become rather dirty and cramped at times when there were six *wwoofers* sharing, but it's amazing what you get used to, and a little initiative towards keeping it tidy always went a long way. We ate our meals during the week in the main house, where water is heated via the fireplace, so no fire, no warm water. This clearly means that the gathering, chopping, and stacking of wood is a good portion of the regular work. A tub was available for occasional use, but, alternatively, there was an outdoor solar shower that was truly luxurious on sunny days.

Of Midges and Bread

I arrived in the afternoon, so chores began the next day. On that first day, I didn't think I would be able to make it. Any further account would be grossly incomplete without elucidating the existence and nature of midges. Imagine a flea-sized insect, only visible on its own as a lazily drifting dark speck. But rarely is a midge viewed on its own. The midge likes to travel in packs, but prefers swarms. These swarms lay dormant until the perfect conditions present themselves, for they are delicate creatures: any precipitation more violent than a drizzle is incompatible with their ethereal wings, any wind fiercer than a breeze too taxing. Yet they're no more resilient to a brightly shining sun, nor to the crisp cold. So they like to make their appearance on that sort of day that needs no help to be horrible—muggy, overcast, still. Low pressure days, migraine days. On these days, they feed, with the intensity of a one and only chance. You'd barely notice one nipping at you, but when it's a dozen at a time, all the time, you do pay attention. At their worst, they instantly cover half the area of your hand. There are measures to be taken against them, but you could never midge proof yourself—unless you were lucky enough to get the one fine mesh midge suit, which the dog ended up destroying. Insect repellant makes a dent when they're not in full force to begin with, but on a really bad day, the only thing to do is smear your face and hair with diesel and cover every inch of yourself, but they'll crawl through the slightest crack, especially around the eyes. And after a little experience with them, no one ever balked from the diesel treatment. My first day happened to be a day for the midges, and I was turning over the soil in a future bed with a shovel, breaking up clumps and picking out stones. Hard work to do for hours, especially as I wasn't yet used to that sort of thing, and didn't at all have the hang of repelling the little minions. So periodically I would throw down my shovel, scratching my face and neck violently while running around to out-pace them. If you move fast enough, you're safe. It speaks volumes that these were the first animals I ever, in all my life, purposefully killed (other than to put some injured insect out of its misery)—wiping my hands down my pant legs constituted a massacre. I really was on the verge of tears that day. But the next day was more merciful on the midge front, and the work a little more interesting.

After being there a while, I could recognize these bad days as simply periodic, and weigh them against the many good and interesting days that were the norm. Common jobs included planting, weeding, *strimming* (the use of a *strimmer*, think very powerful weed whacker), raking and composting the *strimmed* vegetation, and watering the *poly-tunnels* (plastic greenhouses). Twice, we all made cement with a small cement mixer, which involved shoveling a mixture of sand and gravel, and throwing buckets of water into the spinning cement drum. When it was full and mixed, we tipped it into wheelbarrows and poured them onto the building site, which the host proceeded to tamp, level, and smooth. Previously, I had de-weeded and leveled the future foundation, then raked gravel smoothly over it. At one point, I tore out the innards of what had been a goat-milking shed, hammering and chiseling the mortar off concrete blocks and ripping out pallets by any means effective, which basically amounted to hammers and kicks.

The construction-related work wasn't my favorite (except for kicking out the pallets, that was fun); I was always happiest to plant, water, and harvest, and even to weed, when the day was warm and sunny. There were always odd jobs, and several big projects. Creating reed beds was the single biggest and most important collective endeavor, which all the *wwoofers* worked on after only minimal instruction from our host. If you aren't familiar with them (I wasn't), reed beds consist of ponds filled with reeds and other deep-rooted water plants, into which gray water flows and is filtered. Essentially, we built the filtration system for his house (the previous beds were clogged and dead). Sticking the reeds in was the last and most difficult step, as it involved digging them up from distant locations on the property and hauling them away by wheelbarrow. "Digging them up" sounds innocent, but we were after the really colossal clumps, which were probably twice my weight. Luckily, you couldn't kill those giants if you tried, so several people would hack and lever away at the roots, simultaneously and unceremoniously, until the massive network of fibers, soil, and stones came free. Because I was always the only *wwoofer* confident in their bread-baking abilities, I would regularly turn out about fifteen loaves, which was the only scale at which the host considered running their goliath, industrial oven to be efficient. I spent several happy rainy days engaged in this while everyone else had to work outside. I felt a bit guilty, but they seemed to consider the final product worth my lucky break.

WWOOF Tourism

In the surrounding area lie bogs, which have a stark beauty and something like desolation, but are really very complex and, thanks to peat mining, endangered ecosystems. In some areas, the bogs are spotted with quicksand-like patches, which people annually stumble upon to end up asphyxiated. Our immediate area was happily free of such hazards, and I spent many hours traversing them; they were unlike anything I'd walked before. They're uniformly soft but profoundly pocked, up to foot-deep drops and foot-high mounds encountered at every other step. In many places the surface is concealed with tall grasses, so you never know what you're going to get. For this very reason it's great fun to tramp across them quickly and at random; occasional falls are certain, but never painful given the softness of the turf. With a person from the property experienced with the terrain as guide, I once ended up crossing farmyards in almost total darkness. After awhile I learned to trust myself, and let go of the natural fear of losing equilibrium. We kept noticing that the ground seemed to sparkle, and eventually identified the little spots of luminescence as glowworms. Spending the night at a nearby beach, I had the opportunity to witness a similar phenomenon—phosphorescent phytoplankton, which came alive when you disturbed the water with little explosions of brightness like those from dry, green staticky bed sheets.

I should make note of a final local attraction—ring forts. Beginning around the fifth century C.E., inhabitants corralled their cattle—and defended them from raiding parties—within a circle of oak tress, which in turn was girdled by a moat. Nowadays the moats are mostly ditches, but one I visited did still run with water. Sloping upwards from the inner bank is a hillock, the outer perimeter defined by these ancient oaks. They're some of the most incredible trees I've seen. They're the trees of myth, through which you wouldn't be at all surprised to catch a glimmer of *dryads*. They're so densely twisted and bent they give a history of every prevailing wind and each slight breeze they've accommodated. With the girth and sinking *mossiness* of their branches, they irresistibly invite climbing, and offer seductive resting places. The inside of the ring is mostly made of meadow and stands of bracken, but both sites I visited, for some reason, hosted a dense clump of reeds thriving in the center. When you sit still and silent, the atmosphere is a bit eerie—you feel much has happened there, and it's as if the whole place stops and watches while you stay.

It took awhile for me to settle into the rhythm of work, but once I did, I felt I could carry on all my life and be completely happy. But "happy" may not be the right word; while immersed in the work, I didn't have a sense of being happy or really of anything else. In this sense, some of the hours I spent planting, watering, or harvesting brought me effortlessly to the deepest states of meditation I'd known. My sense of self not so much disappeared as exploded; in retrospect, though I didn't contemplate it at the time, it seems as though all I was perceiving was completely unmediated by expectations or interpretations. I was simply aware of that surrounding me, on its own terms. It was a feeling of being filled up by the world.

Conclusion

I'd resolved to *wwoof* because I intuitively felt it was the kind of experience I needed to have to cultivate some sort of psychic balance. Despite this, I had no particular expectations of the experience, nor did I have a clear idea of what it would involve. I think it's quite possible to enter the program looking for something very specific and end up disappointed. I would particularly advise against the almost certainly crushing mistake of coming to it full of idyllic pastoral imagery and notions. The stereotypical picture our society has of country life and farming is a collective construction that, in typical fashion, romanticizes an ailing facet of the culture without even beginning to do justice to the reality of it. Like the perfect mother and the good soldier, the hardworking, honest farmer sticking by good old-fashioned principles is a fiction of cultural consciousness that speaks to the deep-seated need to organize the world with simple, readily understood archetypes. It may be easy to claim exemption from harboring this somewhat archaic ideal, but our conceptions of farming in particular have suffered a renaissance of romanticism with the growth of ecological sensitivity and the desire, in itself well placed and necessary, to "get back to basics." How this truly plays out is at once harsher and more wonderful and varied than any easily formed ideas about it. Because you are responsible for facilitating the growth of life you depend upon, you bring into the fold of your awareness and your scope of sensitivity hidden universes of cycles, rhythms, and patterns which come to define, to be the very measure, of your own inseparable existence. Re-learning the arts of communing with land, water, and sky is among the most demanding commitment anyone can undertake because it can only be embarked upon with your whole self. An innately holistic venture, it cannot be undertaken half way. But this should in no way be daunting. Mindfulness and consistent practice are required above overt effort or skill. Approaching with only these unassuming qualities, demanding nothing and receptive to everything, the rest comes naturally.

Letter From Sneem (a poem for Kaliana)

All seems well in Sneem,
But I arrived after much difficulty:
A traversing of three cultures, four years awaiting, and two-dozen uncertainties
But I AM here.
Their accent helps
To find a match with a dream and song

They are Kerry-stern here.
They farm, no, worship, the sun, the wind and the water like their ancestor druids did
But they call it "alternative technology"

What do I do here, with them?
How can I tell them about my dreams and songs?
Will they hear them?
Will I hear theirs?

But it is MY PLACE now
It is my CHOOSING
And it might become MY SONG TOO:
The song of wind beating sunrays,
The song of water beating wind,
Even all the songs I ever heard dancing to the sun or the wind

I AM HERE!

All seems well in Sneem,
But I arrived after much difficulty:
Try to save money, try not to impose, try to make things better.
I AM here.
Their accent helps
To find a match with a dream and song

They are Kerry-stern here.
I work, they feed me; I work more, they feed me Sneem more.
I am a *WWOOFER* now, I WOLF THEIR FOOD DOWN!
I am also feeding on something else I know not.
No one can feed that to me
Whatever it is, it is soul-rich
Whenever it happens, I will know if satisfied.

I AM HERE . . .
MY PLACE . . .
MY CHOICE . . .
I WILL TIE THE SNEEM KNOT MY WAY.

Chapter Ten

Conclusion: Moving Forward or Staying Behind

I sense that my boat has touched, deep down there something great.
And nothing happens! Nothing . . . . Quietness . . . . Waves . . . .

Nothing happens? Or has it all happened, and we are here, quietly, familiar
with the New?

—Juan Ramon Jimenez[137]

The above poem by the Spanish poet Juan Ramon Jimenez vividly suggests, to me at least, the ambiguity that exists about any great idea. In our journey through life, we are bumped by or bump into great ideas, important movements, or even tsunamis. Or Noah's Ark, like Jimenez's boat, sometimes bumps into the post reality of a universal deluge without definite news that something capital has transpired except for the incessant water that does not seem to go away. Much like Noah, we expect to see a white dove bringing an olive branch, a confirmation that we have finally arrived at a mature and indispensable truth or final address, perhaps even expecting a promise that things will never be this bad or wet again.

I think all has happened. I think that the promise was kept, but that we have screwed things up again. By a lucky accident or as a teleologically expected anthropocentric principle still argued about, we have arrived at our destination: *the malicious ape is now almost the master of his disaster—a vulture on a heap of trash.* With the conquering, bullying, destroying, and contaminating of the world, once awash and clean with promise, we have negated the gift.

More troubling and disconcerting, according to a new Gallup Poll, 57% of the US population believes in the biblical, literal description of the creation of the world,[138] and this was not in their poll, but hypocritically defiles the work of their master. Does that mean that we have developed a convenient amnesia about Noah's Ark, white doves, and olive branches? Is belief in the literal description of creation rescuing us from our own broken promises? Are we so defiant of god, so ungrateful, that six days of his godly work on our behalf means nothing to us? Is our own ecologically manufactured disaster (created by greedy design) BLASPHEMY?

I suspect that a few of us are not "here, quietly, familiar with the new." The new is BAD, is UGLY, and has no SPIRIT—'tis god-less. Most of all, the new is making us very sick and taking the whole world with it. Do we act: jump boat, become agitated, become indignant, and work to save ourselves and the rest of the dying planet, or do we stay in the boat wondering what bumped it? Do we move forward or stay behind, kill everything in sight?

I Am Deliberate: A Recapitulation

I cannot answer any of the above questions for the rest of the world with any degree of confidence or enthusiasm. But I can tell you that the height of my developmental awareness-boat did bump into Buddhism, and then into Deep Ecology, and into Paul Shepard's works, and then into Ecopsychology. And these were BIG ideas, and they were and are GOOD ideas. They are good ideas because they are about keeping mythical promises about the balance of LIFE. They are good ideas because they are about, deliberately, walking a sane path and saving the planet in the process.[139] They are good also because they stand for service—service to us and service to the entire planet.

I believe *"that my boat has touched, deep down there something great."* It is the possibility for renewal, redemption, a way out, a deeper way in, and the opportunity to do my duty. In all these things and doings I take possession of my own *ecopsychological unfolding*, a return trip to ancient life, or life not so ancient but ignored and disrespected. In all these things I make the lives and deaths of my most remote ancestors, Paleolithic or otherwise, worthwhile. I am deliberate in saying that I will not forget their efforts and communion with nature. I cannot forget for my own sanity. I play the didgeridoo for the same reasons.

I see Heinz Droz in me all the time. I talk to him a lot and send him for long walks in the deep freeze of winter when he is being contrary or lazy. That is a start. I also have compassion for the Droz in me as well as all the *androidzes* ambulating through black and white pictures of their own creation or with the assistance of irresponsible leaders and the collusion of profit-driven-only corporations. I have to be compassionate, otherwise nothing makes sense and I injure myself anyway, directly. But being compassionate is very, very hard.

I track animals' minds into the forest. And those actions connect me with a world of entirely new possibilities. They are not-for-profit possibilities. Their tracks end where mine began, in circles, and spirals, and in concentric circles. Their minds begin where mine ends, or my thoughts flourish when they dream. Tracking is definitely a *doing* and also a *thinking*. Tracking is also *wandering* where animals want to *wander* and I must follow. It isn't staying home being gluttonous with food. It isn't cursing at snowmobiles for making noise or spewing fumes. Besides, the "bones" of snowmobiles will never be found. I read between words and under words, especially when the words were crafted with the intention to deceive and with the intention of injuring or taking more of the natural world. I teach others to deconstruct propaganda both from within, setting limitations, and also from without, brainwashing whole generations into being less than human: *inhuman, never becoming the animal we were meant to be.* To be called a beast is no insult to the automaton that forgot what animals are. The human-animal must reject the automaton.

I understood, almost too late, that I was a fabrication of misguided expectations. Someone wanted me to be like him or her, or dance with her, or uphold some second-born law, like obey the first-born. These mediocre selves were recognized as silly homunculi or fake dolls and were destroyed in a joyous bonfire of liberation long ago. Still, the Self needs props on the way to individuation. Totemic identification works for me because, unfortunately, most of the human archetypes that are GOOD are also dead. Their representatives took a long vacation and they have not returned. So I dance like a very specific type of animal. I steal its song and its dance. I carve its image in my chest. I wear a mask that I carved to dance this animal. The mask looks like the animal and me, together in one body. The mask is more real than being a second-born, or the son-of-somebody. Better than a mask is an entire body armor of fur and feathers.

There are cosmic rules, but they are existentially simple. Growth and development are *possibility*, fuel is *energy*, and home is *safety*. Sometimes we stay too long at home and thus reduce *possibility*. Sometimes we consume too much *energy* and become fat, which also reduces *possibility*. Matrices bump into one another, give and take, but when they take too much at the same time, other matrices suffer; other matrices are robbed of *possibility*. *Matricial* existential reality rediscovers the law of interconnectedness: *everything does the same things, except a little bit differently. Humans are not that special.*

I also suspect that future generations will be better Earth companions than we were to the extent that they will have to fix the wrongs we have committed. One lives for the now or one lives for the future. If one lives for the future, then children and forests are first, toys are second. Our daughter, barely 19, worked for food and shelter in order to learn about green technologies on a farm in Seem, Ireland, when her own father barely grasped ecological realities in his late twenties. The future is smarter, they will have to be. The future is stronger. They will have to be to carry their forced upon burden.

I understand why shamans and totemic worship existed. I understand their key socio-ecological functions and why, without those functions, mad preachers of doom seduce us into forgetting our natural origins, and why zoos incarcerate animals, or butchers serve them, soul-less, wrapped in plastic and Styrofoam. When butchering is not part of killing, or when eating animal souls-with-their-bodies is not part of butchering and killing, then, we get mad cow disease or go mad because we are not killing, butchering, and taking our protein sacrament. *I also understand that dreams and visions are part of flesh and that flesh that dreams produces art that dreams of flesh, blood, and spirit.*

All these things that my boat of life bumped into feel right and ring true. The same truth is told the world over, in some fashion or another, by all religions, and consistently predicts whether the bearer of truth deserved to live and die in this wonderful blue bubble. And, finally, to erase the idea that this is just a deep ecological Buddhist story, I will leave you with one of "our own." Father Guye does the talking now. He is tougher and wiser than I so perhaps his words carry more weight than my ecopsychology one-Swiss-Franc tour. Whether a cross, a wolf, a shaman, a raven, a youth pondering these thoughts, LIFE awaits your *actions*.

The Old Church (semi-fiction)

I climbed the polished four hundred year-old stone hewn steps and sneaked inside the old chapel through massive wooden doors. Later, Father Guye told me that when they restored these doors back in 1945, the steel hardware that replaced the crumbling iron came from a wrecked building in *Guernica*, the Basque country. That wrecked building, back in *Guernica*, had been the last refuge of 120 peasant mothers and their children when the Nazis, under Franco's orders, razed the proud Basque town in the middle of their well-attended afternoon market with the most modern destructive war power the world had ever known.

An agnostic ex-Catholic turned Buddhist, I was merely there to get away from the frigid mountain cold after a long hike, and because inside the chapel it smelled like the musty comfort of a Zen monastery. I entered like a thief, dripping melting snow on rock that had received blood and sweat from other criminals and heretics. My guilty eyes, not knowing which saint they should avoid, were drawn to the immense white-gray altar. Majestic under the golden light of a porthole high above it, it reminded me of something, like the ocean reminds one of eternity, or the savannahs bring back the desire to run free and suck blood.

Twenty feet before one could reach the golden altar, there was a bronze plaque that informed any criminal or tourist who could read Swiss French that the altar was made of solid blocks of sea salt mined, by hand, in Northern Africa and carried on the backs of camels to Tunisia to be sold. Not believing what I had read, I approached the altar and was about to lick it when a priest, in a patient but firm voice said: "You do not want to do that, you may get very sick!" Without waiting for my reaction, he quickly went to the opposite end of the altar, and chipped a bit off and handed to me. He made a motion with his only hand, one eye, and single arm that I should put it in my mouth. "This piece is safe, it has not been licked by others." I did what he said and, amazingly, tasted not salt, but an ancient ocean with fish in a far away seabed. He laughed at my reaction, and said, "There, you had your communion."

Father Bernard Guye then asked me to promise him that I would not bring a thousand American tourists to do the same. Since the bequest seemed more like the final word of an informal confession, I nodded to the one-armed, one-eyed, military old priest who could have sentenced me to a lot worse, like five hundred Hail Marys while doing the same number of push-ups. As it turned out, Father Guye had served in the Swiss Army and, used to climbing these mountains every day for almost his entire seventy-years, was intimidating enough to elicit, if not instantaneous conversion, at least a life-long unbreakable promise. I gave it, and so far, I have not broken it even though Father Guye is now dead. He died in his sleep two years after I had met him. Dry salty patches, tears or an ocean once, held on to his wrinkles.

"Out of salt!" I said in my atrocious Swiss-French, and it almost sounded like I had said, "Out of Soul!" "Yes," he responded, "we take faith very seriously in this valley." He was looking back at the altar with an undecipherable expression. "But the porthole, and the rain, and . . .", and he thought but did not say it, "and those desperate, salt-deprived agnostic unfaithful who are determined to empirically confirm the fact that, indeed, this holy table is not merely table salt but the real thing, the skeleton of a pre-historic African Ocean." "Faith is an act, a demonstration, not a phrase," he said enigmatically still looking at the altar. And finally, "We don't tempt God with the altar, rather God invites our trust. The sea-salt was a gift from the poor. They believed that that salt would endure the long desert journey, the thieves, and the camels. I, because THEY believed it, so believe, so we must ALL believe. That altar, minus the chip I just gave you and a few other licks, from humans and rain, has endured at this site for one-hundred years."

That afternoon, I learned many incredible things about this chapel, its crippled priest, and his ministry. When I asked him about the obvious and out of place gigantic First Aid box next to the baptistery, he said that he stored a supply of clotting agent for the babies of a hemophiliac family, just in case. He also bathed babies with AIDS into the Lord who were saved by African surrogate mothers from an earlier death, and who were brought to Switzerland by his fellow missionaries.

The church bells, I learned, were donated over two hundred years ago by all the farmers in the valley who lost over five hundred cows to war and hunger in a single season. They took all their cowbells, added old bronze from broken cannons, from other wars, and forged a triplet of metal voices that still crash with a proud din through the snow and ice. Sometimes, when the autumn wind is just right, and the triplets ring unusually clear and mellow, it seems to their descendants as though a massive herd of unseen animals walks through the fog announcing its return to the wintering stables.

I never asked him directly, but I felt sad about and intimidated by his crippled body. The next day, the old matron who ran the restaurant told me that Father Guye was part of a minority of French-Swiss who had fought alongside the Americans against the Germans. During his service, his best friend had stepped on a land mine and the explosion killed his army buddy instantly and had taken Father Guye's right arm, well, right off. His right eye was hit by a small bit of shrapnel, and for a while, it seemed that he was not going to lose it. But then it turned gray and then white, and one day, it fell out onto his pillow, hard as a pigeon's egg.

"Your timing is excellent," said Father Guye. I thought that he was referring to something serendipitous and quaint like he was about to ring the famous bells or milk the goats and I could help him, when he asked, "You are about forty-five? No? Yes?" "Yes," I said "fortyish-something," not liking the fact that I looked it. "This is when you all return to the altar." He looked at the pile of well-placed salt slabs. "I was just wet and cold and . . . ," He interrupted my excuses, "There is a restaurant down the hill, it is open, it is warmer than this old chapel, and they serve fantastic food." I was puzzled, he was not. He gave me a collusive look and declared with one-eyed mystical certainty, "You all come back to the cross, for the cross." I began to mount an argument, all in bad French, that I was still an agnostic Buddhist, that nature was my goddess and lover, and that I trusted evolution. He said, "None of that matters. I too believe in evolution, my ancestors were Helvetians, Celts, this old Chapel sits on top of old pagan ruins; the entire walls are covered with oak-leaved men and forest dwellers." (They were, and I had thought that very strange.) He saw the confusion in my eyes and added, "What I meant was that you came for what the cross *represents*," and in Latin he said, "*veritas, aequitas, recolitos, maiestas.*"—truth, justice, honor, and dignity.

I later learned that he had used very different Latin connotations for those words. For example the word *aequitas*, although it can be used to signify *justice*, means more *fairness* and *equity* than our English word justice. That is, he could have used the more legal term *justitia* or *justicia*. He also used the Latin word *recolitos*, meaning *venerable* and *worshipful*; and the word *maiestas* means *majesty* and *greatness* more than it means *dignity*.

He continued a well-rehearsed mystic speech for lost fortyish-year-old foreign pagans, the kind of quick sermon one expects to hear in a hundred little chapels and grand churches on the way to Compostela. Only that this was meant for ME.

"The four corners of the cross are the cornerstones of truth, justice, honor, and dignity. This old pagan and Christian chapel is that cross. A GOOD life, a life worth living, is living and growing within those walls no matter who makes the cross." He said this in a conspiratorial and heretical low voice. "Or even whether it is a cross," and now he looked blasphemous "Beyond those walls are error, sickness, and evil." It seemed to me that he indicated the outside of the naves of the chapel but now I am sure that he meant this in a mythical rather than a literal way.

I repeated them, "Truth, equity, veneration, and majesty." Later on, a Jesuit friend of mine said that all those meanings are inclusive. He said, "If it helps, think of them as seven sacred seals instead." But the walled-in room metaphor stuck.

I made a little speech of my own, confident now, dry and getting more comfortable on the hard pew. "But Father, facts, veracity, a true path, do they apply to all things, animate and inanimate and to their interactions?" He answered as if I were no longer there. "Veracity, *veritas*, transcends our species, even the animate or the inanimate. To be holy, to be whole, to be true to one's biological and ontological potential, is to accept the truth, to abide by justice, to acknowledge and cherish, and to have a place in creation where one can express one's potential without robbing that potential indiscriminately. Rob any one thing from creation of these truths and rights and you have evil, *dedecus*. Really, it is easier for mere mortal creatures to act out *fides*, faith, to have it, when we live surrounded by all of them. And if all of us act this way, there is no longer the need for faith. And if we teach and leave this wisdom as our legacy, then we have a good tradition, and the tradition becomes the correct myth."

"If I do not *act in truth*, *re vera*, then *Iniquitas*, injustice, soon follows. My honor is then degraded or tainted, *dedecor*, to a mere ornament, *decus*, blindingly striking my enemy: myself. Human dignity disappears as we sacrifice truth. All four are a grand tautology, seemingly illogical on the surface, connected by imperfect human words as they are, but existentially true nevertheless because all four words stand for existential process-facts, what is and what is not, also, an implication of what should be."

He wiped sweat from his wrinkled brow, and repeatedly, drew geometric schemes on the stone rocks that I now reproduce (Figure 5):

He continued, "In that raw nature of yours, the infirm deer is killed by the wolf, *veritas* and *aequitas*. Equally, the strong deer evades the wolves and passes on strength and ability, again, *veritas* and *aequitas*. Both the herd and wolf pack depend on their leaders' strength and skills to survive and thus they are bestowed *recolitos*, and *maiestas*. A time comes when the old deer knows it cannot outrun the wolf and it is killed, but it saves the herd with its last breath. Or the time comes for the alpha leader to make room for the younger one. Efficient and ordered ascendancy and yielding are also *recolitos* and *maiestas*. Inside our bodies too the cross lives: *Truth* about what the body needs and when, or if at all. *Justice* if we do right by the body and bring it back to its intended biological aims and functions. *Honor* and *dignity* in what a tuned body can achieve, in how it thinks, in what it knows, and in how it moves. Breathing, the right breathing, is the hub of the cross, *Goodness*. Goodness brings *clarity*: PRANA."

I felt as if I had come out of a trance when he slapped his one good left arm hard on my sensationless leg and said, "My chapel is not a motel, is a sanctuary. Go and be *fortyish* somewhere else." Father Guye disappeared behind the blocks of salt looking up to the porthole as it began to rain once again. I took his words to be orders again and left for the warm restaurant and the *Auberge*.

From time to time, I take my own copy of his sweat-drawing when I walk in the woods and when I think about ecology. From time to time, this world seems to be in balance, especially where I am in awe of and understand the natural processes occurring before and within me, one that extends the *good life to all things*, balances *Veritas, Aequitas, Recolitos*, and *Maiestas*. Clarity.

A Poem

I have written poetry for the last thirty years. Most of it I keep for myself and guard as secrets or share with special friends. Other poems I send under pen names, male or female, Slavic or Latino, to publishers around the world as messages in a bottle, as an exercise in detachment, and in order to transcend the boundaries of my smaller self. It is strange and funny to encounter your poem as a Chinese woman living in Poland ten years after the fact. Mostly I write poetry as a transcendental exercise to remove cozy, social "Me" from deeper "I". Lately, perhaps because it's winter, I have been writing a lot in a gloomy quasi-recapitulating sort of way. I wrote one poem that reminded me of life-long transcendental tasks. The poem is now being guarded by a whole lot of electronic demons inside a virtual file. But I thought, after writing this final chapter, and to close in symmetry after Jimenez's better poem, that it was time to liberate it. It is titled,

Screaming at archetypes . . .

. . . feeling at the cusp of some great thing
At the dripping end of an icicle
Dicing ice blue water onto
A dead jay's silent beak

It's been that way since I almost fell
Onto a eagle's back, flying downward
To a valley I once knew:
An oak-green strip of heaven

. . . feeling at the edge of a broken river
When rivers awake to spring
When rivers wake with water green
Onto a salmon's mating memory
It's been that way since I could have
Kissed Isabel, but never did
Since I almost took that trip to India
In the seventies

. . . feeling at the cusp of some great thing
At the dripping end of a rose's thorn
Crying phosphorescent green blood onto
A Buddha's eternal eye

It's been that way since I almost swam
Alongside a dolphin's wake
To an island that was named after me
Inhabited by no one but me

. . . feeling almost tense, like a hero is tense before saving the world
. . . feeling quasi-noble in a yellow robe medicating herbs to *passersbyes*
. . . feeling almost thin, like Gandhi was thin when he threw salt back to the ocean
. . . dancing on the edge of a crystal cup neither falling out nor in
. . . clasping, gasping for quiet air that wants to scream something important
. . . walking on thin ice that never breaks
. . . playing a flute that never sings
. . . running like a three-legged coyote
. . . wearing an old mask that does not scare
. . . walking on shoes that are too small
. . . feeling a body that does not belong
. . . wearing a soul that does not bond
. . . immersed in earth and yet alone
. . . screaming at archetypes that won't wake up

—Odilon Redon, *Head of a Martyr*, photograph of original, 1882

Appendix I

Enrico Passeo on Ecopsychology

"We semioticians owe too much. We are, really, antiquarians. We are always in obligation to the copious foundational ideas of too many writers. Thus, maintaining an original stance and perspective in semiotic writing is as difficult as being a creative historian without the risk of changing history itself. Depending on what we happen to be writing about on a given day, semiotic writing is an interminable and intense labor of annotations, historical references, legends and antiquities . . ."

—Enrico Passeo, *On Singularization*

Some readers may recognize the above passage as a fictional conversation that Enrico Passeo, my heteronym in the footsteps of Fenando Pessoa,[140] might have had with Jorge Luis Borges, when Borges, fictionally, said about semiotics: "es una labor intensa de anotaciones interminables de historia, leyenda, y antigüedades." Enrico is now dead—I "killed" him in Patagonia three years ago. A heteronym is more than a pen name; it is an almost concrete personalization, made much more real by allowing a significant aspect of one's personality to have its own literary life and biography.

Enrico Passeo, being a much older person than I am, could get away with assailing topics that "I" might not have without "his" courage. Also, as I was able to express myself through Enrico, I produced work that I might not have had the courage to present. The three sections that follow were part of a larger body of work that resulted in publications of biosemiotic articles, poems, and aphorisms. This is what is left of that body of work that pertains to ecopsychology proper.

In *Thoreau Misses an Ecopsychological Opportunity,* "Enrico" addresses the accepted notion that Thoreau *ecosophy* is a personal compromise between an idealized pastoral setting balanced against a fairly tame forest, not true wilderness. Not a true cynegetic conversion, Thoreau's is still an enviable ecopsychological role model of seeking, deliberately, simplicity and communion with nature. I thank him personally for having inspired me to extend his "wandering" concept as an ecopsychological practice.

In *I Am Jorge's Heteronym: Here is My "Life"* I attempted to transcend my own ego to produce a living voice. In this section Enrico is making a significant biosemiotic point as it relates to spirituality and the all-out expression of a physical body. Finally, the sketch of *The Ecopsychological and Corrective Force of The "Barbarian"* was crucial to the later development of the *singularization* and the *Lebeinsneid* papers presented earlier.

1.   Thoreau Misses an Ecopsychological Opportunity

I am not a transcendentalist because I cannot imagine what the "higher levels" are supposed to be like, or determine at all if I am moving in "that direction," but I do admire the transcendentalists' intimation with nature and their efforts to connect the 'spiritual,' however defined by each individual, to nature. I find myself quoting Emerson and Thoreau because they often cite a naturalistic and semiotic relationship between everlasting poetry and literature as derived from close contact with the natural. Thus, I am in agreement with both in finding causality between what I have termed in earlier essays as "epiphaneous thought" or as "thinking-in-epiphanies." In earlier essays, I have speculated that the original mind was of nature and so was the source of creative thinking, so long as this mind maintained close physical proximity and was nourished by primordial experiences. This is in agreement with the *pansemiosis* of Jorge Conesa (1999) who argues for a seamless extension between psycholinguistics and matricial existential doings rooted in the properties and functions of three elemental variables for *daisen*: a concern for *Safety*, the pursuit and expression of *Possibility* or opportunity, and both supported by energetic requirements, or the presence or absence of *Energy*.

Thoreau purposely seeks this connection with wilderness, empirically, as if to convince himself of its value and importance. By his active exploration of wilderness Thoreau stands for the metaphor of the civilized pilgrim rediscovering the *barbaric within*—but not quite. He also makes a *pansemiotic* argument when he argues that wilderness is the source of the good and of the creative text in the first place. In one of these trips, maybe the most important one for his environmental philosophy of *balance*, I will argue, Thoreau climbs Mount Katahdin in Maine. At the zenith of this experience he responds with the fear of all civilized humans to this desolate experience and writes:

"She (the mountain) does not smile at him as in the plains" and describing the mountain as "a place for heathenism and superstitious rites, to be inhabited by men nearer of kin to the rocks and wild animals than we."

From this and other experiences that Thoreau did not leave in writing or speech evolves his notion of an ideal dialectics between a limited scaled down civilization (as in the Concord of the mid 1800's) and wilderness as forest or woods: rural existence, the pastoral. This harmonious balance for Thoreau still allows the mind to construct new things, to tap into two worlds of creative sustenance. Living as I do partly in Patagonia and partly in Rio de La Plata, and deriving dual compensation from inhabiting both creative realms, I too identify with his insight. The deep ecologist in me though will also argue for the intrinsic value of raw, impenetrable nature that neither Thoreau nor I will (should?) ever venture into.

But going back to Thoreau's experience atop Mount Katahdin as the springboard to the conclusion and title of this essay, Thoreau's sentiment can nowadays be scientifically explained as the reflection and fear of a truly African mind encountering mountainous high places for the first time. Empirical evidence from *biophilic* authors such as Ulrich, Kaplan & Kaplan, and Orians have convinced me at least that the origin of the mind-text is more African, from its savannahs, than from Mount Everest or Ararat. Thoreau's Concord mind first evolved in the African savannah, according to these authors, thus one would expect it to react with aversion and fear to finding itself lost in a zenith of rock. Ulrich, Kaplan & Kaplan, and Orians would smile, if they have not already, at Thoreau's comment that "She (the mountain) does not smile at him as in the plains."

Mountains are awesome and sacred places precisely because they are inhospitable and distant. They are awesome because the proto-human mind did not evolve there nor can it procure an easy living on their granite slopes. They become mythical (Olympus, Ararat, Kulshan, Rainier, etc.) entities where only infrequent visitors such as aboriginal teenagers, Moses, or Thoreau are willing to risk death and discomfort while grasping transcendental truths or in order to achieve manhood after a prescribed puberty ritual only to return to the valleys or "plains." Now, many cultures, and in contradiction to Thoreau's sentiment, dwell in high abodes and their response to altitude is far different than fear. Perhaps these are new, unique or desperate adaptations and represent only a minority of preferences.

Thoreau's environmental, philosophical, and religious compromise—a balance and harmony to be found in rural or pastoral living—is, I believe, a consequence of this event and a confirmation that a distant African mind-text and message was received in Maine, atop Mount Katahdin. The semiotician in me cannot help assuming that evolutionary adaptation as text has reached over millennia into the tired body and sensitive mind of Thoreau and offered (re-wrote) an ancient signifier, safe-plain, while using the oldest sign: emotional foreboding and fear. Thoreau himself embodies an ancient Piercian triad, or at the very least, the sign, fatigued-and-fearful-in-the-mountain, resonated with his interpretant limbic system to understand that his ancestors never did this sort of sport.

However successful Thoreau is in interpreting this African message by reacting with dread, this trans-generational communication leads to another textual confusion that engenders his philosophy: the rejection of the truly wild and awesome as potential inspiration for further text! That is, Thoreau will never again risk these wilder experiences or allow an incursion into further dialogue with mountain. If he did, he might not have secured a literary place as a Transcendentalist but might have become instead a wilder Muir or a Whitman.

2.   I Am Jorge's Heteronym: Here is My "Life"

Jorge Conesa has forced me to write this introduction! The following text is an involuntary act on my part. Jorge is asking me to remember a time or place when/where semiotics begins for me. I tell him he does not know anything about semiotics or *multidetermined signification* because otherwise he would not ask such a stupid thing of an old man. However, he is also posting some of my work on "the web," mostly for his amusement I think, so I will concede to the guilt of writing something so intimate. Here it goes.

People who, like Jorge, are foolish enough to come to me and ask me about my field of continuous learning, semiotics, and ask for a succinct explanation and justification for my livelihood usually end up hearing the following real account which, as a manner of an introductory koan, stays with some as a bothersome idea, or becomes an instant revelation and understanding of my devotion to what I do. I don't care either way.

After this very short tale, I will add definitional components that come from the field of *ecopsychology* and give a fuller view of the semiotic and biosemiotic enterprises as I pursue them. This personal story is easy to prove because I have a remarkably long and thin scar running down the left side of my face from the end of my brow to the end of my lip. This sign/symbol is at least three inches long.

I have been a trail runner since when I was about 13 years old, and on an early summer day, I ran down a rocky hill and olive grove on a farm belonging to my Uncle Tito, near Sorrento. On that particular occasion and sibling race, for a moment that seemed a lifetime, I experienced my first and only runner's *oceanic* or *peak moment*. Running carelessly downhill, as fast as my skinny Italian legs could carry me, I heard my brother's and sister's voices and cries growing dimmer and distant as my gallop, it seemed to me, slowed down to a kind of timeless glide or floatation. All sounds ceased, even the sound of my didgeridoo-like breathing (Jorge forced me to make this analogy). As far as I can recollect this experience now, I don't remember a self experiencing all this. In front of me, replacing the view of the sea below was a lighter blue sky, tunnel-like. From that lighter space and contrast emanated a vortex, and from the vortex, two hooded human figures (gigantic heads) came out like faster clouds and took positions on either side of me.

I remember exactly what they said next: "This is the emotion of thinking without words." Then, after positioning themselves on either side of my arms, they lifted me higher and higher into this kind of timeless glide with my legs gently and slowly beating the airless and soundless sky. I only know what the word bliss means from this singular experience. What happened after that, given the description of this event by my siblings, is highly contested even today. I remember hearing a loud thump and slowly, as if waking up from a dream, becoming aware that my face and head hit a large old olive tree, the gushing of warm blood down my cheeks and mouth, its coppery taste, and then a dark olive-green blackness. I vaguely remember waking up to a cacophony of human voices expressing their own pains in a hospital room in Sorrento. I was in and out of consciousness several times. So I have several fragmented memories of my parents as they sat or walked about in the room smiling and talking to me. I remember not being able to talk because of the stitches and bandages and the pain in my face and mouth. I wanted to tell my parents what I had experienced, about the flying, and to let them know that my pain was not that bad. I tried to smile and that brought an expression of concern to my mother's face because, as she told me later, it looked to her like I was in terrible pain.

The memories of being in the hospital are few and imprecise. But I do remember going back to the hill with my siblings and listening to their account of my "incredible leaping fall." My brother (Bruno) and sister (Marcella) concur that at one point during our downhill race I indeed leaped into the air briefly only to land against the tree with a terrible and brutal force. My sister remembers crying and running uphill to get Uncle Tito. My brother remained there where I was bleeding, holding me on his lap. My uncle Tito remembers me muttering something about hooded men. This is the end of my personal story.

I have (and do occasionally as an adult) run down the same Italian hill and stopped by the same tree. I have spent many times thinking about that day while sitting by that olive tree which also wears a scar from my teeth and bones. I wonder what stories it tells to other trees and to sensitive humans about that day. I wonder if this tree "saw" the hooded beings or was part of a supernatural conspiracy playing the role of a catcher-of-faces-after-epiphanies. I have not experienced an oceanic moment like that in ten thousand subsequent runs. At most, sometimes on good runs, I pretend that my legs beat the thin air instead of the ground and that someone supports my weight while I fly. But since that day, other knowledge has come to replace that memory, and now we come to the subject of semiotics proper.

I said earlier that I am a trail runner (less so at this moment of arthritic pain). Partly, I run in the hills and countryside hoping to recapture the event in Sorrento. But mostly I run on rugged terrain in forests, sand, or grasses because *I believe I am in conversation with a sentient topology.* This sentient topology is no *Gaia.* It is only sentient in the sense that my primate-complex brain, with the rest of its body running, is being fed extremely complex, variant and fast changing information; my body and the ground are in semiosis. In that interpretation, my feet have to accommodate an uneven terrain full of small pebbles, larger rocks, thorny bushes, soft grasses, mud, water, sand, dust, uphill and downhill slopes, and a myriad of countless other terrain features. The ground receives from me: a trail, pounding, scrapes, the dispersion of seeds and bugs, and its flattening and commercial ornamentation by my plantiferous Nikes.

Unlike treadmill exercising or city block-pavement running, trail running demands immediate perception as well as sharper and instantaneous decision-making. One false move and one might find himself/herself kissing an olive tree, or worse, a rock! In this sense, trail running is closer to authentic, in-your-face discourse and communication than to ornate and regulated formulaic conversation. In short, my primate brain has thus to interpret, accommodate, and make fast decisions based on these multiples and fast occurring sensations and perceptions. My primate brain is performing and ancient hunter-gatherer chase and dance. It is doing what it evolved to do even though Enrico, presently, is not chasing big game or being chased by a leopard. All these running computations and experiences are combined into a more or less unified experience, my consciousness, itself dynamically changing moods and reflecting on a larger, more abstract experience. Finally, running on cross-country trails is all about relating the cognitive-physiological system to an immense world of raw and untamed data-possibilities, which on a country trail are rich and diverse, pregnant with its potential to inform and to adhere to the interlocutor part of a natural dialogue. This possibility and richness can in turn be recoded only as history with language.

And here comes an important biosemiotic point: *Even before language editorializes the last details of my experience "running," the unconscious cognitive-physiological system has already been involved in an authentic semiotic transaction.* Externally, the intelligence and brain that inhabit my body are forced to reckon with a natural *Telos* that must be interpreted continuously and authentically at that primitive level if the resulting experiences-as-gains are to be real. Additionally, my body is communicating within, *endosemiotically,* when hormones, neurotransmitters, receptors, muscles, and firing impulses are maintaining a certain level of athletic performance in response to my behavioral choices. Kinesthetic intelligence is in this sense pre-verbal. *This is the ontogenetic continuity of Piaget's sensorimotor stage preserved in the adult, where the logic of space and what the body senses and experiences in space give rise to intelligence at large*. The secret revealed to me by my fantastic air giants, namely that my conscious elation was "the emotion of thinking without words," is *a kind of preamble to the semiosis of human language*. It is ultimately *biosemiosis* because so much information has been exchanged already about experiencing the world, being one with the world before uttering disgusting words.

In short, *interpretation is demanded naturally by existence, interdependence, and survival*. Thus *interpretation* precedes language production, and most of the time, acknowledging understanding requires *any behavior* not exclusively speech or vocalization. The great British actor Anthony Hopkins can convey a huge repertoire of emotions and internal states with a few gestures and hints of behaviors. As far as I know, all children are natural runners and many might have experienced the pre-linguistic moment I described earlier. I will speculate that most mammals are capable of experiencing oceanic moments as well. Capturing ancient Being to me is one of the tasks of semiotics.

My now deceased friend and American Ecologist Paul Shepard was fond of using the English word and modifier "*telluric*" when *adjectivising* the powers and effects of nature. Heiddeger used the word '*telos*' to differentiate a heightened, more meaningful speech from what he referred to as '*gerede*' or noise. The latter he described as self-centered, anthropocentric and ultimately casual forms of speech: dull. I am now struggling with this introduction and essay by citing these superb and deep ecological thinkers and connecting their ideas with a person, and purely fictional self, a semiotic idea or exercise in the making. The scar communicates many things: it is *multidesignated, multidetermined, multisignified* because it was created, it developed and it now resides in the enormous space between the "telluric" and "gerede" and beyond, into the Peircian 'Possibility.'

3. The Ecopsychological and Corrective Force of The "Barbarian"

Barbarians in any age are the natural people with a foreign accent that live "out there" by their own wits. The self-sufficient human is a non-citizen and therefore a threat and an aberration to the necessary codependency of polis. Hive protocol demands hive mentality only: a few figure-eight wiggles of the abdomen to signify a food source. In this sense the hippies, the Vikings, the environmentalists, the ancient Germans, the Mongols, or the Native Americans are/were threats to the status quo of stiff linguistic interpretation and dominance. Barbarians do not need the hive. They rest and eat atop another beast, a horse, or on the folds and embroidery of Earth's mantle. It may be true as Merlin Donald writes that language development comes second to the cognitive organization of interpreting the world in a mythical sense. If so, then there is always a "danger" that within any civilized orthodoxy and linguistic straightjacket there is a small flame of new myths waiting to appear.

The epiphany always threatens with illumination and a desire to interpret the real world, nature at large, as opposed to accepting a prefabricated version of existing orthodoxy in social reality.

The price human existence risks paying when its *daisen* is embedded in complex, literate culture is that limited, pre-ordained, and premeditated language usage may engulf the mind and dull the ancient sensitivities of looking toward nature for creative answers. This is the beginning of the end. The mind risks becoming obese with circular ornamentation that never nourishes and the body soon follows. The antidotes for the orthodoxy of language and mental models are the same as they have always been: new poetry, multilingualism and multiculturalism, the return and the exposure to natural cycles. Civilization-in-balance pays homage to nature by incorporating it in its folklore and existence and when each generation is taught 'out there' the *primeval values*. In Hermann Hesse's Magister Ludi, Joseph's last existential act is a swim in the frigid waters of a mountain lake, a symbol of a return to the simple and the real. Joseph's sophistication in the mastery of the Glass Bead Game, its ornate meditations and protocol, and its connection to a literate elite are engulfed in the end by natural space. This last scene in Hesse's book can be used as a metaphor for the fate of civilized human condition in general if harmony is not found.

Henry David Thoreau described this intimacy and early authentic connection better when he reminded a Concord audience in 1851 of the myth and origins of the city of Rome and the consequences to future and civilized generations of 'disconnection.' He wrote, "It was because the children of the Empire were not suckled by the wolf, that they were conquered and displaced by the children of the children of the northern forests who were." The return to the barbarian, in the 'noble savage' and romantic sense of this phrase, is a return to expressing thinking-in-epiphanies in new language and thinking forms. Language becomes magical once again when both the incantations and the cantors are real and authentic in their contact to the original matrix of experience and being. The sin of civilization is always in danger of being rescued by the barbarian. No sooner has civilization become cozy with extremes of safety and the usurping of individual rights than another myth appears in the horizon atop a dark horse waving a banner with an animalistic emblem. The rider usually speaks a foreign tongue and has unusual table manners. Farting and burping, an earlier and more authentic form of speech and symbol, threaten a comeback. Only the civilized world prohibits farting and burping as linguistic expressions of joy and release since eating is done indoors and in close quarters. Contamination is the greatest fear and ultimate alienation of the civilized mind and speech. But the barbarian eats and sleeps outdoors in the company of horses that happily fart and burp into the wind. "May the wind be in front of you and me in front of the wind," could be an ironic phrase to signify luck only understood by the natural human of prairies and steppes.

In closing, there seems to be no other way for human existence but three manners of being. Either civilization provides a space for barbarism to co-exist with its creations, as in a dialogue in a state of equilibrium and harmony, or barbarism will correct the extreme version of civilized orthodoxy with bloodshed and rock-and-roll music (I choose the former death). Or barbarism reigns alone without some of the advantages and products of civilization, themselves a source of creativity and nourishment for the barbaric.

As in Walden Pond, I believe that the harmonious society sits surrounded by vast natural spaces, human dwellings modestly situated as if not to intrude on nature. The philosopher-as-human and barbarian ekes out a necessary existence from this plenty. She has a cottage, not a useless palace. But the ultimate reward is always inspirational: the ripples on the pond from wind spirit stir intimations within and provide ancient thinking-in-epiphanies. The final philosophy is BALANCE.

—Odilon Redon, *La fleur du marécage:*
une tête humaine et triste, photograph of original, 1885

Appendix II

Prometheus' Curse: Fire as Humanity's Worst Invention

Therefore, humanity has paid a psychological price as well. Today, more and more, we are all ecopsychologically ill, disconnected from Nature-at-large and can no longer read her original bonding instructions. Fire stands between Her and us and burns the manual that could extinguish our anger, instruct our arrogance, and mitigate our deficiencies as a limited species, one more, no more no less.

—Excerpt from this essay

I entered this short essay in a literary contest for the *Ecologist Magazine*'s Annual Essay Competition (2006). Although I did not win this competition, I was happy to use this opportunity to think deeply about the course of human evolution and to ponder about significant "forks on the road." It seems to me, and I still make this argument, that the invention, discovery, and control of fire were a drastic and decisive turn in our proto-human evolution. The argument is one that is uncomfortable to make or to hear because of the obvious virtues of this invention-innovation. But like many obvious things, when one thinks deeply about them, they turn out to have a more sinister, elusive, and unfamiliar element to them.

Prometheus' Curse

Long ago in mythical time, Zeus warned that a humanity who possessed fire would become arrogant and destroy itself. He was quoted then saying something like, "Let humans eat their flesh raw." According to Greek legend, Zeus created the brothers Prometheus (meaning "foresight") and Epimetheus (meaning "hindsight"). Both brothers proceeded to create humanity and animals respectively. Epimetheus bestowed the best gifts to animals leaving his brother Prometheus with only the lesser gifts for the humans. Chided and frustrated, Prometheus went to Olympus and stole the sacred fire and gave it to humanity against Zeus' warnings and prohibitions.

In hindsight, Epimetheus was right, had it, and Prometheus, untrue to the meaning of his name, had no foresight, for humanity has been abusing "the gift of fire" ever since. An entire planet, too, has suffered the consequences of mastering fire. Also in hindsight, Zeus was right in that arrogance is an automatic consequence of power. If anyone knew, it was Zeus, the most arrogant of all the gods.[141]

Making and keeping fire, a discovery, invention, and innovation, are causal and fundamental antecedents that gave rise to humanity changing and destroying entire ecosystems since probably the time of Homo erectus. The invention of making and keeping fire was/is a catalyst for the discovery of basic chemistry that subsequently allowed for technological advances that came to pollute, erode, and ultimately upset naturally occurring geo-biological balances. Even when multiple species benefit directly or indirectly from the consequences of naturally occurring fires, its anthropocentric use and calculated manipulation goes beyond these predictable or avoidable cycles.

Having gained control over fire, even when for a long time slash-and-burn hunting and agriculture were only small sores on planetary natural history, and minimal were their impact, it was difficult for humans *not* to have insights that eventually led to the discovery of ceramics, glass manufacturing, and combustion technologies that gave rise to all sorts of modern-day industries which have had a greater disrupting impact on geo-biological balances than promoting new plant growth in order to attract and kill game ever did.

More specifically, fire, its replication and maintenance by humans, is *humanity's worst invention* to the extent that basic understanding of combustion, oxygenation, oxidation, evaporation, and metallurgy (all phenomena connected with fire manipulation and familiarity of materials thus affected), gave rise to humanly created wars, chemical, and petrochemical industries that eventually supersede the stability of geo-biological balances. A good thing can be spoiled or abused, and so it was with fire and its catalyzing properties.

Finally, the phosphorous match becomes the lethal and quick *simplification* of the need to flick a fire at will based on thousands, even millions, of years of innovation. Thus, a match represents an encapsulated history of humanity's further control and miniaturization or compression of the potential destructive power of the sun on a single red head, making the question possible: *how many devils dance on the head of a match?* An innovation from flint-sparks or even bow-frictional technologies, the match is emblematic of using fire and also of the maturity of the chemistry of combustible substances. It was an Englishman, Robert Boyle, who in 1680, experimented with and noticed that sulfur and phosphorous would, when struck together, burst into a flame.[142] Applying Boyle's discovery, another Englishman, John Walker, in 1827, invented gigantic matches. Safe 'red' matches, however, did not make an appearance until 1855 when a Swede, Carl Lundstrom, invented them. Finally, the matchbox was the serendipitous discovery and further development of an American lawyer, Joshua Pusey, in 1889, who finally sold his idea to the Diamond Match Company. Given our argument that fire was humanity's worst invention, the 1836 term for matches "locofocos" (by match American innovator Alonzo D. Phillips) may be the most apt name for their deadly use and for carrying the *meme* of fire one step further.

It would seem that lighters, not "locofocos", should be emblematic of fire "power" in a increasingly pampered modern world that wraps technological advances around itself as a panacea for all its evils and juvenile demands. However, in the UK alone, children under the age of five playing with matches start more fires, and cause more injuries or deaths, than when playing with lighters.[143] Matches are simple and lethal: light a match and PUFF! there goes the planet. Even a motorically clumsy child can burn a forest with a single match.

The statistics become more dire and grim when we look at the number of deaths caused by cigarette smoking, a fire in one's mouth, second-hand smoking, and forest fires caused by cigarettes or by modern-day and inept hunter-and-foragers. And moving away from this selfish concern, it is un-quantifiable perhaps to even consider the consequences of entire forests going up in flames to clear the way for mono agriculture, burger-cattle, cities or towns, or because the forest, the ultimate bogeyman, stands in the way of "civilized clarity." Fire is an actual and material Kundalini not burning to enlighten but to diminish. Its ashes are simpler to understand, it seems, than entire and complex ecosystems whose intricate LIFE dialectics demands attention and patience.

I readily admit that a roasted pig tastes better than raw and potentially *Trypanosomic* meat. Reading a book by the hearth or singing Cumbayá around a campfire beats freezing in the cold, no doubt. If we concentrate only on the obvious "gains"— personal comfort, gourmet cooking, the rise of civilization, agriculture, the development of chemistry, automaton rovers mapping Martian territory—we might miss the fact that, on balance, these "gains" have come at a greater and real cost—to the planet and other animals—than their purported and publicized superiority by anthropocentric propaganda.

To sum up, the abuse of fire in planetary holocaust against other animals (humanity's envy of Epimetheus' greater gifts to animals), other humans, and entire ecosystems, has changed the face of Earth fundamentally and extensively so, in ways that no other invention has. Killing by holocaust has finally dehumanized us, making for a steeper and more degraded gradient between the "beasts" and the false "demigods," to the extent that a Golden retriever is a better representative of nobility than the primate who went *ashtray*.

Therefore, humanity has paid a psychological price as well. Today, more and more, we are all ecopsychologically ill, disconnected from Nature-at-large and can no longer read her original bonding instructions. Fire stands between Her and us and burns the manual that could extinguish our anger, instruct our arrogance, and mitigate our deficiencies as a limited species, one more, no more no less.

Zeus condemned Prometheus,[144] for giving away the sacred fire and other transgressions, to be accosted by and suffer great physical pain in perpetuity by liver-devouring eagles. According to Greek legend, Prometheus' liver would heal during the night, every night, only to be torn, masticated, and ingested again and again by eagles from sunrise to sunset. That Prometheus was delivered from this unsavory situation and freed by Hercules, is, as they say, another Greek story. But barring a compassionate Hercules on the way to killing more lions, who will deliver the Earth from Prometheus' curse? Can fire even be extinguished anymore?

Robert Graves, (1955). *The Greek Myths.* NY: Moyer Bell Ltd

—Fuseli, *Prometheus*, photograph of original

Appendix III

Elsbeth's Farm Montessori /English Middle School

Day School and Day-Overnight
Neuchâtel, Switzerland

Education in Neuchâtel

The City of Neuchâtel (and surrounding region and cantons) provides the opportunity to immerse the international student, as well as the local student, in a culturally rich, traditionally pastoral, and modern-diverse educational milieu. These cantonal values and opportunities, when combined with a superior and internationally competitive curriculum, have the potential for creating a long lasting cultural bond that connects the present student to the region during developmentally impressionable years and for years to come. The backbone of this heritage is the rural life and long-held customs that support the rich culture of the communes. The founders of Elsbeth's Farm (EF) believe that it is this unique environment and heritage that attracts visitors to our area and helps them decide to stay in our region. It is for that reason that EF has crafted its educational goals and curriculum to maximize these opportunities for educational and personal enrichment. Equally important, EF creates many exploratory opportunities where families from abroad can discover the riches of our canton and city and participate fully in the educational experience of their youth. The availability of many and diverse museums, an extensive natural trail system that can be used in all seasons, and the proximity to our beautiful lake makes education in Neuchâtel an endless adventure.

Mission Statements

1. To assist and train youth learners in acquiring specialized scientific methodology without which students cannot evaluate personal, socially complex, and natural information accurately.

2. To involve learners in epistemological criticism (a critical dialogue about ways of knowing) in all skill areas and fields of inquiry (*metacognitive reasoning*).
3. To inspire learners to contribute their personal commitment and reasoned judgment so they can solve, or inspire others to solve, real problems in the real world: economical, humanistic, artistic, environmental, social, or political.

CONTENTS

I

Introduction

Elsbeth's Farm School (EF) is a continuation of 40 years of combined teaching, counseling, Montessori education, and ecological science education school experiences. Based on Maria Montessori's pedagogical and philosophical ideas of the cognitive, personality and social benefits of immersing the youth in practical living and natural surroundings, **EF** complements her insights with a developmentally current, detailed, and extensive participatory natural history curriculum, round-the-clock educational-psychological counseling, and greater participation and activities in natural or wild spaces. These practices adhere to the highest of American Montessori Society's (AMS) educational standards where youth meet and usually exceed performance standards as compared to children in mainstream academic settings.

The academic demands of global education require that the **EF** youth not only meet Swiss curricula standards (DIPAC objectives and schedule), but will be prepared to meet IB and American AP standards, given diverse educational needs. All along, he/she continues the integration of his/her scientific and personal ecological knowledge, in different fields, with a larger-than-self world and perspective.

Additionally, the instruction and guidance found at **EF** aspires to instill a deeper understanding of the role of nature in forming a healthy and mature individual. This is achieved by fostering authentic interactions with natural spaces and developing affectively mature and scientifically sound relationships with the physical world and its human community in general.

Thus concepts, discussions, and scientific learning of a Montessori and integrated curriculum for grades 4-6 are learned, acted upon, and reiterated during the next developmental phase. This second phase, the focus of **EF's** instruction (Grades 7-9- ages 12-15 years), is more abstract, *and it aims at integrating a perfecting idea of self with social responsibility while entering an introspective, reflective, and physically demanding stage of development.*

This youth-centered scientific and human cultural orientation is integrated across an academically strong curriculum, and continues during international visits. The pedagogy and personal interactive aspects of instruction are carried out with great sensitivity and with the utmost respect for individual differences (physical size, age, gender, talents, temperament, intelligences). These interactions are based on mutual respect, sensitivity to the rights and needs of others, and while adhering to expected and agreed upon norms of civility that characterize healthy camaraderie. With ample parental support, the EF youth, at the end of our program, becomes a confident, sophisticated, and independent individual learner eager to continue to explore (athletically, scientifically, humanistically, or artistically) his/her role in and responsibilities to society, to natural spaces, and to him/herself.

Preliminary Assessment of Cognitive Development With Achievement of Primary Program (Ages 9-12) Mental Skills : (Classification, Concrete Experience-based Learning)

This assessment will determine competency in taxonomic and classificatory knowledge of the natural and human worlds, answering the basic developmental-cognitive needs of this age group: "How many things are there?" "How are they related?" "What is it?" "What does it do?"

"How does it do it?"

II

Secondary Program: Ages 12-15

(Abstract Thinking, Philosophical Inquiry, and Problem Solving)

GOALS: The integration of knowledge within an emerging sense of self and the responsibilities to society. The epistemological quest of asking questions about knowledge itself.

- **Main Subjects**
    - Languages (English-Spanish—the primary languages of instruction, with 2nd language programs In French, and/or German)
    - Math and Geometry (Introduced and integrated as a means toward, and as a practical tool in, discovery and quantification—statistical math, related to other subject areas and includes Introduction to Algebra)
    - Biology (Natural History, Ecology, Anatomy, Physiology, Taxonomy)
    - Earth Sciences (Geology—soils and active landscape; Astronomy; Water sciences—including land-locked hydrology and oceanography)
    - History (Pre-historical, Classical, and Modern History)
    - Geography
    - Civics (including social sciences)
    - Informatics

- **Arts**
    - Drawing
    - Sculpture
    - Pottery
    - Dancing
    - Music making
    - Weaving
    - Sewing
    - Drama (Mimicking, Skits and Plays)

- **Enrichment**
  - Horticulture (See mushroom farm)
  - Gastronomy (Cultural and natural)
  - Tutoring (Taking care of others)

- **Physical Activity**
  - Basketball
  - Soccer
  - Games
  - Skiing
  - Swimming
  - Cynegetic Training: Excursions into the forest (ecological wandering or hiking, tracking and orienting)

- **Basics/Mechanics**
  - Reading
  - Writing
  - Speaking (effective and constructive discourse, dialectics, as opposed to rhetoric)
  - Literature appreciation and discussion

• Rationale for EF Curriculum

The secondary school curriculum addresses the development of abstract thinking, and the deepening of the complexity and the meaning of earlier learning is sought. The above subjects are now breached in philosophical-analytical as well as practical terms. Societal problems are considered and the natural altruism and idealism of this age group is galvanized toward community, environmental, or humanistic goals and problem solving.

For example, while exploring literature, *poetry* becomes a personal exercise and a means of expressing complex emotions and ideas now becoming more important in a self-conscious mind. Reading and writing skills are further developed and utilized while completing and sharing reports, essays, and PowerPoint presentations for the benefit of students and guides. *Understanding philosophical and psychological modes of inquiry and scientific methodology in an attempt to further define a sense of self, who naturally asks existential-personal and ultimate reality questions.* This inquiry includes ecological thinking and lessons about LIFE and interrelatedness to arrive at a location of a healthy and responsible self in the universe as well as in human society.

• Math

All math at this level has a practical aim. It includes the use of statistics and statistical design with the goal of assisting experimental design and final analysis. Data gathering, data organization, data interpretation (Excel, StatView, SuperAnova) are all honed as skills in a variety of projects, studies and presentations. Specific math skills are taught to prepare individual transitions into different academic programs in Switzerland or abroad (could include beginning and/or intermediate level of college math when needed).

• Arts and Enrichment

All these activities are explored and exercised with the aims of discovering and rediscovering individual talents, interests and expertise and can be pursued in earnest as part of other reading, writing and community projects. Understanding artistic expression, in general, becomes an intellectual exploration of understanding its manifestation in religion, social, political, propagandistic, or personal means for communication. Tutoring each other or younger children is an integral component of service to the community and fosters patience with nascent intelligence and behaviors.

• Physical Activity

Playing all the sports mentioned in the primary section continues to be part of maintaining a healthy body and a peaceful mind. Increasing expeditions are taken into natural spaces and wilderness as a means of achieving the further integration of natural historical lessons and as a way of testing skills and knowledge. Early in this program youth is trained in orienting, basic safety-medical-survival, tracking, and foraging in the forest. Mushroom identification and mycological studies of native species are part of a natural gastronomy unit. Within the boundaries of individual physical capacity (never coerced) and under strict supervision, youth is naturally disposed to test its wits and budding physical confidence in a real landscape of rocks, water, forest, and in the presence of other non-human intelligence. Extended, two-day and week-long wanderings into forest and mountain, water and plains not only provide the means to be physically active, but it is part of the life of a natural sciences scientist in the field, or an artist in the field, gathering information and inspiration for further study, reflection, or for archival needs for specimens.

• Basics/Mechanics

Individualized *test tutoring* and preparation is provided, based on individual decisions and choices with respect to transitioning into other schools (for example, practicing tests such as the TOEFL for native non-English speakers or emphasizing DIPAC curricula in transitioning to modernity or lyceum requirements).

• Additional Learning Activities

• Communication.

It continues basic learning of effective discourse but now it includes the semiotic analysis of text itself and the inquiry into the originator of the text and the intention of the text (Who wrote this? For what purpose? In what context?). It also includes the examination and deconstruction of propaganda as one of many uses of language for communicative purposes.

• Book Club
A group exercise of reading and sharing books chosen by students.

• The Socrates Cafe
A dialectic and rule-bound weekly exercise of philosophical inquiry based on topics of personal interest, topics that happen to be salient in the media, or continued from class discussions. Each youth takes a turn leading the discussion of the day.

• Seminars
Bi-weekly university instructional method that demands the reading and discussion of articles relevant to all of the disciplines of study. Seminars are led by an instructor/guide with specific learning objectives and instructional goals in mind. Since seminars demand constant student participation and preparation of materials it is a far superior method of learning. It replaces the uni-directional and passive listening, passive learning mode of the typical lecture and obligates students to stay current in their studies. Seminars also foster the practice and habit of the long-life learner.

• Senior Project : A graduation requirement
The project commences (and continues during) six months before graduation. A cross-curricula synthesis that includes choosing a preferred topic, doing a science-based unit, one artistic component, one cultural or historical unit, PowerPoint or other visual presentation, and a written paper. In addition to preparing the youth for future educational situations where long-term projects lead to specific degree requirement (senior theses, master, or doctorate), the senior project combines diverse learning opportunities and taps into multiple intelligence modalities. Each youth is able to select a set of informational media that best suits his/her capacities and interests while at the same time making sure that basic skills are honed.

III

Special Learning and Recreational Activities

- **International trips (England, Spain, and Italy).** This is an optional trip to a selected country. The trip coincides with week-long local holidays. This is an opportunity for immersing the child in a different culture, language, geography and ecology.

- **Mushroom Cultivation.** Conservation and preservation efforts to save rare mushroom species of our area and cultivation of gourmet species. The cultivation of mushrooms is a multi-curricula effort where children/youth are taught biology, chemistry, botany, economy (mushroom stand and sale), and gastronomy.

- **Skiing.** Two ski resorts are nearby: Les Bugnenets and Crêt du Puy. Additionally, access to the Chemin des Crêtes for cross-country skiing.

- **Horseback Riding.**

- **Windsurfing.** Once a year at lake Neuchâtel.

IV

Additional Services/Activities

- Psychological Counseling

- Day Student Overnight Resident Option

- Professional and Educational Retreats (Summer)

V

Timeline

✓ Tested curriculum in place
✓ Meeting with additional investing parties
✓ Initial securing capital investment in conjunction with additional party available
✓ Principal staff available to prepare and coordinate the purchase of materials
✓ Properties nearby have been visited and real state agents contacted
✓ Tentative permission requested from the city of Neuchâtel for one of the proposed sites
✓ Second language instructors in agreement to teach next year
✓ Agreement with the XXX XXX Center (XXXXX Community College, WA, USA) has been procured to commence foreign student and teacher exchange
✓ Two three-year business and financial plans have been prepared contingent on a decision about one of two properties that seem promising
✓ Meeting with Mme.XXXXXX to coordinate curriculum and identify common educational goals and needs
✓ Technical advisors (e.g., MycoXXX/MycoXXX—mushroom farm project) contacted
✓ Physical education and natural history instructors contacted

Still in progress . . .

• Meeting with representatives of canton or cantonal educational authority in order to assess cantonal needs
• Meeting with industry representatives to assess their institutional needs
• Final decision to purchase one of two properties (or consider alternative sites) based on the following criteria:
    • Attractive natural surroundings that are conducive to learning
    • Proximity to forest, or other natural setting for botany and biology laboratory
    • Possibility of triple use/function for educational needs of XXX and workshop site

- Proximity to the city of Neuchâtel or the procurement of daily transport for students if property is not so centrally located
- Sufficiently large to accommodate managing residence, classroom, dormitory space, and garden

VI

Mushroom Cultivation

An Example of Teaching Across the Curriculum:
Environmental, Ecological, and Cultural

The following is an example of an integrated, meaningful, and contextualized approach to teaching different subjects areas.

Growing Mushrooms. The practical life emphasis of *Erdkinder* pedagogical ideas is galvanized in running an enterprise based on a natural product, mushrooms, that has, at least, the following learning objectives:

1. To understand the life cycle of different mushroom species
2. To acquire the horticultural/mycological skills to grow successful cultures
3. To understand the natural history and ecological relationship of specimens
4. To contact expert growers in order to improve skills and understanding
5. To harvest and sell the produce and receive an income to be re-invested
6. To present and clearly explain the results of any aspect of their operation to the public

Subject Areas Covered for Achieving Learning Objective #1:
Math, Biology, Chemistry, Botany, and Microbiology

Subject Areas Covered for Achieving Learning Objective #2:
Math, Soil Technology, Horticultural sustainable practices, Chemistry, Physical Sciences (understanding of the interactions between temperature, humidity, and sterile cultures)

Subject Areas Covered in Achieving Learning Objective #3:
Math-statistics, Ecology, Traditional Cultivation Methods, Culture, and History

Subject Areas Covered in Achieving Learning Objective #4:
Communication skills in order to enter into meaningful and relevant peer dialogue with the mycologist experts at Mycotech/Mycorama (Mr. XXXXX, Site de Cernier) and The University of Neuchâtel.

Subject Areas Covered for Achieving Learning Objective #5:
Economics, Interpersonal Skills, Accounting, and Nutrition

Subject Areas Covered for Achieving Learning Objective #6:
Speech/Communication (with PowerPoint and Scientific Poster delivery), Nutrition, Gastronomy (cultural and natural)

Note: Any aspect of the ***Mushroom Cultivation and Economics Exercise*** can be used by any student as a way to probe deeper into the knowledge of different subject areas acquired with the aim of satisfying their ***Senior Project*** requirement.

List and addresses of primary, secondary, and professional training schools that adhere, if not to ecopsychological curricula, to a strong back-to-nature, wilderness, or environmental programs:

USA
Nature's Classroom Institute
Environmental Science and Montessori Schools
P.O. Box 660
Mukwonago, WI 53149
(800) 574-7881
http://www.nciw.org/nci.htm

Fletcher Farm School for the Arts and Crafts
611 Route 103 South
Ludlow, VT 05149
Telephone: 802-228-8770
Fax: 802-228-7402
http://www.fletcherfarm.com

The Cornerstone School: A Montessori Approach to Learning
146 High Street Stratham,NH 03885 USAph:(603) 772-4349
http://cornerstoneschool.org

SWITZERLAND
La Grande Ourse School
18 Recrêtes Street
2300 La Chaux-de-Fonds
Switzerland
Telephone: 032 926 01 66
(from abroad: +41 32 926 01 66)
Telephone: 032 926 01 66
http://www.grande-ourse.ch/a_index.htm

ITALY
Scuola di Ecopsicologia: associazione culturale Inventare il Mondo
via Marconi 18
23875 Osnago (Lc)
Tel. 039 9280269
ecopsicologia@ecopsicologia.it—www.ecopsicologia.it

Endnotes

[1] Narrow in the sense that a human-nature connection predates this recent history and in view of the fact that poets and philosophers, often contributors to the questions that psychologists ask, have written equally abundantly about ecopsychological themes.

[2] Cross-culturally, in its exclusion of female psychology, and its obsession with single-issue psychology

[3] Theodore Roszak's phrase and construct

[4] Or other esoteric forces conceived

[5] Kuhn, Thomas S. 1962. *The Structure of Scientific Revolutions*. Chicago: University of Chicago Press.

[6] Ibid: 1962

[7] Reprinted with permission of the European Ecopsychology Society ® © www.ecopsychology.net

[8] Used almost interchangeably we shall consider only *ecopsychological alienation,* the condition more likely to produce psychopathies. On the other hand, *ecopsychological estrangement*, *Nature estrangement*, and *Nature dissociation* are less extreme or permanent nature-psyche disconnections, but they too can produce the neuroses most likely to be seen by ecopsychological counselors and therapists.

[9] In my mind, when I say "Heinz Droz," the two names blend together to sound like "android".

[10] From the point of view of human development, at an excessively and unthinkable premature age of 10 or in sixth grade, respectively

[11] The primary and fundamental function of language that assists self-definition and gives rise to ego-driven and rational assessments of information for the benefit of survival and adaptation

[12] Or in genuine experiences

[13] Engels' *Commodity Fetishism*

[14] I would grant that "freedom" is relative to begin with, but at the same time that we also have the power to stretch the relative conditions of its personal existential form.

[15] In "1984"

[16] I place my trust on collective and well-orchestrated and managed efforts.

[17] From Mark Kurlansky's excellent book, *The Basque History of The World*, pg. 242

[18] Under the more absurd name, *Ecological Psychological Outcome Theory*

[19] See full-fledged thesis in this chapter under "Main Thesis."

[20] However, the foundations of Ecopsychology are found in Environmental Psychology, Deep Ecology, Ecology, and Ecosophy.

[21] Recent only in that its progression and its more marked effects have coincided with and have been exacerbated by the globalization of an industrialized and corporate ethos and their merchandizing culture.

[22] Ralph Metzner's phrase

[23] Some do, such as naturalists, but they now belong to the group "human in the fringes."

[24] Hence the larger font for the right side of this analogy

[25] "Wandering" in the sense that American naturalist Henry Thoreau meant it, being a spontaneous walking and discovery of the natural spaces on their own terms. "Wandering" can even be practiced in urban areas.

[26] According to Bill Devall, Gary Snyder, and Arne Naess, by insight acquired while in these wanderings

[27] Conesa, J. (2001). *A Semiotic Metalanguage Based on Existential Ontologies*. Presented at the International Summer Institute for Semiotic and Structural Studies in Imatra, Finland (June10-15, 2001).

[28] In actuality, and biosemiotically speaking, anything could be a *matrix* as long as it meets the definitional requirements of even being perceived as one. The idea of God is therefore a matrix and so is currency.

[29] By the way, I do believe that *incommensurability* is pervasive for less complex organisms with respect to more complex ones to the extent that mind is absent in the former. An insect, for example, cannot understand the concept or idea *humanness;* but an intelligent dog, for example, an organism with a fairly complex mind, can sympathize in many non-commensurable moments with its human partner.

[30] The problem of "passing" presented and dealt with in the Mead article in this book

[31] Joseph Chilton Pearce (1971 and 1977) first laid out the developmental sequence just mentioned, and proposed the ideas that are foundational to SMT. Even his idea and use of the term 'matrix', used in this developmental sense, makes a better case for this progression than I am making here. I encourage readers to revisit his thought provoking and controversial book, *Magical Child* (1977).

[32] Based on the psycholingusitic experiments presented in *Ecological Outcome Psychological Theory,* (1999). The seven categoris and elements alluded here are: Matrix, Energy, Safety, Possibility, Generativity, Control, and Power. Each one has five behavioral/existential levels, thus, 7 x 5= 245 *being* levels.

[33] From *Ecological Outcome Psychological Theory,* (1999)

[34] This is an existential-functional premise, unlike Peirce's metaphysical use of the word "possibility."

[35] Manuscript made public in January of 2005

[36] He is equally critical of the reality spin of a capitalistic lingo that judges and decides what thoughts are sellable and which are not, as well as communist demagogy.

[37] I don't think this is an original pun. I have tried to locate its source to give due credit to the author without success. Do claim it! My guess is that it is a pun that Jesper Hoffmeyer wrote.

[38] That is, even hunter-forager-horticulturalists today are, to some extent, influenced by the material and conceptual goods of civilization. Those groups that were or are not must deal with this intimacy in an inescapable way, without access to an alternate semiosis for comparison, acceptance, and/or rejection.

[39] This is only a small concession on my part because I will take sides with Paul Shepard's view that it is the hunter-forager (even horticulturalist) text that is the more authentic and biosemiotic.

[40] **Zero nature**: Original, pristine wilderness, untouched by and independent of human activities; **First nature**: the "nature we see, identify, describe" and interpret; **Second nature**: materially changed or interpreted nature; and **Third nature**: a "virtual nature, as it exists in art and science."

[41] Some readers may recognize this passage as a fictional conversation that Enrico Passeo, my heteronym in the footsteps of Fenando Pessoa, might have had with Jorge Luis Borges, when Borges, fictionally, said about semiotics: "es una labor intensa de anotaciones interminables de historia, leyenda, y antigüedades."

[42] There is ample evidence to suggest that Jung may have known and also that Freud did not.

[43] Symbols of Transformation, II, pp.20-21

[44] This is also, in Mannheim's terminology, a *noological* progression.

[45] Symbols of . . . , p.16

[46] Symbols of . . . , p.20

[47] The word *google* was "Coined in 1940 by mathematician Edward Kasmer's 9-year old nephew when asked for a name for an enormous number; a 1 followed by 100 zeros—perhaps influenced by comic strip character Barney Google." Online Etymology Dictionary, www.etymology.com.

[48] As of this writing, Changazi et al. have reported great regularity in the visual structure of writing and symbols throughout human history and across languages. The particular subset of recurring angles and shapes employed across most languages, they argue, speaks of evolutionary adaptation of the human visual system to natural signs. In, Changazi et. al., (2006). The structures of letters and symbols throughout human history are selected to match those found in objects in natural scences. *The American Naturalist*, 167 (5), E117-E137.

[49] Freud himself makes a similar case when he argues for the *Thatanos* instinct as the built-in desire of all organic life to go back to its simpler, inorganic origin.

[50] Camouflage "lies." But all sorts of deceptive phenotypic as well as behavioral "deceit" can be, and has been, accommodated by the hunter-forager mind. Besides, these forms of "deceits" are easily manageable constants or invariant percepts. A camouflaged moth does not, in fact, cannot, in fact, rationalize its "lie."

51   Throughout this paper I am making an assumption that other biosemioticians may not accept, namely that the human culture-nature semiotic interaction of true hunter-gatherers, even when using natural language, might have been closer to the definition of biosemiosis as "living systems as sign systems." This thesis can stand if we agree that there is a crucial qualitative difference in the semiosis of city dwelling urbanites with respect to their surrounding "Zero nature" as contrasted to the relationship of present-day hunter-foragers to nature; a biosemiosis.

52   The ecologist, the LIFE loving and, equally, scientifically-trained professional

53   Search for Extraterrestrial Intelligence

54   They did not call it an ecological unconscious, ecopsychologist Theodore Roszak does.

55   The subject of the last triad of articles examining, proactively, the remedies of the sick text

56   Shepard does not refer to his theses as semiotic or biosemiotic; I interpret them as such.

57   See Roderick Nash 1982, *Wilderness and the American Mind, 3rd Ed*, for a historical example of this progression in the opposite direction, toward biocentric sensitivity.

58   Heinz Werner, an admirer of both Jacob von Uexkull and of Martha Muchow (Crain, 2000), calls it synchretic thinking/perception.

59   A cognitive-semiotic term described by Karl Mannheim (1936, pp. 349): "Noology (= the study of the contents and forms of thought in their purely cognitive interrelations)"

60   1976 U.S. dollars!

61   There I go again, singularizing psychologists.

62   They won't like ideologs of any persuasion, nor the old *intelligentsia*.

63   Once again, excepting transpesonal psychology

64   One could argue that 19th century and turn of the 20th century thinkers lived surrounded by, still, so much nature and wilderness that the thought never occurred to them.

65   It has been suggested that multiple personalities disorder, MPD, is an exaggeration of this flexibility.

66   My thanks to the editor of *Sign System Studies*, Dr. Kalevi Kull, and reviewers for making the original manuscript more sleek!

67   Sick! . . . when the generic and arbitrary turns out to be the literal as well.

68   My paraphrase of John Dewey's personal evaluation of Mead's literary productivity in his prefatory remarks in *The Philosophy of the Present*, 1934.

69   This universal and biosemiotic sounding description was written in 1932, a good seventy or so years before Jesper Hoffmeyer's *Signs of Meaning in the Universe*, in 1996. This comparison is made partly out of respect to J. Hoffmeyer's work and also because his name is associated with a canonical-now in biosemiotics providing a useful historical frame of reference.

70   But realistically speaking, the majority of social agents cannot pull this off, and humans, in our example, are more *ergodic* than *non-ergodic,* thus being limited to only finite sets of relatedness by their genotypic and phenotypic boundaries, and by their experiential and psychological experiences and limitations.

71   Or even mark him as an ecopsychologist like Kurt Lewin (1935; 1936; 1939; 1951) expressing a similar, non-topological description of *Life Space*.

72   In concordance with Heinz Werner's (1934; 1963) developmental description and move from juvenile syncretic, sensorial, and affective (implying faster and unreasoned limbic processes) processes, to more mature mental states that are discrete, objective and language based. Also Ernest Schachtel's (1959) distinction between an earlier developmental experiential realm dominated by *autocentric* senses, or the intimate senses of touch, smell and taste, toward, with increased maturity, to an ascending dependency on *allocentric* or distal senses such as vision and hearing and the mediation of reality through language.

73   I am co-opting the term *historicity* from its other uses, in semiotics and biosemiotics. Within semiotics itself it has been used as a term used to move away from a decontextualized Saussurean (1916/1983) Synchronic analyses. See page eleven in this work for my own qualified biosemiotic meaning of *historicity*.

74   Mead specifically mentions a semiosis of hormonal functioning, "There is in the physiological system such a system of communication carried out by hormones." (*The Philosophy of The Present*, pg. 83.)

75   One person's multireferential insight is all it takes. After the fact, an entire culture can benefit from this insight without a thorough understanding of this accomplishment or what it REALLY means.

76   In actuality, and biosemiotically speaking, anything could be a *matrix* as long as it meets the definitional requirements of even being perceived as one. The idea of God is therefore a matrix and so is currency.

77   By the way, I do believe that *incommensurability* is pervasive for less complex organisms with respect to more complex ones to the extent that mind is absent in the former. An insect, for example, cannot understand the concept or idea *humanness;* but an intelligent dog, for example, an organism with a fairly complex mind, can sympathize in many non-commensurable moments with its human partner.

78   Joseph Chilton Pearce (1971 and 1977), first laid out the developmental sequence just mentioned, and proposed the ideas that are foundational to SMT. Even his idea and use of the term 'matrix', used in this developmental sense, makes a better case for this progression than I am making here. I encourage readers to revisit his thought provoking and controversial book, *Magical Child* (1977).

79   I see it as and call it a problem, Mead may have not thought of it as a problem. His writings assume and are hopeful that the *generalized other* would be passport enough (pun intended) between umwelten.

80   Peter Kropotkin's (1914) name must be added as a precursor to this list of ecopsychologists (Roszak 2001) for he contributed, to the budding concept of an 'ecosystem,' being dependent on mutual, intespecies aid.

81   SMT traces the existential doings of organic matter and of life to inorganic, energetic beginnings. Thus, in this more inclusive sense, the terms *pansemiosis* or *biopansemiotic* are used.

82   As my grandmother Carmen Sevilla Perez from Cadiz told my Catalan mother, Montserrat Sevilla de Conesa, born in Paris, and my mother continually reminds us

when we unjustly, stereotypically, compare the ways and customs of diverse peoples and countries: "En todas partes del mundo se comen habas", or "Everywhere, everyone eats [some sort of] beans." "Just a little bit differently," I add.

83   My own *awe-sense* of spirituality while in communion with natural spaces but the spirituality of others as well

84   One can read it as the antithesis to E. O. Wilson's **Biophilia,** 1984.

85   By embracing the natural and wild I also mean acquiring the necessary statistical know-how to be able to assess, often-subtle changes, long term, or when data are copious and overwhelm commonsensical but false notions.

86   I am using this term metaphorically, to emphasize our consumer-driven and thoughtless relation with nature, excluding a grander biosemiosis of cooperation and interrelatedness.

87   We can, however, study present-day hunter-forager-horticulturalists and judge afterwards whether they are prototypes of psychological wellness.

88   Please refer to the last synnomic phase, Phase Three, which describes the ecological scientist-as-a-shaman in Conesa-Sevilla, 2005b.

89   My suspicion is that these "flashes of insight," as Sigurd Olson describes them—Appendix C at the end of this chapter, are a far more common experience in *nature wanderers* than reported.

90   In my hierarchy "Wolf" should be capitalized and "chihuahua" should not. But alas, my spelling program insists that chihuahua dogs reign grammatically supreme over Wolf and Wolves.

91   For more about the re-enactment of the African Savannah in urban spaces please refer to the Kaplan, Orians, and Ulrich citations.

92   Enter your own sect, order, or religion here, as long as there is an historical precedence and continuity of this natural relatedness.

93   In Theodore Roszak's recent re-release of *The Voice of The Earth* (2001), he explains how when asked for an interview the reporter wanted to confirm that Dr. Roszak had "objective evidence" about ecopsychological illnesses or objective proof that nature-estrangement could affect human psychology. I believe he got tired of amassing a great heap of social scientific interdisciplinary data pointing to the obvious: we are natural beings.

94   See above Section 2: *Wolf Religion Versus Chihuahua Religion*

95   A prelude to this developmental tradition, at fourteen, I ran away from home looking for a life in Tahiti among glistening bodies and colorful fruit only to realize that I already lived in Venezuela. So began my daring wanderings and brushes with cynegism.

96   When my students and I were asked to do an analysis of the pattern of complaints logged by the citizens of a Puget Sound area community we found that one of the most common entries were noise of various sorts.

97   An admonition form the past might be found in Rousseau's Emile, Book One [24:] *Natural man is everything for himself. He is the numerical unit, the absolute whole, accountable only to himself or to his own kind. Civil man is only a fractional unit dependent on the denominator, whose value is in his relationship with the whole, that is, the social body.*

[98]   It is impossible to quantify the effects, the regression in years, and the consequences of convenient denial of the present American republican administration with respect to a wide range of environmental issues. Whether it is a matter of convenient denial, outright deception, environmental illiteracy, or the fact that a significant number of ontogenetically arrested adult males--who make decisions which impact the entire biosphere--lack the cynegetic awareness to assess the complexity of these problems, is not for me to judge. However, their actions and decisions speak for themselves.

[99]   See above Section 2: *Wolf Religion Versus Chihuahua Religion*

[100]   Paper presented in Barcelona, Spain, at the International Anthrozoological Society meeting (2006)

[101]   In the above passage used as a metaphor for higher and more abstract forms of understanding. Technically speaking, is refers to inferred and projected tracks or the easy and lazy way of tracking.

[102]   And Paul Shepard brilliantly expanded in Animal Intelligence and The Others . . . (1996)"

[103]   From 1985-1988, under the kind and sage-like tutoring eye of Dr. Joe Lesh . . . thank you!

[104]   This animal is the biggest chamois I have seen in Switzerland.

[105]   A close relative of the red fox, the gray fox, does not have this feature, making the tracking of both foxes fairly easy.

[106]   A term that Paul Shepard uses often that is central to his description of the ideal human-Nature relationship: a hunter's life.

[107]   Many Inuit songs are *pranatic,* wolf-like panting. The Finnish-Swedish folk group "Hedningarna" plays many songs utilizing this technique, resulting in an eerie and primal sound.

[108]   Some seasoned trackers use self-given nicknames such as Kim Cabrera's "Beartracker," or "Buckshot." Even when not rising to the experiential designation and implication of "Beartracker," I recommend the habit of using a "forest name." A sound ecopsychological practice, a transpersonalized name may get you into the habit of thinking beyond the self you are used to (thanks to Dr. Margaret Riordan for getting me started in thinking along these lines).

[109]   Unless we are talking about "*Green* Economics," or "Green Economists."

[110]   I recently found out that the president of a prestigious Environmental college, Green Mountain, VT, decided that the first graduate degree to be offered would be in business. That this would happen in an environmental college is sad enough, but that students and faculty did not protest this decision is heartbreaking!

[111]   An excellent, contemporary and far more ecopsychological restatement of these ideas can be found in Richard Louv's *Last Child in the Woods: Saving Our Children from Nature-Deficit Disorder*

[112]   In, "British Colleges Seek Quantity and Quality," March 16, 2006, The Christian Science Monitor.

[113]   International Baccalaureate degrees. See also IBO, the International Baccalaureate Organization, based in Geneva, Switzerland, it began producing a curriculum designed

for children of diplomats who moved around quite a bit. The local politician was impressed by the historical fact that the IB curriculum was originally designed to meet the exclusive needs (of perhaps MBA-bound) of rich children and that it seemed to provide some sort of distinction or clout to the city of Neuchâtel.

[114] According to Paul Shepard's widow, Dr. Florence Shepard, and coincidentally, Paul also went to school briefly at the University of Neuchatel. Personal communication.

[115] Freire's phrase and pedagogy implies "environmental workers" or even "eco-educators" in the context of our own emphases.

[116] John Dewey should never be a footnote.

[117] The subtitle for Bill Devall's and George Sessions' book Deep Ecology (1985)

[118] (ibid, 1985) *Deep Ecology*

[119] (ibid, 1985) *Deep Ecology*

[120] AMARANDA, The Journal of The European Ecopsychology Society (EES), November 2005, Vol 1, 1.

[121] The arguments presented in these sections were the seeds for, "The Intrinsic Value of the Whole: Cognitive and Utilitarian Evaluative Processes as They Pertain to Ecoethics, Deep Ecological, and Ecopsychological "Valuing." The Trumpeter, Vol 22 (2), 2006.

[122] *The 'Is-Ought' Problem Resolved*, American Psychological Association, 1974, pp. 34-61

[123] *Ecological Outcome Psychological Theory*, Forbes Publishers, 1999, pp. 1-33, 84-103

[124] *The farther reaches of human nature*, 1971, Penguin.

[125] Daniel Dennett's phrase in *Consciousness Explained*.

[126] *Ecological Outcome Psychological Theory*, pp. 19-23

[127] *Principles of topological psychology*, 1936, McGraw-Hill; and *Field theory and social science*, 1951, Harper.

[128] By a statement of fact is meant any capricious claim, not empirically corroborable, that can be asserted such as "there is a god" or "there is a hell" (Is), which leads logically, therefore, to *ought* prescriptions. Hence moral behavior is rationalized and to act in such a manner that is consistent with the desires of a god and avoid punishment is good. The potential fallaciousness of "Is-ought" arguments is illustrated by the slippery move from supernatural claim to moral dictum. My premises are not statements of fact of this sort but observable law that can be corroborated by empirical methods.

[129] A green ecologist or ecopsychologist who still keeps his ancient "bag of tricks" is the respected Ralph Metzner.

[130] I still don't get this. If a clinical psychologist looks like and acts like he/she is about to have a power lunch with corporate America, is he/she really ready to get dirty and deal with my nasty Id—or his/her nasty Id? Is she/he indicating by this gracious attire that she/he is committed to my well being?

[131] Conesa-Sevilla, J. (2004), Wrestling with ghosts: a personal and scientific account of sleep paralysis. Pennsylvania: Xlibris/Randomhouse

[132] A manifestation of what Theodore Roszak calls the *ecological unconscious*

[133] Including, emotions-as-thoughts

134 Based on an original article written for The Lucid Dream Exchange, November, 2005, and reprinted here with permission from its editors

135 Then 19 years old

136 I have made Berlin sound like a pretty bad place. I was tempted to change her name to protect her identity. So in fairness, I have to include a disclaimer: I'm describing the effect living in the city had on me, which would have been similar in any city of comparable size. Had I merely visited Berlin, in the spring perhaps, I'm sure I would have loved it. Right before I left, as winter was starting to break, I discovered that it is in fact among the greenest and most park-filled cities I'd ever encountered, and the center of life shifts to these spaces for many Berliners.

137 Siento que el barco mío ha tropezadeo, allà en el fondo, con algo grande. Y nada sucede Nada . . . . Quietud . . . . Olas . . . . Nada sucede? O es que ha sucedido todo, y estamos ya, tranquilos, en lo nuevo?

138 "Gallup: More Than Half of Americans Reject Evolution, Back Bible--By *Editor & Publisher*," . . . "The report was written by the director of The Gallup Poll, Frank Newport." . . . "Published: March 08, 2006 10:15 AM ET."

139 In view of the widespread and catasthropic effects of environmental defiling, it is more accurate to continue thinking of "saving a planet" and of "service" to the extent that we are working under a *therapeutical* as opposed to a truly *sustainable* model.

140 The reader is encouraged to read anything by Pessoa. His *sensationalism* can be construed as a keen ecopsychological perceptual attitude. Thanks to Mr. Jeff Hipolito for introducing Pessoa to me.

141 Arrogance begets other evils. After all, Zeus' servants were 'Force' and 'Violence'

142 The Great Idea Finder: http://www.ideafinder.com

143 Source: UK based National Economic Research Associates (NERA) doing research for the Consumer Safety Unit.

144 Zeus servants 'Force' and 'Violence' seized and chained Prometheus.

Printed in the United States
70129LV00005B/52

9 781425 723149